COUNTRY BOUND!

◆

TRADING YOUR BUSINESS SUIT BLUES FOR BLUE JEAN DREAMS

MARILYN & TOM ROSS

Upstart
Publishing Company
Specializing in Small Business Publishing
a division of Dearborn Publishing Group, Inc.

This publication is designed to provide accurate and authoritative information in regard to the subject matter covered. It is sold with the understanding that the publisher is not engaged in rendering legal, accounting, or other professional service. If legal advice or other expert assistance is required, the services of a competent professional person should be sought.

Executive Editor: Cynthia A. Zigmund
Managing Editor: Jack Kiburz
Interior Design: Lucy Jenkins
Cover Design: Rohani Design
Typesetting: Elizabeth Pitts

97 98 99 10 9 8 7 6 5 4 3 2 1

Library of Congress Cataloging-in-Publication Data

Ross, Marilyn Heimberg.
    Country bound! : trade your business suit blues for blue jean
dreams / by Marilyn and Tom Ross.
        p.   cm.
    Originally published: Buena Vista, CO : Communication Creativity,
©1992.
    Includes index.
    ISBN 0-7931-2358-5 (pbk.)
    1. Urban-rural migration—United States.   2. Career changes—
United States.   3. United States—Rural conditions.   4. New
business enterprises—United States.   I. Ross, Tom. 1933-   .
II. Title.
HB1965.R59   1997   96-38085
307.2'612'0973—dc21   CIP

Dedication

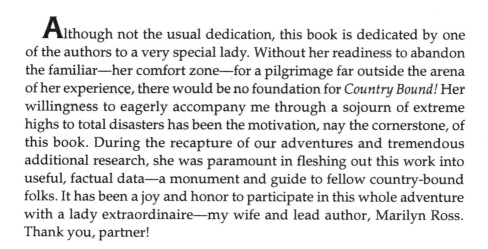

Although not the usual dedication, this book is dedicated by one of the authors to a very special lady. Without her readiness to abandon the familiar—her comfort zone—for a pilgrimage far outside the arena of her experience, there would be no foundation for *Country Bound!* Her willingness to eagerly accompany me through a sojourn of extreme highs to total disasters has been the motivation, nay the cornerstone, of this book. During the recapture of our adventures and tremendous additional research, she was paramount in fleshing out this work into useful, factual data—a monument and guide to fellow country-bound folks. It has been a joy and honor to participate in this whole adventure with a lady extraordinaire—my wife and lead author, Marilyn Ross. Thank you, partner!

Praise for *Country Bound!*

"The *What Color Is Your Parachute?* to making a transition to smaller cities and towns in rural areas."

Bill Seavey, Greener Pastures Institute

"*Country Bound!* is an excellent guide for the bewildered seeker of a new life in small towns. Its treasury of ideas and painstaking research will rescue readers from many potential mistakes."

Jack Lessinger, author of *Penturbia*
Professor Emeritus, Real Estate and Urban Development
University of Washington

"Includes criteria for selection and steps for investigating potential places to live, the logistics of moving, adapting to small-town life, social activities, business opportunities such as franchising or professional practices, home-based employment or entrepreneurial possibilities, and job hunting in small-town and rural markets . . . helpful maps, charts, and graphs are also included."

Booklist

"More than a guide to changing careers, *Country Bound!* is about radically remaking your entire life in small town U.S.A. Well thought through and jam-packed with specific resources, helpful information, and useful advice. Don't leave your current lifestyle without it."

Small Press Magazine

"Their experiences in adjusting are shared with a great deal of 'down home' wit and candor—the good and the bad—and there's very little of the latter if you follow their advice."

John Austin, *Books of the Week*

"An incredibly complete resource. Offers exhaustive, down-to-earth guidance on everything from deciding where to move, to buying the real estate, to earning a living in the new environment. This husband-wife writing team has turned out several other memorable products prior to this effort. When they do a job, they do it right."

The Real Estate Professional

"*Country Bound!* spurs you to dream up fun ways to spend your time."

The Rocky Mountain News

"A one-of-a-kind book showing disgruntled urbanites how to turn avocational pastimes into regular paychecks; telecommute to their existing jobs; set up an 'information age' home-based business; buy an existing rural enterprise; or create their dream job in the country."

The Midwest Book Review

"A business book as well as a lifestyle guide."

Nation's Business

"If you want to get out of the fast lane the Rosses have penned a book with hundreds of practical ideas of just how to go about it."

Alan Caruba, *Bookviews*

"They (the Rosses) walk you through the logistics and costs, as well as the psychological aspects."

Chicago *Daily Herald*

"Comes to the rescue with hundreds of practical, thought-provoking ideas to help people prosper in paradise."

Cindy Bartorillo, *Reading for Pleasure*

"Everything you need to know to successfully escape. Includes maps and charts that compare crime rates, property taxes, and household income for various locations."

Log Home Living

"A good read whether or not you are ready to exit metropolitan madness. This is an invaluable resource guide."

Barbara Garro, *Corp Talk*

"As the executive director of the Chamber of Commerce and a member of the Partnership for Economic Development, your book has become a major source of reference."

Pegi Brown

"How to regain control of your life, to launch new adventures easily, quickly, and profitably."

Best Books

"Chock-full of quizzes, exercises, and checklists, *Country Bound!* helps make the urban to rural transition easy and fun."

Tourism & Commercial Recreation Update

"This exciting new concept will benefit rural economic development, tourism, retirement, small business, and women/minority owned enterprises. It's an excellent manual that takes you from A to Z. What a fascinating encyclopedia for anyone who wants to live in a rural area!"

Martin J. Darity, Governor's Liaison
Alabama Advantage for Retirees

"If you've been trying to flee from big city stress and pollution to a more relaxed country setting, *Country Bound!* is your book."

Environ

"Successful 'Countrypreneurs' tell how to fulfill your dreams. They share their experiences with wit and candor, telling readers what *not* to do as much as what to do."

Simple Living News

"Certain to attract numerous city-weary dwellers who can see in self-employment their own key to freedom from the 9-5 hassles. The blend of practical financial savvy with a rural focus sets this apart from similar titles which focus on either country living or entrepreneur opportunities."

The Bookwatch

"Hundreds of entrepreneurial ideas for living in the country."

My Generation, American Association of Boomers

"In their new book, *Country Bound! Trade Your Business Suit Blues for Blue Jean Dreams,* authors Marilyn and Tom Ross offer step-by-step advice on how to earn a good living in the country and have a better quality of life. They're full of thought-provoking ideas."

Newsmaker Interviews

"Case histories show you what works and what doesn't. Includes quizzes, maps, tables, charts, and checklists."

Workamper News

"Strategies to become successfully self-employed, 23 gutsy tactics for finding the right rural job, tips for tapping into the information age and telecommuting, and much more."

United Country

"Shows disgruntled urbanites how to effectively escape the big city rat race, create a successful business in the boonies, and experience an enhanced quality of life."

Downscaling 46510

"If you relocate employees to rural areas, check out *Country Bound!* It offers pre- and post-move advice for coping with the personal side of small-town life, such as what to consider when contemplating a move, adjusting to the rural 'mind-set,' and cultivating a satisfying social life in a small town."

Runzheimer Reports on Relocation

"An amazing book and an absolutely great gift."
Doug Benton, WACV Radio

"Provides answers for rural economic development problems."
Pueblo Chieftain

"In addition to counseling readers on rural business opportunities, much of the book focuses on cultural adjustment . . . lots of down home advice."
William Charland, "Skills Update"

Contents

PART TWO
Business Aspects

PART THREE
Resources to Ease Your Relocation and Strengthen Your Business

Preface

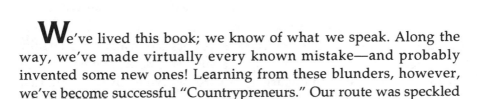

We've lived this book; we know of what we speak. Along the way, we've made virtually every known mistake—and probably invented some new ones! Learning from these blunders, however, we've become successful "Countrypreneurs." Our route was speckled with hardship, humor, and hard work.

First, the mistakes. In 1980, we left a suite of offices overlooking the Pacific Ocean in La Jolla, California, to buy a 320-acre ranch in Colorado. We had a thriving consulting business in San Diego. But, while it is indeed America's finest big city, we'd arrived at a point in our lives where more bucolic surroundings beckoned. A vacation in a mountain log cabin at Big Bear Lake—surrounded by God's natural wonders, blessed silence, friendly squirrels playing on the roof, and deer grazing by the front door—made us realize our values had shifted. Since our writing, book publishing, and marketing clients were all over the country—and we worked with them primarily by mail and phone—it became obvious our business was portable. But, oh, the things that weren't so obvious . . .

We bought raw land: lush meadows with two bubbling creeks and surrounded by craggy mountains. There were aspen groves, blue spruce, and pine trees galore. Deer and antelope cavorted in our meadows. What we didn't have, however, was a house, telephone lines, a well, or a power source.

Never ones to back away from a challenge, we figured we'd be self-sufficient: build our home, develop our own potable water source, and generate our own power. Mistake number one.

Lunching in the historic hotel dining room in the nearby town of 500 people—which we will call "First Try" throughout the book to avoid offending the folks who find it to their liking—our real estate agent mentioned the hotel had recently fallen out of escrow. You can't run a consulting business from a tent on bare land . . . Marilyn looked around and the wheels started whirling. *Gee, this would give us a place to live, plenty of office space, and phone lines. Besides, we're entrepreneurial souls. Certainly a 16-room hotel and restaurant can't be that hard to run. And the price is a steal compared to California real estate!* You know what comes next. We bought the place. Mistake number two.

We don't, however, want to overwhelm you with all our foibles at one time. Stupidity, like castor oil, is best tolerated in small doses. So we've sprinkled what we've gleaned throughout these pages with the hope our lapses in logic will serve as your bridges to happiness.

A few words of redemption: We later made a second move to Buena Vista, Colorado. It's a town of 2,000 people nestled in a beautiful valley surrounded by 14,000-foot mountain peaks. This relocation has proven both soul satisfying and financially rewarding. We'll tell you about that too, including how to make a successful move and find professional and personal fulfillment. Let's get started!

Acknowledgments

We are indebted to many competent people who helped bring this book to fruition. Suzanne Miller orchestrated a multitude of tasks—coordinating, researching, getting permissions, and applying her "eagle eye" to catch mistakes before they became embarrassments. Bridget Wallace did endless research on the phone and via the Internet. Cathy Bowman entered and checked data. Thank you each for your caring and capabilities.

We also want to gratefully acknowledge several people who gave so generously of their time and expertise to read the manuscript. Those who shared their insights and feedback include Kathy Black, Alley DeVore, Ken Waddell, Jack Lessinger, and Pegi Brown.

A book of this nature can only come about as a result of intensive research. Countless people answered our pleas for help. Certainly we've overlooked some, and for that we apologize. Among those who contributed greatly were Dewitt John, Marci Levin, Judy Krueger, Lou Francis, Bill Seavey, Patricia John, Louise Reynnells, Scott McKearney, Cindy Murphy, Jim Henderson, Calvin Beale, David Savageau, Mary Pekas, Dan Gibb, Peggy Counce, Jeff Ollinger, Lew Lowe, Patricia Mokhtarian, Cheryl Chepeus, Bill Obermeier, Gil Gordon, and Jack Niles.

Last only in the chronological life of *Country Bound!*, we thank Christine Litavsky, acquisitions editor at Dearborn Financial Publishing, Inc., for her vision in seeing the potential for this book. And we're excited about working with Eileen Johnson, whose special sales acumen is the reason we placed the book with Dearborn.

Thank you each and every one for your energy, enthusiasm, and encouragement!

PART ONE

◆

Personal Considerations

1

◆

Your Future Awaits

"The boonies are booming," reported the October 9, 1995, issue of *Business Week*. Do you dream of getting away from it all? Or maybe of having it all? You're not alone. Three out of four Americans say they would prefer *not* living in a metropolitan area. After all, don't thousands of people take to the road each weekend to escape the city? A Gallup Poll revealed that given their druthers, 29 percent would live in a city of 10,000 to 100,000 residents, and 52 percent prefer a rural area or small town. While trading the fast lane for a country road is the dream of countless millions, until recently lack of job opportunities thwarted most. They simply couldn't earn a living outside the city.

Now *Country Bound!* comes to the rescue with practical, thought-provoking ideas you can use to prosper in paradise. Picking up where back-to-the-land books left off several years ago, it proposes viable strategies to help you trade Wall Street for Main Street—strategies everyone contemplating leaving the big city scene and taking charge of their destiny in Small Town USA can use. Finally you can follow your dream . . . without tripping over a nightmare!

In this one-of-a-kind resource you'll find not only advice, but also phone numbers, addresses, and Web sites to help you track down every bit of information you need to make a successful rural relocation. Substance and a dash of humor rule here. This is a candid, detailed, and specific relocation kit like no other. In 19 information-dense, yet lively, chapters you'll discover everything you need to know to make a pain-free move and earn a comfortable living.

David Birch, the head of Cognetics, Inc., and a guru on small business, recently told *Inc.* magazine: "With modern telecommunications facilities, far-reaching parcel delivery service, [the national] interstate highway system, and a U.S. Post Office, the possibilities for growing a successful company in the boondocks are quite real."

Combine that fact with a career poll reported by the *Wall Street Journal*, which showed the majority of people asked to describe their dream job responded overwhelmingly: "Head my own business." After buying a comparable house in a rural area, most folks have enough money left over to do just that. They become "Countrypreneurs" (the word we've coined for entrepreneurs who work in the country). This book is for them.

It not only shows how to *get started* in a small-town business, but how to *stay in business and be successful.* Big-city types must learn how to deal with less cosmopolitan folks, fit into Small Town USA, and prospect for business in new ways. *Country Bound!* covers this and much more.

Of course, whether urban transplants find what they're looking for depends on how realistic their expectations are. We're the first to say that small town life isn't for everyone. Our mission is not only to point the way for those who want slower paces and friendlier faces, but also to caution others who aren't suited for this transition.

Frankly, some people would feel stifled in rural America. For them, saying *sayonara* to sophisticated civilization makes about as much sense as mice getting together to chase a cat. We'd like to spare these individuals the heartache, frustration, and possible financial ruin such a relocation could entail.

WHY THIS BOOK AT THIS TIME?

Faith Popcorn, founder of BrainReserve—a forward-thinking marketing consulting firm—addresses the primary reason in her book, *The Popcorn Report.* She identifies "Cashing Out" as one of the ten top trends for this decade. This is when men and women leave the corporate rat race in search of quality of life. "It's not copping out or dropping out or selling out," explains this nationally acclaimed trend-spotter. "It's cashing in the career chips you've been stacking up all these years and going somewhere else to work at something you want to do, the way you want to do it." Popcorn feels the Cashing Out movement will signal no less than the economic decentralization of America—for the better. People are anxious to get away from the masses of strangers in the city. "More than the romance of the country, it's a promise of safety, of comfort, and of old-fashioned values . . . and the living costs are lower," she observes.

The editors at Research Alert, whose book is titled *The Lifestyle Odyssey: 2,001 Ways Americans' Lives Are Changing,* also feel career-obsessiveness is on the wane. They expect less emphasis on "things" and increased pleasure in the simple aspects of life. "While this scaling back of the traditional American Dream may feel frightening or depressing, I see it as an entrance into another kind of Dream," says author Eric Miller. "This new ethic will open the door to another kind of optimism and activism—the era of quality of life."

There is no question materialism was the mantra of the acquiring 1980s. It was the decade of overconsumption. The successful drove Mercedes with vanity license plates, had cosmetic surgery, and shopped at expensive clothing boutiques. But today people are beginning to realize their joy isn't dependent on status symbols. They are questioning their values, reprioritizing their lives. They strive to *be* the best . . . and are not satisfied just to *have* the best. They have composted the greed weed into beautiful blossoms. Greater self-reliance, a wish to take control, a slower pace, more time with one's family, a closeness with nature, a hunger for great spirituality: These are shaping up as the preferences for the future. Quality of life has become more important than quantity in life.

Dr. Jack Lessinger, a frequently quoted real estate and urban development expert, has been studying America's migration cycles all his adult life. "The 20th century gave us suburbia," he says. "The 21st will shift the nation's center of gravity in a massive swerve . . . from suburbia to penturbia." Penturbia (a term he coined) is an emerging region of growth and opportunity consisting of small cities and towns interspersed with farms, forests, lakes, and rivers.

"The present migration is no flash in the pan . . . the decision to leave suburbia is part of a long trend that will continue for decades," he says. His theory is that we're well along on the fifth great migration since the beginning of industrialization. This forecast is being borne out daily.

The workforce is in tremendous transition. Massive downsizings continue. According to the *Kiplinger Washington Letter,* an estimated 400,000 Americans were laid off in 1996. And that's in addition to the more than 4.5 million workers who already lost their jobs during this decade. (Some say IBM has downsized so much that they're now called

IB.) Middle managers and professionals are the hardest hit, leaving the once-secure "corporate career" in tatters.

With the Internet becoming an ever-larger presence in our lives, an awesome global resource has emerged. Participation in the World Wide Web doubles almost every month. According to estimates from Webmaster, Inc., by the year 2000 business and consumer transactions over the Internet will exceed $21 billion. We talk throughout *Country Bound!* about how you can use this extraordinary tool to your advantage: both as a research tool and to level the playing field as a far-flung Countrypreneur. And even if you're not personally online, most libraries are connected—so all the wonders we'll be discussing are available to you.

SOMETHING FOR ALMOST EVERYONE

Using this book as a road map, disenchanted baby boomers, squeezed out by downsizing, may well discover a better lifestyle and the bonus of more rewarding work. Middle- and upper-level managers trapped by layoffs, career plateauing, or early retirement can create meaningful new careers. Many are individuals who formulate their own flight plans, prepare for a different future, redefine priorities, bring their loyalty back to self and family.

Phil Burgess, president of the Denver-based Center for the New West, has given these individuals a name: Lone Eagles. Their ranks include consultants, writers, analysts, stockbrokers, lawyers—anyone who lives by their wits. They remain connected to the outside world by faxes, computers, modems, telephones, express mail, and airplane tickets. These Lone Eagles have spread their wings and taken flight. They can live anywhere because they export their work. Give them five acres and a modem and they're in business.

And what of individuals who voluntarily unshackle themselves from the mighty achiever's ball and chain? Frequently these are men going through the male menopause. Tired of what they've been doing for 20 or so years, they want to relieve their boredom and find new zest in what they do. They're discovering less stressful ways to earn a living with fresh pizzazz. Management guru Peter Drucker says we're likely to form a new breed of older, more sophisticated entrepreneurs who bring skills and competitive expertise to start-ups—not to mention existing enterprises.

Owners of many home-based businesses and cottage industries located in congested metropolitan areas are ideal candidates for small-town life. If they specialize in information management, their slogan might be "Five acres and a modem." Not being location-specific, they can create "virtual companies" and conduct business from anywhere with a personal computer, modem, phone lines, fax, and overnight delivery service.

Another burgeoning group fleeing the city includes employees of large companies who work in information management fields. They "telecommute" via a satellite home-based office complete with computer, modem, and telephone—plus an occasional trip into corporate headquarters. Today, workers from such companies as Travelers' Insurance, AT&T, Citibank, Pacific Bell, J.C. Penney, New York Life, and Blue Cross/Blue Shield telecommute.

This innovative approach to the workplace is growing rapidly as employees cut deals with their bosses to perform tasks ranging from collection to marketing and from billing to inventory control. It's a win-win arrangement that offers the parent company savings in office rent and other benefits. *The Futurist* magazine recently reported, "Work will move to unconventional sites and arrangements. Employers are becoming willing to consider almost any work arrangement that will get work done at less cost. Businesses are seeking to contain costs and are responding to the need for flexibility."

Retirees represent an additional group who can benefit from the message in this guide. They are more physically fit and energetic than ever before. A satisfying later life may mean leaving a crime-ridden, congested metropolitan area for a personal oasis in some recreational wonderland. Adventuresome mature people welcome a change of scene as much as their younger counterparts. Some seek the challenge of entrepreneurship and have money to invest in their own businesses. For folks in their golden years who seek to augment Social Security, income-supplementing ideas abound.

Parents who dream of raising their children in a safe, healthy environment will find they can do so—and even afford to own a comfortable home without a crippling mortgage. What was a convenient location before you had kids becomes congested and confining after they come along. More important, mothers and fathers worry about busing, violence, and drugs, or overcrowded, overspecialized, and undersupervised classrooms.

Children of the corporate ladder grow up with a whole different set of experiences. While they can regale you with tales of the nearest fast-food restaurants, they don't experience the excitement of harvesting wild asparagus; seeing a mare with her newborn, spindly-legged foal; or eating fresh radish snacks from seeds they personally planted.

People considering the purchase of a vacation home or second home will also find useful information here. Weekend farmers do everything from growing Christmas trees to raising goats on their spare-time spreads. For some, their country place is a simple farmhouse or cabin, a few acres of pasture or woods, perhaps a pond or creek. Others buy undeveloped land and visit it frequently in their campers, trailers, or RVs. Recreational property ownership will rise dramatically over the next 20 years. Fully a third of current owners of such property say they see it as an investment or a source of income. The expanding affluent sector that stays in metropolitan areas will be all the more anxious to have a country hideaway as cities and suburbs further deteriorate. The theme song for many may be "Visit Now, Retire Later."

"Death sucking lemons," someone once said in describing the face of a person caught out during a smog alert. Swollen, teary eyes. Furrowed brow. Downturned mouth. (And this says nothing about the sore throat and rasping breath.) Yes, health is another major reason prompting many to flee metropolitan madness. Where you live affects more than your sense of beauty and your wallet. It can also determine how long you will live. The two top killers are cardiovascular disease (including strokes) and cancer. Carcinogens proliferate in big cities. So do stress-provoking situations. How can people feel laid-back when they're fighting to maintain their place on a clogged freeway, clawing their way up the corporate ladder, or having their private space invaded by their neighbor's blaring stereo? Good health is our greatest blessing. Do we dare continue to jeopardize it?

Environmentalists will also welcome the option presented here. They recognize we don't inherit our land from our parents—we borrow it from our children. Countless urban nests have been soiled beyond repair. Those concerned about ecology and the environment may want to disperse to unspoiled places.

Country life affords special opportunities for grassroots environmental activism. Your voice is heard; your actions are felt. Issues surrounding clear-cutting, dams, road building, endangered species, mining, waste disposal, soil erosion, overgrazing, pesticides in the water supply, and many other causes can be lobbied effectively. It's easier to be a master of your own fate in the country, to truly practice stewardship of the land. Clearly, one individual *can* make a difference.

Decision makers at all levels of government will benefit from this breakthrough book. Rural economic development is one of this nation's greatest challenges. It is being addressed at all levels: by the towns themselves, counties, states, and the federal government. But they view it from the *inside out*. Towns ask how they can help existing farms and businesses, keep their young people from leaving, and establish a more reliable tax base. They hold conferences, launch pilot projects, write bulky reports. Yet no one is looking at this issue from the *outside in*. The out-migration from major cities is a trickle now. Forecasters predict it will be a steady stream by the year 2010. Smart towns and counties are addressing how they can capitalize on this trend to attract more than their share of the new residents.

In fact, anyone who wants to escape to the hinterland will find this book a useful tool for locating their special Eden. Do greener pastures beckon you? Do you want to unplug from the system to avoid being victimized by it? Are you ready to liberate yourself from your limitations? Then read on. Our vision is to connect people with their futures.

One caution however: Make sure you're not running *away* from anything, but rather that you're running *to* something. Changing location to solve one's problems is like sitting on a cheap waterbed: The problem, like the water, just pops up somewhere else.

NEW TREND: CALL OF THE COUNTRY

The covers of magazines sport lead stories detailing this trend. Major newspapers carry articles. Americans are flinging open the doors and revolting against the big city mind-set. Tired of trendiness and materialism, they are rediscovering the joys of home life, basic values, and things that last. They abhor the megalopolises that stretch from Boston to Washington, D.C., and from San Diego to Los Angeles.

They want to get out of corporate cultures that know them only as a number and ignore the dignity of the individual. They're tired of perpetual, meaningless memos, rigid dress codes, and endless meetings. They understand that when the work is done, real satisfaction is not in what you end up with, but in how much of yourself you've left behind. These Renaissance souls are founding a silent revolution.

What spawns this trend? The confluence of new technological, social, and economic forces. Information management is emerging as the engine of our economy, fueling job creation and making possible exciting new choices. Affordable high-tech equipment has released people from traditional ways of working. Many now run technologically sophisticated and highly profitable rural businesses. Others, while still employed by Fortune 1,000 companies, telecommute from their homes—going into the office perhaps once a week. Naisbitt and Aburdene say, "Technology has evolved to a point that workers are no longer location bound. This will contribute to the decline of the cities. There'll be a new electronic heartland."

There's another way of looking at this migration, say Paul and Sarah Edwards, authors of *Working from Home* and *Making It on Your Own.* "People who make major moves are not motivated by what they don't like. They are searching for a better life." Circumstances such as a safer setting for raising their children, lower living costs, and environmentally safe surroundings attract these folks. The Edwards have found that many who ditch the city are couples in their 40s and 50s. They've had their fill of the fast lane and are ready to sell their California holdings, move to Montana, and start a business of their own. Those who own pricey real estate can sell their expensive urban residences and move where their property dollars stretch much further. (We'll explain how later.)

For the first time in 200 years, more people are moving to rural areas than urban. Recent data compiled by Dr. Kenneth M. Johnson, a demographer at Chicago's Loyola University, shows that more than 1.6 million people moved into rural areas and small towns during the first 5½ years of this decade. According to the U.S. Census Bureau, small towns are growing three times faster in the 1990s than they did in the 1980s. Social experts expect the trend to escalate. People crave roots: a place to feel at home, a sense of security and community. They are abandoning cities for quality of life and trading the boardroom for the backyard.

This migration is not proceeding unnoticed. Foote, Cone & Belding, a large national advertising agency, placed undercover researchers in a Midwest community of 12,000 people. The mission of this unusual social laboratory? To learn what makes the townspeople tick. The information they gleaned is being used to develop future consumer ad campaigns for their clients.

This movement is pervasive, according to sociologist Stephen Warner of the University of Illinois at Chicago. "This is not something simply happening to the burnouts from Wall Street. There is an American phenomenon going on that crosses all social lines." Displaced and disenchanted Americans have fallen out of love with their lifestyles.

We're in the early throes of a migratory flux. People are trading demanding careers for more rewarding lifestyles. Executive dropouts are deciding their kids went to bed one too many times before dad or mom got home.

People are leaving the executive suite to become fishing guides, schoolteachers, shopkeepers, or to run bed-and-breakfast inns. Most of us are eager to leave behind smog, noise pollution, congestion, crack houses, youth gangs, terrorism, school busing, street people, corporate politics, and endless gridlock.

DEFINING THIS RURAL RENAISSANCE

When we talk of a rural Renaissance, we don't mean agriculture. Sadly, many of our nation's small farms have been gobbled up in foreclosure sales. Farmers and ranchers trying to hang onto homesteads that have been in their families for generations experience ever-growing frustration.

The rural Renaissance to which we refer is the out-migration from urban centers and crowded suburbs. In the 13th century, cities were vibrant but sparsely populated. They served primarily as trading headquarters and cultural centers. Most of the work was done elsewhere. We may see this pattern occur again before the year 2000. In their book, *American Renaissance: Our Life at the Turn of the 21st Century*, Marvin Cetron and Owen Davis predict that 88 percent of the labor force will be employed in the information industry. Twenty-two percent of these people will be working at home. Estimates put these numbers at more than 24 million. This opens enormous new options.

Here's a breakdown to define sizes of places this book addresses:

Medium cities	50,001 to 100,000 population
Small cities	25,001 to 50,000 population
Big towns	5,001 to 25,000 population
Small towns	5,000 or fewer people
Rural locales	Hamlets, farms, ranches, remote retreats located 60+ miles from a metropolitan hub

HOW TO SQUEEZE THE MOST FROM THIS RESOURCE

This hands-on guide is loaded with practical advice to help you cope triumphantly with change. In it we challenge you to ask, and answer, the hard questions. And we encourage you to take a *realistic* look at your skills, capabilities, expectations, and values. In addition to our experiences, we've interviewed dozens of Countrypreneurs to develop a sourcebook of practical information and friendly advice. The subject is explored in depth—warts and all. You'll find a wealth of specific resources here contained in no other book on the subject

Part One explores personal considerations: cashing in on your urban equity and picking the ideal location. You'll discover how to understand small-town attitudes, cultivate a social life, and become involved in your new community.

Part Two deals with rural business aspects. You'll learn how to turn avocational interests into vocational pursuits, create a new career focus, or purchase an existing establishment in a small town. Business start-up considerations are addressed, as are tactics for successful ongoing operation. Scores of proven profit-making ideas are offered. And for those job-hunting in Small Town USA, Chapter 18 tells you all about "Finding a Rural Job: Gutsy Strategies Mother Never Told You."

Part Three encompasses a resource section worth its weight in bullion. It's full of useful governmental and private sector sources. This unique collection overflows with data to help you make informed decisions, have a more pleasant experience, and live a more fulfilled life. You'll also find a list of hard-to-locate books we've tracked down for you.

This is a compendium of hundreds of facts found nowhere else. We've tried to eliminate the frustration of locating all this information yourself. Far from the typical "how-to" book, it's more like a cross between a friendly chat of homespun wisdom and a unique reference book.

Here you'll discover checklists, exercises, surveys, maps, quizzes, examples, and case histories to help you determine if you want to swap yesterday's boondocks for today's "boomdocks." We also include references to many Web sites on the Internet to boost the efficiency of your quest—and we show you how to use cyberspace to boost your bottom line as well.

The ideal approach is to read *Country Bound!* from start to finish. That will give you a complete overview, plus creative options you probably never thought of. Next, go back and review those chapters that pertain specifically to you. Really apply what's here; you can't make scrambled eggs without breaking the yolks. *Use* the various checklists and research aids provided. Get started. Get thinking. Get involved. You just may be embarking on the most exciting, rewarding adventure of your life!

2

---◆---

Contemplating the Great Adventure

Americans are searching. We're looking for answers. Our senses are assaulted, our energy invaded, our peace of mind threatened. The culprit? Big City Stress. (You know you're pushing too hard when you drop your bank deposit in the mailbox instead of the bank's deposit slot.) If you feel unsettled, exploited, stifled—journey with us in exploring a new option. It may not be the right path for you. On the other hand, it may offer a pilgrimage to freedom. Freedom is, after all, a matter of choice.

EXPLORING THE PLEASURES AND PITFALLS OF RURAL LIFE

Should you choose to live out in the country, in a small town, or in a smaller city where the pace is slower and the costs are lower? Or will this make you feel like a salmon constantly hurling herself against the current? Let's evaluate the tradeoffs and examine what you really want from life. This chapter will titillate any desire you have to move to a more bucolic environment. We'll investigate the pros and cons of living and working in the "boonies." Keep an open mind. What you initially perceive as a limitation may actually be an advantage. This will help you get clear about your intentions, to focus on what you want from life.

What's causing this new migration? Why are people in their prime turning their backs on bright lights, big cities, and hefty salaries? While the reasons are diverse, they center on certain issues. Values are becoming more important than things. We're starting to demand quality time with our children and emotional relief for ourselves. "The search for community, safety, and meaning will preoccupy boomers in the 1990s," predicts David Meer, a senior vice president at Daniel Yankelovich Group, Inc., a market research firm.

After the extravagance of the 1980s, baby boomers have discovered that time with family is priceless. They're finding the long hours at work required to maintain the standard of living they thought was necessary just aren't worth it. As these people reach middle age, their children are growing up. Precious moments are being lost. According to a Gallup Poll, 43 percent of women ages 26 to 45 will reduce their job commitments in the next five years, and 23 percent expect to quit altogether. As for the men, 33 percent also want to reduce time spent at work and 64 percent want to take more long weekends.

ADVANTAGES OF THE RURAL LIFE

Rediscovering Our Roots

Rootlessness is one of the most pervasive and least publicized problems of modern life. Today many people feel lost, cut off, powerless. In the old days, generations lived together or families stayed near each other. They had a tightly woven psychological and emotional safety net. Now we've become a restless, migratory society. Twenty percent of us move every year. Yet many of us crave a place to call home and a community to feel a part of.

While pining for one place and living in another is a typical American state of mind, today's urbanites are missing something. We don't have the sense of community and permanence our ancestors had. Qualities once taken for granted—trust and honesty, regional and ethnic heritage, clean air and friendly neighbors—are special treasures. As the news highlights the emerging global economy, many of us simply hunger for a supportive local network. We need to feel *connected*.

Community is the *soul* of a place. It grows out of discovering and nurturing the things you share with your neighbors. It doesn't happen overnight. Most good things don't. It's often an accumulation of little, almost insignificant details—learning the history and ambiance of a town, knowing who to go to when you need something, joining a group that works for civic betterment.

In rural areas you can become personally involved in the government, get acquainted with local and regional legislators, and take an active role in area affairs. Roots require commitment, nurturing, and a willingness to give of yourself. The personal pride small-town residents have in their communities is apparent when the downtown area blooms with flower boxes overflowing with colorful blossoms, and inviting redwood benches welcome shoppers to rest a spell.

Big is not always better. Some of us are loneliest in the busiest of places. We cling to talk radio, seeking human interaction with complete strangers. What a poor substitute when we could put down roots and cultivate a true celebration of life!

After we were settled in First Try, a prospective client hunted us down without remembering our names or the title of the book he had read (our *Complete Guide to Self-Publishing*), which introduced him to us. How did he do it? Luckily, he remembered the town where we lived. So he traveled to our little village, went to the post office, and inquired as to whether the postmaster knew anyone who did this sort of work. The postmaster did and even drew the man a map.

In 1981, Peter Moyer and his wife made a life-changing decision. They completely restructured their priorities and opted to live in a place that was smaller, simpler, and less expensive. That's not surprising, until you realize Moyer was an attorney with the venerable Wall Street law firm of David, Polk & Wardwell. Not only that, had he stayed he would be earning $1.2 million a year and would have achieved partner status. Is he sorry he pulled the plug on such a promising career? Absolutely not. Moyer figures that money "would probably be spent on alimony, taxes, and private schools."

Today he, his wife, and their three children live in Jackson, Wyoming, a trendy town of about 6,000 people. Despite a drastic drop in earnings and an initial verbal thrashing from the local judge, he soon had enough clients to hang out his own shingle. All kinds of entities now turn to him for legal counsel: banks, the local hospital, corporations, even some big resorts in the valley.

Feeling Safe and Secure

We would all agree that our personal safety, and that of our families, is a paramount concern. Gang wars and drive-by shootings are foreign concepts in Small Town USA. You don't find skinheads, crack houses, or high rape and homicide rates in Muskogee. In our village, the law enforcement officers' biggest challenge is teenage mischief and occasional vandalism or petty theft. Yet *Public Opinion* magazine recently reported that 59 percent of U.S. citizens feel it's risky to go for a walk in their own neighborhoods after dark.

Are vicious felonies an overriding concern for you? Then listen up. According to figures from the Department of Justice, those wishing to avoid violent crimes should stick to the upper Midwest and shun coastal cities. The top five safest areas they've identified include Grand Forks and Bismarck, North Dakota; Eau Claire, Wisconsin; Parkersburg-Marietta, West Virginia; and Saint Cloud, Minnesota. We'd bet most small towns fit in the elite group. The violence hot spots are New York City; Miami–Hialeah; Los Angeles–Long Beach; Jacksonville, Florida; and Flint, Michigan.

James Kennedy escaped all that. He publishes two highly respected newsletters for consultants and executive recruiters. You'd think such canny advice would emanate from New York City, Los Angeles, Chicago, or maybe Boston. Rather it comes out of tiny Fitzwilliam, New Hampshire (population 1,795). The Kennedy family moved to their New England vacation home full time because they "liked the country and conservative values. . . . It was the height of drug times in suburbia," Kennedy explains.

Today, he sounds like a man in heaven. This Lone Eagle and his wife live in a red colonial house across from his office, which overlooks a panorama of woods and hills. Classical music wafts on the breeze. Upstairs is a whirlpool bath, downstairs a fully appointed kitchen. The $1.5 million he rakes in annually from his newsletters and directory publishing allows him to indulge in his fancy of traveling. Recent jaunts included Brazil, Switzerland, Canada, Austria, Germany, and Italy. Not bad for a country boy!

Enjoying True Quality of Life

Quality of life is a catch-all phrase that has different connotations for different people.

The current reawakening of environmental concerns is drawing many out of metropolitan hibernation. They are tired of polluted air, tainted water, dangerous landfills, littered streets, and blaring ghetto blasters. They want natural, quiet, unsullied surroundings—to walk a gentle path. To reach that goal, many are heading for a rural setting.

Along with those who want to heal the environment by consuming fewer natural resources are people highly motivated to live long, healthy lives. There is a proven link between country living and greater longevity. "Living in a large city shortens life expectancy," states Norman Shealy, MD, PhD, founder and director of the Shealy Institute for Comprehensive Care and Pain Management in Springfield, Missouri. Cancer incidence is *6 percent higher* in urban areas such as Los Angeles and Houston, where petroleum refineries emit carcinogens into the atmosphere, says the *Atlas of Cancer Mortality*.

The three places in America with the cleanest, driest air are Sedona, Arizona; Boulder City, Nevada; and Greeley, Colorado. And the healthiest states? According to Northwest National Life Insurance Company, they are predominantly rural: Utah, North Dakota, Idaho, Vermont, Nebraska, Colorado, Wyoming, and Montana.

Healthy bodies also need healthy minds and spirits. Those of a rural persuasion enjoy a serenity seldom found in the city. When you get away from the metropolis, you get to quietude. While it may not be hundreds of miles in distance, this quest for peace is a galaxy apart in emotional terms.

In the country you can find a quiet spot away from the shrill disorder of modern ambition and the urgency of ongoing power struggles. Solitude is the well into which you dip for refreshment of the soul, a laboratory in which you distill the pure essence from the raw materials of your experiences.

Well, perhaps your refuge isn't totally quiet. Crows may caw their opinions or woodpeckers tap out their messages. Quaking aspen trees may whisper a secret known only to them and God, as a gurgling creek reveals its confidences to those who listen. If you're exceptionally lucky, you may hear the mating bugle of a bull elk. This is the silence of nature, awash with the sound of living things. To be alone, yet part of it, is awesome.

Along with quietude comes a simpler lifestyle. Wearing apparel is more functional, less glitzy. Escargot and oysters on the half shell give way to meat loaf and mashed potatoes. Pickup trucks outnumber sports cars. Entertainment centers on people rather than places. Spiritual ties are stronger and the church often plays a social as well as a religious role. Parades, band concerts, and school events replace ballet, opera, and gallery openings.

That's not to say you must give up the social amenities of a big city. Seldom will you locate more than a couple of hours from a major metropolitan hub. We're two-and-a-half hours from Denver. We frequently go in for the weekend, sometimes catching a play Saturday night, then meeting friends for a gourmet Sunday brunch. Museums, art galleries, and festivals are never more than a short trip away. Before you start feeling deprived, be truthful with yourself: Just how many cultural events do you attend now?

In many country environments, the most beautiful works of art are right outside your door. Mother Nature puts on a touching and constantly changing show. Take a good look at yourself and your family. What's your bliss?

Let's try a little experiment. Think about activities you particularly relish. Are you an avid golfer? Do you get absorbed in the *New York Times* crossword puzzle? Do "moonlight madness" sales at the mall get your heart pumping? Or would you prefer an easy chair, a fireplace, and a good book? What are the specific joys in your life? Do they lie in the realm of "city happenings" or can they just as easily be enjoyed in the country? As the days go by, keep a running agenda and see which column fills up faster. What must you have to feel complete and what is a rural counterpart? Don't try to evaluate these pros and cons in a day; take time to step back and ponder.

One alternative is to locate in a college town where a vibrant cultural climate exists. Here you can see plays and attend film festivals, hear guest lecturers or chamber music concerts, and spectate at collegiate sporting events. A college brings a continuous supply of new blood and intellectual stimulation to its locale. (Additionally, the students it attracts provide an eager workforce.)

Of course, with today's technology you can stay informed, entertained, and educated as long as you have a satellite receiving dish. Old movies, operas, and sporting events abound. Plus PBS and some of the other channels offer a potpourri of fun and learning. Today, a Digital Transmission Satellite (DTS) the size of a pizza will bring the world to your doorstep. And there's always the VCR.

Even in tiny towns entertainment thrives. Here in Buena Vista, we have an eclectic and artsy mix of people. Our little theater group, the Pick and Shovel Players, puts on a melodrama and olio each summer. It's a wonderful evening of boos, aaahs, and laughs. And what makes it especially fun is you know most of the cast. The woman who wrote the play selected one year is a friend. So we got to share her opening night glory.

Furthermore, your social diversions may change drastically! Being a couch potato could give way to hikes, bird-watching, photography, hunting, snowmobiling, skiing, fishing, picnics, or white-water rafting.

And these are just some of the natural attractions awaiting rural recruits.

Another advantage of a small town is *living* the country life instead of merely emulating it. The "country look" is now a chic way to decorate and dress. Country cooking is in. Perhaps this is part of the move back to a more basic, sensual, tactile existence. What many of us want is to go back to dinner at Grandma's. There's is nothing like a functional wood fireplace on chilly winter evenings and the goodness of a "from-scratch" cake just plucked from the oven.

Rural rhythms are definitely slower. Time is *not* of the essence. While a more laid-back lifestyle is one of the attributes that draws people to the country, old habits die hard. Appointments and time constraints govern rural folks less than their urban counterparts; this may take some adjustment on your part.

Quality of life dramatically affects those of us with children. We want to raise them in a more wholesome atmosphere. We want them to grow up valuing themselves and others more than material possessions. In countrified settings, families are more likely to do inexpensive, family-oriented activities together, rather than hiring a baby-sitter while Mom and Dad go out with other couples. Parents are more involved with their kids.

The Loughlin family lives in a town of 17,000. Says Paulette, "Anytime my children do anything—win an award in school, score the most points in a basketball game—they're in the daily newspaper." That fosters pride and self-esteem. So does participation in such organizations as the 4-H club. Nothing outshines the smile of a kid whose heifer or lamb has just captured a blue ribbon at the county fair. Youngsters raised on farms and in small towns seem to have more self-reliance. They gain an education from *doing,* not just book learning. If you want to influence the quality of education personally, chances are you can—by getting elected to the school board, helping coach a sport, or doing informal tutoring.

Here's another plus for city-weary parents: no more playing chauffeur! In Small Town USA you don't have to carpool the youngsters halfway across town for lessons or sports. The kids can hop on their bikes (or horses) and take themselves.

A Natural Stress Buster

One of the biggest reasons for escaping the city is burnout. It takes enormous energy to live in a place like Los Angeles, Chicago, New

York, Detroit, or Houston. Unfortunately just *surviving* takes a lot of effort. Yet such energy is the lifeblood of the cosmopolitan connoisseur of urban living. The only outdoors Mr. and Mrs. True Sophisticate want to experience is what they pass through to get from their condo to a taxi.

For most of us, such a lifestyle translates into tension: too many people too close together and too much corporate politicking. We'd just as soon *not* cope with hailing a cab in Manhattan, navigating LA freeways, or flying out of O'Hare Airport. We'd rather see a country sunrise than a downtown high-rise.

That's what Christian and Lea Andrade finally decided. They traded engrossing jobs in San Francisco for a new life on San Juan Island off the northwest coast of Washington. They are now the proprietors of Olympic Lights, a bed-and-breakfast that overlooks the sea. "It was as though we were obsessed," recalls Christian. "Wound up." Another couple also left San Francisco to run the B&B with them. As a parting gift to his brother-in-law, the other husband gave him his prized collection of 150 neckties. "Take them," he urged. "I'll never use them again."

"Our guests bring us all the company and outside stimulation we need," remarks Lea. Not that they didn't like San Francisco. "But it was the pace, the pressure, that finally got to us," she says. "That and the freeways and fast-food chains and all the craziness about making as much money as possible."

Hours of commuting to and from work each day take a toll on our health. Raymond Novaco, PhD, of the University of California at Irvine has been studying the stressful effects of commuting on a group of Southern California drivers. Novaco has shown that traffic congestion is a threat to physical and psychological well-being. He has further confirmed that traffic induces antagonistic behavior. On the other hand, in a rural community you can often walk or bike to work. Instead of concentrating on avoiding wrecks and traffic jams, you can mentally prepare yourself for the day ahead. Furthermore, many people start cottage industries right in their own homes. We address this in depth in Chapter 12, "Home Suite Home: The Information Age Option."

In big cities, gridlock is creating wall-to-wall cars. In some metropolitan areas, rush hours no longer exist; traffic constantly clogs freeways. And this is not just happening in Los Angeles, Atlanta, and Dallas. One reporter quipped that the only way to change lanes on the Texas LBJ freeway is to "trade cars." Workers in San Francisco; Washington, D.C.; Portland, Oregon; and even Charlotte, North Carolina, suffer varying degrees of frustration and terror as they creep from the far reaches of suburbia. For them, being stuck in traffic has become a way of life, and a dangerous one at that.

"Due to congestion," reports *The Futurist* magazine, "the average travel speed on roads in Southern California is expected to drop to 15 mph by the year 2000." Author and futurist Alvin Toffler says, "Commuting is the single most anti-productive thing we do."

The worst rush-hour traffic is in Washington, D.C., according to just-released statistics compiled by the Road Information Program of the Transportation Construction Coalition. Seventy-six percent of major roadways are clogged there during rush hour. Other areas with incredibly congested freeways—listed worst first—include San Francisco–Oakland, New York, Los Angeles, Phoenix, Seattle, Houston, Chicago, San Bernadino–Riverside, and then Miami

Other work-bound urban dwellers must cope with this dilemma in a different way. They descend into the bowels of the city to grapple with thousands of other bodies crushed into a subway. What a way to begin and end each day. Wouldn't you rather have a more *stretch-ful* life than such a *stressful* one?

Slashing the Cost of Living

If you enjoy a six-figure income that you consider "barely making a living," you'd better stay put. In a nonurban environment, people typically earn less. Other factors, however, balance this lower income. People also spend less. The gap in real estate prices could span the Grand Canyon. In 1996, a typical four-bedroom family home in San Francisco cost $566,750; a comparable house in Mesa, Arizona, could be had for $130,725. And what you'd pay $641,625 for in Greenwich, Connecticut, you could buy for $133,250 in Dalton, Georgia. With today's interest rates and taxes, this alone changes earning requirements drastically.

If you're looking for a starter house or want to retire to something less spacious, the price drops dramatically. Bargains in the $30,000 to $40,000 range are not unusual in some small communities.

Other financial considerations include groceries, gasoline, and miscellaneous goods. Usually these cost a bit more in rural areas. That's because they are trucked into the more out-of-the-way locations, plus local merchants lack the volume buying power their big-city counterparts enjoy. Also look at state and local taxes, especially if you're going into business. The April 1996 *Trendsetter Barometer* indicated that "CEOs at small and mid-size firms say rising state and local taxes greatly influence where they locate their businesses." Some places have no taxes, while in Milwaukee, for instance, they're as high as a Halloween cat's back. Many areas offer inviting tax inducements for new businesses as well. (We'll talk more about that in Chapter 15.)

Your clothes budget will definitely shrink. There is little call for a fancy wardrobe, and clothes stay in style longer. The pressure to sport designer jeans, Gucci loafers, or Oscar de la Renta suits diminishes in direct proportion to a town's population. Unless you're a professional (and even then, perhaps not) you won't need a coat and tie—nor dress and heels—unless you're going to church, a funeral, or a special event. On the other hand, if you enjoy dressing fit to kill, do it—but prepare for some stares and whispers. What we do is save our more cosmopolitan attire for recreational trips into Denver and for business trips when we travel to lecture or consult with clients around the nation.

DECIPHERING THE DRAWBACKS

Are there disadvantages to less citified ways? You bet. Practiced though we are in the feint and parry of debate, we won't dance away from this issue. Some people who move away from the big cities feel as though they've been exiled to Siberia. Living—and making a living— in rural America isn't a magic talisman that banishes all cares. It can feel as uncomfortable as walking around in someone else's shoes. So study this guide carefully. Hindsight is a painful and exacting science.

Unless you originally hail from a small town, you'll suffer some culture shock. In the country, you can't go to the grocery store looking your worst without running into friends or neighbors. Nor can you check trashy novels out of the library without people being privy to your reading taste. And it's virtually impossible to carry on an undetected affair. On the other hand, you're unlikely to be stranded on the side of the road while stoic-faced passerbys look the other way and ignore your plight.

On a more practical level, transportation may be a problem. If you frequently travel by plane, you'll find some inconvenience in not having a major airport handy. When taking a commuter flight to connect with an airline servicing a metropolitan area, prepare yourself for skyway robbery. Many tiny towns don't have taxi or bus service, so those without a car could feel stranded. Of course, you may be within walking distance of where you need to go anyway.

When shopping, you won't always find what you want. Some things are like a slippery bar of soap: You can't get a handle on them. There are not as many retail stores, repair facilities, or personal services. This does subdue impulse buying, however, which can be a real plus if you're on a tight budget. In smaller towns you have to shop through the *mails* instead of the *malls*, tap into the Internet, or travel to bigger cities where shopping becomes an adventure instead of an ordeal. Many outlet malls are being built in rural areas, because manufacturers insist on distance from major shopping areas for competition reasons.

Some recreational facilities are scarce. If you are into a specific sport—racquetball, for instance—be sure your new locale has a court.

A sudden shift in their personal support system is difficult for many people at first. Letters and phone calls just aren't the same as a warm hug. While any move interrupts relations with friends and loved ones, changing from an urban to a rural environment can provide those you left behind with an occasional escape to "the good life." We had more company from San Diego the first year we moved to Colorado than we had the previous five years when San Diego was our hometown! Sure, change tends to cause discomfort; but should we stay miserable in an environment that no longer serves us personally just for the proximity to friends and relatives? (More about that later, plus how and where to meet new prospective friends.)

Another countrified drawback is that reaching sophisticated medical facilities usually requires extra driving. On the other hand, rural areas frequently have terrific volunteer systems. Because emergency rooms are not always close by, you'll often find well-trained local EMT crews ready to respond at a moment's notice.

For the person setting up a business, having an adequate labor pool is another major consideration. Some small towns don't have a lot of highly skilled potential employees. Computer specialists may also be hard to come by. We found this in the village of 500 where we lived before moving to Buena Vista. Many of the residents were either retired or on welfare. Others frequently worked seasonal jobs, then relied on unemployment the rest of the year. After generations of partaking at the public trough, they had little concept of a true work ethic. Consequently, we had to import employees from other cities to staff our small historic hotel and restaurant. This proved to be about as practical as a mud fence in a rainstorm. (We share more about this experience in a future chapter.)

Our attempt at total self-sufficiency also left much to be desired. While this book is not aimed primarily at people who want to be back-to-the-landers—those who generate their own power and pioneer in the purest sense—this certainly can be one facet of doing business in the boonies. We'll share those trials, tribulations, and elations shortly.

Oh, one other point. Small towns don't boast Marriotts, Hiltons, or Four Seasons hotels. Clean, relatively comfortable motels, yes. Maybe a Holiday Inn. If you require urbane conference facilities or need to impress clients or customers by putting them up in luxury accommodations, you'll need to be more creative—or settle for a mid-sized city. On the other hand, a cozy log cabin or historic bed-and-breakfast might be a refreshing change of pace for the travel-jaded—and certainly less expensive for you.

For those of you who feel the pleasures outweigh the pitfalls, or who remain undecided, let's move onto the next section. There, we'll explore in detail what it's like to trade concrete for country.

SHARPENING YOUR FOCUS ON WHAT'S INVOLVED

Small Town USA is stripped of glitz. It's a place where less is more—where life's frills are streamlined and values telescoped. A place where little joys abound: the smell of freshly cut hay, the majesty of a fiery sun setting over rolling hills, the nicker of a friendly horse. A place where things can still happen on a handshake.

Some say time will be to the first decade of the 21st century what money was to the 1980s, that leisure will replace the treadmill. Community will be the cultural backdrop of this decade, a balanced life the new currency. The previous money-making binge left us with spiritual hangovers. Many of us got drunk on greed one too many times. Now we want to return to God, country, and family.

Pinpointing Priorities

Take a hard look at your priorities. Getting clear on what you value is fundamental to deciding if country life is for you.

When psychologist Abraham Maslow developed his needs hierarchy, he put survival on the bottom, meaning that it was the most fundamental need of humans. Above that he listed needs that were important but less fundamental—security, then belonging. Above that is self-esteem. Most people reading this book are either entering—or comfortably established at—this level. Upon reflection, however, those who are comfortable may find their self-image tied to what they *own*. Some people feel it is paramount to live in the right part of town, belong to the right country club, drive the right car, tour Europe in the right way, and wear only the right designer clothes. And many are miserable, especially if they measure their personal worth by material possessions. Keeping up with the Joneses is a vicious trap. Superficial paraphernalia may appear glamorous, but it often makes a wasteland of the soul.

Earning the money to support such habits becomes another trap. Children grow up while their parents are at work 12 to 14 hours a day. Workaholics find peace and personal serenity unfamiliar turf, so entangled are they in earning a living.

On the other hand, those who approach self-esteem in a more healthy manner may be ready to step up to the top of the pyramid, to move onto self-actualization. If you are in this group, you're inclined to follow your bliss. You know what excites you, what it is that makes you feel vibrantly alive. Having this kind of handle on your individual needs gives you an immense advantage. It allows you to fulfill your life's purpose and express your full potential instead of teetering on the brink of overload.

Of course, fresh beginnings can have sad endings unless we refuse to bring along the corpse of yesterday's mistakes. We can move from one side of the globe to the other, find a new life partner, create another career, and be in the same rut. Why? Because we take ourselves with us. Unless we handle problems as we meet them, we'll likely find ourselves looking at the same scenario—simply played by a new cast of characters in a different setting.

The Small Town Viewpoint

Marilyn discovered there is a world of difference in *how things work* and *how folks treat one another* in the country. First off, in tiny towns and farm areas you get in the habit of waving at every vehicle that passes. Chances are you know the occupant, or at least their kin. And speaking of being cordial, don't be surprised if you're saying "hello" to the same person in the market, then the video store, and finally at the hairdresser's. This universe is much more finite.

People go out of their way to be helpful. We had a new employee who was moving from one mobile home to another. Though she had been in the area only a couple of months, men from her church turned out in a snowstorm to haul the heavy objects for her. Another employee had an emergency and couldn't reach her sister by phone. So a coworker drove to the adjacent town where the sister lives (a round-trip of more than 70 miles) to convey the message. Local grocers sometimes extend credit if they know you're in a bind. When tragedy strikes a family, residents rally immediately to raise funds through auctions, bake sales, collection jars at area merchants, etc. In small towns, such caring flourishes.

Barter is also big in the boonies. We had extra frozen homemade butter left over from when we were milking a cow. Our neighbor had a robust garden. Soon she was spreading our butter and we were crunching her veggies. And recently we created an advertising flyer and news release to announce a grand opening for a local merchant, in exchange for credit to purchase merchandise at her shop.

The country can also humble you. If you think individuals must have initials like PhD, MBA, MD, BA, or BS behind their names before they're worth much, you're in for a big surprise. Ranchers with barely a grade-school education have held us spellbound with their knowledge about animals, weather patterns, and the land. Rural life also offers a wonderful mixture of folk wisdom found nowhere else. Additionally, many country people can fix virtually anything with almost nothing. (What a priceless gift this resourceful, can-do attitude would be for city kids whose self-esteem is shattered!)

Rural people also are a lot more trusting. Roadside stands are sometimes left untended. Money boxes perch on the counters waiting for customers to pay for the produce or flowers they take. It's the honor system at work. People usually don't lock their cars and many leave their houses unlocked at night.

There is also a special sense of *coming home* we experience here in Colorado that never touched us in California. When returning from out of town, we find ourselves eagerly straining to catch that first glimpse of the majestic mountains and feel a peace encircle us as we head into our lovely little valley. Previously, we were too busy coping with the freeway traffic that held our lives hostage to even think of our natural surroundings.

Allowing Kids to Be Kids

Children of industry, sophistication, and science (the city) are often strangers to the world of other living things. Does this deny them their birthright? Urban life has a tendency to make kids conceited, self-centered, and exploitive. Many demand expensive techie toys, rebel against doing chores and being responsible, and insist on hanging out with friends who give their parents the creeps.

Country kids have a different lifestyle. Rather than staying glued to the television, they're more likely to be outdoors doing something adventuresome. They enjoy roaming in wide open spaces—discovering a fox's lair, a bird nest, or a beaver dam. A day's outing might include admiring the delicate work of a cobweb or finding a berry patch and overdosing on sweet, ripe raspberries. These youngsters create special hideouts, hike, swim, fish, or skate on a winter pond.

If they are truly rural, they'll learn to drive a tractor and pilot the family pickup far before the legal age. These kids don't need field trips and expensive summer camps to understand what life is all about. Nature is their friend and their teacher. They become worldly in a different way: hearing gunshots ringing from the woods during hunting season or observing an orphaned lamb raised on a bottle. Thus they take for granted a whole range of experiences from caring for livestock to killing an animal cleanly when it comes time for butchering. This gives them a sense of perspective; it reminds them of what matters and what doesn't. In most cases, it makes them stouthearted, resilient, compassionate adults with lots of self-reliance.

Metropolitan life, on the other hand, teaches kids to be streetwise: savvy in negative ways. Country kids have fewer limitations imposed on them—which, in a way, makes their world larger. They are less protected, less fussed over. Adults in sophisticated suburbia are more like security guards. In small towns, folks look out for each other's children.

Another bonus of country life for kids is the consistency of long-term friendships. Michelle Worthey, one of our past associates, grew up in a town of 5,000. She says one of her most treasured memories is of going to school with the same people from kindergarten through 12th grade. It gave her a sense of extended family and belonging. Now when she goes back to Texas for holidays and vacations, she returns full of stories of old friends, families, and new babies.

In a rural environment, you also have more control over your child's education. You can talk to the principal and teachers personally before your youngster ever enters school. And probably you already know several of those serving on the school board. Want to give them direct feedback? (Or run for that position yourself?) Go for it!

In higher grades, kids get very specialized in large metropolitan schools. Competition is fierce. If a youth goes out for football, the pressures are such that he won't have time for band. And he'd better be an outstanding athlete, or he'll spend most playing time warming the bench. Interests like drama, music, art, and athletics collide. If you do one, there's no time to accommodate another. Why must children suffer this stress and conflict at such an early age? Don't they deserve a lifestyle free of unnecessary anxiety and tension as much as we adults do?

In rural school systems, athletic teams and theatrical groups need every able-bodied student. Each person has a chance to contribute and shine. The environment for developing leadership in young people flourishes. Because fewer students are available to carry the load, each person can make a significant contribution to the whole. Students, by necessity, learn to wear many hats. In turn, we publicize and applaud these feats in local newspapers and service clubs.

Criteria for Making a Decision

Realism, backed by knowledge of self, is the key to happy relocation. Carefully evaluating what you want will allow you to glide from pressure to pleasure.

Kathy, who has close family ties to Atlanta, didn't want to be far removed from those she loved. So she got a map and drew a radius of 200 miles around the city core. This gave her freedom, yet placed reasonable boundaries. Kathy located a charming smaller town about 170 miles away and can get home easily for weekends.

Leonard, another rural transplant, was concerned he would feel mentally stifled in a small town. When he talked with a local merchant, he discovered that small-town social life and business life are interwoven. The merchant told him that customers, who have also become his friends, provide him with stimulating conversation, as well as a livelihood.

The Jamison family was worried about the overall cost of living. While they knew real estate prices were typically much lower in rural areas, they wondered about other items. According to the Bureau of Labor Statistics' 1994 Consumer Expenditures Survey, the average annual spending in rural areas is $28,724 versus $32,247 in the urban or metropolitan statistical areas.

What this says is that you definitely can live on less in the country. And even that may be an inflated figure. Say, for instance, you start raising your own food or create a home office and no longer have to pay for child care. Such actions dramatically slash what it takes to live.

How do you pinpoint your own fears and concerns? One of the best ways is by taking a personal inventory. Grab a large pad. Title your list "my personal inventory." Now write the numbers 1 through 15 down the left side of the paper. Think about the activities or pastimes you enjoy that you have done within the last year. (Only list those things you've actually *done*. While you may love sailing, if you live far from a body of water and haven't indulged during the past 12 months, it doesn't count.) Next, note how often you do each thing—once a week? Twice a quarter? Then assign a value to each item. It may be easiest to just rewrite your inventory in priority order. Save this sheet.

Now we're going to start your "joy list." Again number from 1 to 15. (Sailing might be the first entry on this one.) Here, you'll put down everything you love to do, whether or not you've had the time or opportunity recently to actually do it. Again, give each entry a value so you get a clear picture of your personal priorities.

Naturally you should do this in conjunction with your partner if you're in a committed relationship. Consider both parties' needs. School-aged children should also become a part of this planning process. From about eight years up, a child can create inventories and joy lists of his or her own.

Compare your two sheets, plus any feedback from your children. Are you living your bliss? Let's say you're an opera buff. If you only go once or twice a year, does it really make sense to stay in the city for that reason? Does that offset the rush-hour traffic jams? The crime? The turf battles at the office? If you're candid, you may discover what limited use you actually make of metropolitan facilities. This isn't a graded test, so only you can discern what your priorities are. But it's worth taking a look and making some evaluations.

Let's do another exercise. Pretend you're trying to negotiate a beautiful stream in a canoe, but several large boulders are in your way. Do a rough sketch of water and scatter four or five large rocks in the way. These represent the things that scare you about moving to the country. Think about your apprehensions. Now name the boulders. One might be "leaving my family," another could be "boredom." You might label other rocks "fear of change" or "missing my friends." If you need more boulders, add them.

Now get a fresh piece of paper and draw another stream. Add the boulders. This time we want you to label the rocks with the things that bug you about the city. Your stream may be strewn with such comments as "crime," "drugs," "traffic congestion," "street people," "noise," "unfriendly people," "my boss," "this neighborhood," "smog," etc. Add more boulders as needed. Compare your two streams. Interesting, eh?

Using this method to clarify our reservations and concerns helps us face our fears. Then we can deal with them effectively. We can look for healthy ways to cope, recognize there is little holding us back, or decide the risk is too great and we want to stay where we are.

Another way to tune into what you really want out of life is to pay attention to your daydreams. Not necessarily aimless mind wanderings, daydreams are small windows that allow us to get fleeting glimpses of our inner selves. They can help us plan for the future.

Thinking Through Your Work Alternatives

With our longer life span, people are more likely to have more multiple careers than ever before. During the last half of the 1990s, this country's 70 million baby boomers are beginning to enter mid-life—a time when, according to popular mythology, many people make the break and go for a career change. The entire second part of this book is devoted to business aspects of moving to Small Town USA and evaluating options, but let's touch briefly on this topic now. (If you're retired and have no interest in working, simply skip to the next heading.)

Do you seek a job, a career, to have your own business, to homestead, or to become a farmer or rancher? Each of these groups has its place in Small Town USA.

Those who just want a job are looking strictly at the bucks. They are more concerned with the wage than with performing mentally stimulating tasks or anticipating long-term advancement. Temporary, part-time, or seasonal work often falls in this category. We have a friend who just retired. To flesh out his meager monthly income from Social Security and a little business he just sold, he drives a potato truck for two months during the summer.

Career seekers, on the other hand, want to affiliate with a company that offers growth and personal fulfillment. They are much more selective. And if they bring well-honed skills and strong managerial ability, they are likely to be welcomed in the country. Life in a big business, however, doesn't prepare you for life in a small one. Part of our later mission is to help you see why not—and to help you correct for that.

More and more career people will remain with their companies, yet operate from countrified settings. Telecommuting is the wave of the future. In seconds, personal computers can link us with headquarters offices anywhere on the globe. All that's required to merge office and home is a PC, printer, modem, fax machine, and phone lines. The home office will soar to new zeniths as workers operate from their houses, clad in comfy running suits and gazing out at restful, pastoral country scenes. We devote Chapter 13 to the topic of telecommuting.

Entrepreneurial types who want to call their own shots—either by purchasing an existing business or creating one of their own—are prime candidates for out-migration. *Country Bound* is primarily intended for those who want to do their own thing. Twenty percent of all discharged managers today start their own businesses. (That figure is almost triple the number ten years ago.)

This is possible now in ways that didn't exist a decade ago. Many of the new opportunities hinge on the electronic marketplace. Computers and fiber optics, faxes and phone lines—these are the currencies as we move into the new century. Professionals operate at a distance from their clients. Businesses learn new ways to court prospects and service their customers. A new group of entrepreneurs and freelance professionals, called Lone Eagles, run their knowledge-based businesses from pristine remote locations.

Telephones will take on new business roles as 900 numbers become more responsive. For a fee, these numbers will put consumers in touch with everyone from an expert who can coach them through fixing an overflowing washing machine to a therapist who offers instant family counseling.

LOOKING AT HOMESTEADING

Homesteading, farming, and ranching can be a wonderfully rewarding lifestyle—or it can drive you bananas! It takes courage to unplug from the system. It also takes a huge measure of hard work. Frontier fantasy sounds romantic. In reality, there is little romance when you collapse into bed dead-tired after 14 to 18 hours of physical labor.

Farm routine is unlike office and factory work. As you do the daily chores, there are no ringing telephones or clattering machines. Usually you're alone. You'll actually have time to think, to ponder, to speculate! Yet there is an unending parade of things that need fixing: the water pump, the generator, the tractor, the fence, etc. It's also different in another way: if you have animals, many require care every day, 365 days a year. Cows can't wait to be milked.

On the plus side, there's nothing like plucking your own veggies from the garden for the noon meal, or making peach pies with your own fruit. Then there's the pride you feel when you open your root cellar and show off scores of canning jars filled with the bounty you grew. Many would say, "This is the country God has made. Rejoice and be glad in it."

But let us also take a practical look at farming. Why do you want to do it?

- Does it represent some form of escape for you?
- Do you see it as an investment?
- Are you doing it because your parents or grandparents did it and you're following family tradition?
- Does the lifestyle appeal to you?
- Do issues like your family's health and welfare play an important role?
- Do you feel you are "called" to do this work?
- Are you going into farming because you feel forced to?
- Are you going into farming because you should be able to survive if you grow all your own food?

Once you've thought through your motivation, you can begin to analyze just how logical moving to a rural area really would be.

Don't set out to buy a farm or ranch until you know what you're getting into. Will you grow corn? Raise poultry? Grow truck farm vegetables, herbs, or exotic fruit? Have an orchard? Raise horses, beef, or hogs? Breed earthworms, sheep, llamas, or catfish? Actually, it's a good idea to combine two or more of these. Mixed crop and livestock operations spread the risk, and they benefit from interrelationships.

Have you researched thoroughly to learn about your chosen animals or crops? Do you know how long it will take to get a cash crop? Is there a market handy for your product? Can it be shipped or sold through mail order? Have you talked to other growers? Also consider whether you have experience at farming or are educated—either through schooling or by being self-taught—in farm matters. If not, get informed or team up with someone who is—before taking the plunge!

No matter which way you go, it takes guts to leave your ruts. But the rewards can be delicious. With this in mind, let's proceed by using seven standards to measure your "move quotient."

3

◆

Seven Criteria to Use in Measuring Your Move

What walks in four directions at the same time and speaks Spanish while chanting in Latin? You guessed it: statistics. They say everything and nothing. Statistics can be extremely misleading indicators. Statewide averages, for instance, hide local realities. Nonetheless, having various facts at your disposal is useful. Just realize they must be weighed with caution when applied to your individual needs. And what precisely are your needs?

Measuring quality of life is an inexact science, to say the least. What is significant to one person may be trivial to another. Characteristics refuse to line up neatly like a can of Pringles potato chips. Don't let all this overwhelm you—if it does, skip it and come back later. It's all downhill from here.

In this chapter we will examine seven yardsticks for measuring an area's quality of life. They include: cost of living, crime, weather (climate), health care, environment (pollution), leisure (culture, arts, recreation, attitude, and entertainment), and infrastructure (education and transportation). To aid you in this appraisal, several tables and maps are included: everything from the location of nuclear power plants to hate-group strongholds, earthquake fault areas to hurricane-prone locations. With these, we hope you'll get the whole story. Thoroughness is an important trait, as the following story proves:

If you've ever lived on a ranch or farm, you may remember that when a horse is infested with larvae of the botfly—"has bots," as they say—you have a serious problem. Several years ago, a farmer in west Texas came to his neighbor's house and asked him, "Joe, didn't you have a horse come down sick with the bots one time?"

"Yep," replied Joe.

"Well, what did you do for it?"

"Fed him turpentine," came the answer.

"Hmm, thanks," the farmer said and went back home shaking his head in wonder.

A few weeks later the farmer returned and asked, "Joe, what did you say you gave your horse for the bots?"

"Turpentine," Joe replied.

"Hmm," said the farmer. "That's what I thought you said. Well, by golly, I fed mine some turpentine—and it killed him!"

"Yep," Joe said dryly, "killed mine, too."

We hope the following information gives you the *whole story*, and that these seven gauges supply remedies for your urban blues.

DECIPHERING THE COST OF LIVING

Most of us are trying to do more with less and slipping a little further behind each year. Economists come up with elaborate formulas and detailed explanations for what things cost in different locales. There is no question that it's cheaper overall to live away from metropolitan centers. How much cheaper, and in what ways, we'll examine here.

Analyzing Expenses

In a recent study, Runzheimer International (800-558-1702), a relocation consulting firm, analyzed a family's expenses in four areas. Their typical family had a couple and two children, an annual income of $62,000, and a four-bedroom house. The segments analyzed encompassed housing (including the mortgage, insurance, utilities, maintenance, and real estate tax); transportation (maintenance and insurance for two relatively late-model vehicles); goods and services (which includes food, clothing, medical care, and recreational expenses); and miscellaneous (such things as savings and life insurance).

They found huge disparities. In Los Angeles, for instance, it costs $70,296 to buy what $55,500 buys in Small Town USA!

If you want to do serious comparisons, hire a cost-of-living consultant for current information and guidance. While these companies usually serve large corporations in analyzing proposed relocations, some also will work with individuals. Economic Research Institute was especially gracious in talking with us. They provide comparisons for more than 4,000 destinations and charge a $150 fee for a one-page comparison (see the "Relocation Assessment"). Reach them at 800-627-3697.

Right Choice, Inc. does comparative analysis and specializes in working with individuals. They include commuting costs and even day care expenses in their customized proposals for site evaluations. The one-time fee is $190. Reach them at 800-872-2294. For computer-literate people, they also sell a software program called ReloSmart that contains data for hundreds of cities and towns. It calculates the financial impact of moving, based on your own financial information, and is available for either DOS or Macintosh platforms for $79.95.

If you're online, a great site to visit is the Economic Research Institute. Here you can find free and quick estimates of both cost of living and competitive salaries. Although you can pay them for detailed data, initial analysis is available at no cost. We discovered, for instance, that Dakota City, Nebraska, has a cost of living 85.6 percent of the U.S. national norm. Log onto http://www.erieri.com/~eri and do your own comparisons.

Another source of information is the U.S. Chamber of Commerce. Every quarter, they survey costs of housing, food, services, transportation, and health care at approximately 300 sites around the country. For $120 you can order an annual subscription to their newsletter, or subscribe to the last quarter for $60. If you belong to a local chamber of commerce that participates in this program, they may have a copy on file; some libraries also subscribe. Reach them at 703-998-0072.

Housing Costs

Curious about what your house would cost elsewhere? You can hire an appraiser to check in the *Residential Cost Handbook* by Marshall and Swift. Using multipliers, the appraiser can compute values in some 500 locations around the nation. Generally, the most affordable homes are in the Midwest and the South. According to the National Association of REALTORS®, the median home price of a single-family resale house in the Midwest was $102,000 in the summer of 1996. Of course your home isn't the only consideration.

Relocation Assessment			
Original Data:			
Annual earnings	$62,000	$62,000	
Number of autos: Used Auto values	2 $23,000	2 $23,000	
Square feet, three- bedroom house Family size	1,800 4	1,800 4	
Areas Compared	Denver, Colorado	Trinidad, Colorado	Difference Denver– Trinidad
Consumables: Other	$15,662	$16,188	($ 526)
Housing: Utilities/ Property Taxes/Other	$20,892	$ 9,413	$11,479
Health Services	$ 1,704	$ 1,722	($ 18)
Income + Payroll Taxes	$15,452	$17,579	($2,127)
Transportation: Public/ Automobiles/Other	$ 4,978	$ 4,781	$ 197
Miscellaneous	$ 3,312	$ 3,312	0
Total Cost of Living	$62,000	$52,995	$ 9,005
Compared to U.S. national average	109.2%	93.3%	15.9%

Source: *ERI Economic Research Institute, 16770 N.E. 79th Street, Suite 104, Redmond, WA 98052, 206-556-0205, Fax: 206-885-5091; http://www.erieri.com/eri; e-mail: eri_redmond@ msn.com. (1996 data.)*

Information based on a family of four owning their own home, with estimated earnings of $62,000.

Power and Other Expenses

Power bills vary considerably, especially if you're moving into an area that requires air-conditioning or is colder than you're used to. Electric bills may zoom. (Or a wood stove may cut them to almost nil.) Publicly owned electric power companies, those that are municipal, typically have much different rates than their privately owned cousins. For instance, to purchase 750 kilowatt hours of monthly service in Cowlitz, Washington, costs $160. With San Diego Gas & Electric, however, the same hours go for a whopping $1,144. Telephone bills are often higher in the country because they bill many calls as long distance.

Speaking of power, in the country you need to be prepared for outages that are more frequent and last longer than in the city. If you'll be using a computer in your business, it is wise to buy an uninterruptible power source with a lot of battery capacity.

There are other less obvious variables when moving to the boonies. While you're saving on commuting expenses, your gasoline mileage may plummet. Why? Because the terrain is uneven and the top speed might be 35 mph. Auto insurance, however, is typically much cheaper in rural areas. But fire insurance may be higher if you're served by a volunteer fire department with an engine headquartered several miles away. Groceries may also cost more. You pay 13 percent more for them in Medford, Oregon, for instance, than you do in Los Angeles. On the plus side, you'll spend less on clothing and entertainment. Much of what country people do for fun carries no price tag.

If you're retired military, locating near a base or post where your military ID card gives you exchange or commissary shopping privileges could be a major consideration. Ditto on health considerations. Being near a veterans' hospital can pay big dividends. Where you relocate can also dramatically affect college tuition and expenses. Moving to a college town where there is an appropriate institute of higher education may allow your son or daughter to live at home while attending classes.

Taxes as Taskmasters

Most people are about as fond of taxes as Federal Express is of fax machines. Taxes take a big bite out of everyone's income. According to the Tax Foundation, the average worker spends two hours and 48 minutes of every eight-hour work day earning enough money to pay all federal, state, county, and local taxes. Social Security taxes and federal personal income taxes are constants no matter where you live. Others, like gasoline taxes, differ immensely. For a comparison of taxes, see the following "1995 Homestead Property Taxes—Nonurban Areas" and "State and Local Taxes, Fees, and Assessments."

Retired people have other incentives. In Alaska, for instance, once you reach 65, you escape property taxes completely. And we understand that eight other states allow special exemptions or credits to older

1995 Homestead Property Taxes—Nonurban Areas

$70,000 Land and Building; $10,000 Fixtures

National Rank	State	Property Tax	National Rank	State	Property Tax
48	Alabama	$287.00	22	Montana	$1,022.00
23	Alaska	$912.00	11	Nebraska	$1,445.00
42	Arizona	$510.00	40	Nevada	$541.00
38	Arkansas	$570.00	45	New Hampshire	$1,727.00
34	California	$715.00	1	New Jersey	$1,944.00
36	Colorado	$612.00	5	New Mexico	$415.00
4	Connecticut	$1,728.00	2	New York	$1,906.00
15	Delaware	$1,340.00	32	North Carolina	$756.00
9	District of Columbia	$1,216.80	17	North Dakota	$1,079.00
16	Florida	$1,137.00	29	Ohio	$801.00
19	Georgia	$1,065.00	39	Oklahoma	$565.00
50	Hawaii	$83.00	21	Oregon	$1,051.00
37	Idaho	$602.00	8	Pennsylvania	$1,564.00
9	Illinois	$1,506.00	12	Rhode Island	$1,399.00
26	Indiana	$816.00	27	South Carolina	$813.00
13	Iowa	$1,377.00	3	South Dakota	$1,890.00
10	Kansas	$1,485.00	43	Tennessee	$501.00
35	Kentucky	$707.00	7	Texas	$1,651.00
49	Louisiana	$119.00	41	Utah	$512.00
33	Maine	$747.00	14	Vermont	$1,345.00
28	Maryland	$801.00	31	Virginia	$771.00
18	Massachusetts	$1,068.00	24	Washington	$876.00
20	Michigan	$1,053.00	46	West Virginia	$362.00
25	Minnesota	$840.00	6	Wisconsin	$1,675.00
47	Mississippi	$359.00	44	Wyoming	$452.00
30	Missouri	$798.00			

Source: The Minnesota Taxpayers Association's *50 State Property Tax Comparison Study: Payable Year 1995.*

State and Local Taxes, Fees, and Assessments*
per $1,000 Personal Income

State	Taxes per $1,000 Income	State Tax Burden Ranking	State	Taxes Per $1,000 Income	State Tax Burden Ranking
Alaska	$227.36	1	Oklahoma	$139.17	26
New York	$178.93	2	New Jersey	$139.12	27
Hawaii	$170.86	3	Kentucky	$136.99	28
Wyoming	$167.17	4	Georgia	$136.83	29
Minnesota	$163.24	5	North Carolina	$135.83	30
Wisconsin	$157.24	6	Indiana	$135.31	31
New Mexico	$156.18	7	Alabama	$133.99	32
Delaware	$154.67	8	Kansas	$133.76	33
North Dakota	$154.60	9	Pennsylvania	$132.22	34
Iowa	$153.65	10	Colorado	$132.01	35
Vermont	$153.42	11	Ohio	$131.51	36
Utah	$151.21	12	Massachusetts	$131.37	37
Oregon	$150.14	13	Florida	$130.97	38
Washington	$146.04	14	Arkansas	$130.82	39
Nebraska	$145.12	15	Texas	$130.72	40
Arizona	$145.09	16	Connecticut	$130.54	41
Michigan	$144.39	17	Rhode Island	$130.35	42
Louisiana	$143.97	18	Nevada	$130.24	43
Maine	$143.21	19	Virginia	$125.86	44
Idaho	$143.15	20	Illinois	$122.70	45
South Carolina	$142.80	21	Maryland	$121.98	46
California	$142.52	22	Tennessee	$119.77	47
Mississippi	$141.18	23	New Hampshire	$117.87	48
Montana	$140.63	24	South Dakota	$116.93	49
West Virginia	$139.71	25	Missouri	$111.76	50

*(The higher the number, the lower the taxes)
Source: Courtesy of the California Tax Payer's Association, based on U.S. Census Bureau information 1991–1992.

homeowners, no matter the size of their incomes. These include: Hawaii, Illinois, Kentucky, Mississippi, New Jersey, South Carolina, Texas, and West Virginia. Furthermore, 17 states permit the elderly to legally postpone paying some or all of their property taxes. Under these programs, the state puts a lien on the property. The money becomes due when the home is sold, given away, or when the owner dies.

If you anticipate incorporating in your new locale, also consider state annual fees and corporate income taxes. This is often less in states trying to attract new industry.

For additional information on the cost of living, plus greater detail on the next six criteria, we recommend you get a copy of *Places Rated Almanac* by Richard Boyer and David Savageau. Savageau's *Retirement Places Rated* may also be useful.

COPING WITH CRIME RISKS

For the first time in the history of humankind, it's safer to live in the wilderness than in civilization.

Violent crimes, which involve bodily injury or the threat of injury, are the most feared by everyone. They include murder, rape, robbery, and assault—and make up 10 percent of all crimes committed in the U.S. In some cities, your chance of being the target of one of these terrifying acts is more than one in 100. In Miami and New York City this escalates to one in 61! Grand Forks, North Dakota, on the other hand, is 30 times safer than New York City. *Public Opinion* magazine reports that 59 percent of the population feels it's risky to go for a walk in their own neighborhoods after dark. This fear inhibits our freedom as surely as does a barbed wire fence.

The Threat of Gangs, Hate Groups, and Terrorism

Street gangs and drive-by shootings have grown into a major menace, especially with the proliferation of crack cocaine. A University of Chicago study identified 1,439 gangs, of varying sizes and influence, that exist in 45 cities. They are no longer isolated in major crime-ridden cities. Youth gangs—with a tragic average member age of only 13½— are also proliferating in Seattle, Cleveland, Denver, Phoenix, Milwaukee, and even some smaller cities.

Another expanding threat is hate groups. Recruitment has swung into high gear and racially motivated crimes are on the rise. Membership in skinhead and neo-Nazi groups and the Ku Klux Klan is mushrooming in certain parts of the country (see "White Supremacist Groups in the Unites States—in 1991"). Experts see the flood of hate crimes rising in proportion to economic difficulties.

We never know where terrorism will strike next. The families of those killed in the Oklahoma City bombings will never be the same. The only comforting aspect is that terrorists want lots of visibility so they aren't likely to perpetuate their horror in very small, obscure towns.

Afraid for their safety, some Americans are becoming prisoners in their own homes. According to the *New England Journal of Medicine,* this is affecting their health. An increase in obesity, hypertension, and diabetes is the result of people missing needed exercise.

City size has a direct bearing on crime. So does a transient population and even a hot climate. Perhaps this is why the Miami-Hialeah, Florida, area leads even Los Angeles in violent crimes. Cops and crooks are busier in warmer parts of the nation. And areas where there is high immigrant relocation and racial strife are hotbeds of illegal activities.

Property Crimes

Property crime is defined as something directed against a person's possessions. It includes burglary, grand larceny, auto theft, and vandalism. Property crimes, while not life-threatening, are expensive and unsettling. When your home is broken into, your privacy is invaded and your sense of security is destroyed. Auto theft, traditionally considered a nonviolent act, has taken a vicious turn.

Carjacking has given new meaning to Detroit as the Motor City. Over a six-week period, nearly 300 Detroit drivers there were forced to abandon their cars at gunpoint. Instead of heisting *empty* vehicles, thieves are walking up to motorists at stoplights and shopping malls, demanding cars—and killing those who hesitate. While there is no set pattern, carjackers are also at work in Atlanta, San Francisco, Los Angeles, and Houston.

A recent TV special reported that some New York teenagers are better armed than the police force! The kids tote deadly 9-millimeter semiautomatics. Searches before school are becoming commonplace in big cities. But junior high school students in Indianapolis were shocked recently when they climbed off the school bus—and were confronted with security guards and metal detectors before being permitted to attend classes. A Centers for Disease Control study revealed that more

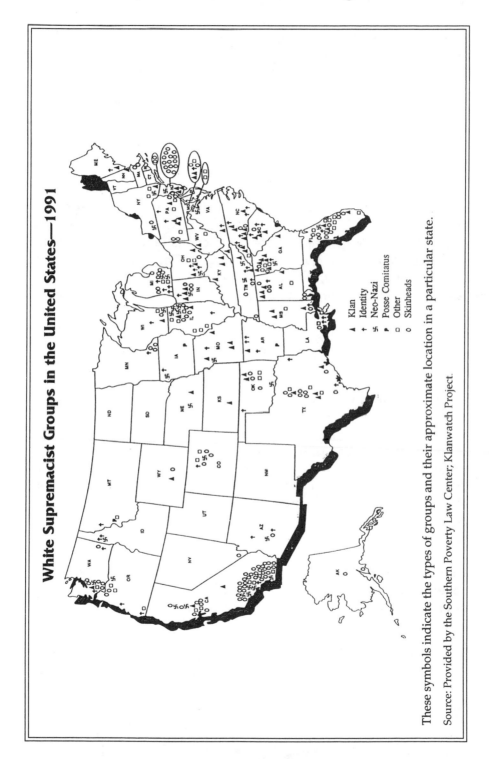

White Supremacist Groups in the United States—1991

Klan ▲
Identity †
Neo-Nazi 卐
Posse Comitatus P
Other □
Skinheads o

These symbols indicate the types of groups and their approximate location in a particular state.

Source: Provided by the Southern Poverty Law Center; Klanwatch Project.

than one in three high school boys admitted to carrying a gun, knife, or club within the prior 30 days.

There is no simple solution. But removing yourself and your family from potential everyday contact with the criminal element is one obvious remedy. Metropolitan areas average 28 percent more offenses than do small cities. Want to be safer? Go rural, young man, go rural. In small towns, people look out for each other.

Ferreting Out the Figures

The FBI publishes a detailed report that shows figures for law enforcement jurisdictions across the country. Approximately 16,000 jurisdictions are registered. Those jurisdictions reporting will include the number of months their data represents. This computer printout, called *Crime by County,* can be ordered for $40 from the FBI Criminal Justice Information Service Division, Attn: Communication Unit, D-3 1000 Custer Hollow Road, Clarksburg, WV 26306.

Suppose you're interested in locations within a particular state or want figures for such crimes as narcotic sales and possession, gambling, prostitution, commercial vice, fraud, or driving under the influence. The FBI publishes county and city arrest figures for these offenses in a report called *Crime in the United States.* You can call 202-324-3000 and ask for the press department. It costs around $25 and also can be found in most major libraries.

Another way to determine the scene of crime in towns you're considering as relocation sites is to check out the rate of reported criminal offenses. What's the total crime rate? How much of it is violent crime? How strong is the police presence in the community? Are they adequately staffed? Does the town provide enough financial commitment so the police force can do its job?

These statistics dramatize the extent of violent behavior in the United States. Fortunately, such occurrences are far less frequent in the country. So making good choices about where you live and watching out for your own personal safety become more and more important.

WENDING YOUR WAY AROUND THE WEATHER

Don't knock the weather. Many people couldn't start a conversation if it weren't for the weather. And, yes, sometimes it's so hot there's nothing left to do but take off your flesh and sit in your bones. Other times, it's so cold that when you open your closet, your spring coat is wearing your overcoat. If you suffer from either of these extremes, maybe it's time to consider making a move.

What Determines Climate

When speaking of weather, we use the word *climate* interchangeably. Climate is determined by five geographic factors: water, latitude, elevation, prevailing winds, and mountain ranges. Towns near large bodies of water tend to be cooler in the summer and warmer in the winter. The higher (more northerly) the latitude, the more severe the weather is likely to be. As to elevation, you can figure the temperature lowers by 3.3 degrees for each 1,000 feet of elevation. Thus, if you were considering moving to Arizona, there would be a substantial difference in temperature between small towns near Flagstaff and those in the vicinity of Tucson.

Prevailing winds in this country blow from west to east. Towns along the West Coast get the benefits of the Pacific winds. (For wind speeds, look under "meteorology" in the *World Almanac*.) Mountains also play a role in various climes. They serve as barriers to divert nasty weather or channel winds. The climate on one side of a mountain range can be quite different from that of the other side. To find your ideal climate, you probably will want to answer the questions in the "Weather Watch Questionnaire."

Most people, if they were considering only climate, would prefer to live in mild, sunny locations, especially as they age. Such locales are abundant on the Pacific Coast, along the South Atlantic, in Florida, and along the Gulf Coast Shore. But settling for such moderate climes also has disadvantages. Those who love the blaze of autumn color when the leaves change, and the miracle of a distinct spring, will miss experiencing the four seasons. And people who love winter sports will also feel cheated. Additionally, real estate is expensive in these highly desirable locations.

Weather Watch Questionnaire

How many days does it fall below freezing (32°F)?
How many days does it fall below 0°F?
How many days does it get over 90°F?
What is the average annual rainfall?
What is the average annual snowfall?
What is the average January temperature?
How about the average July temperature?
How long is the growing season?
How many days during the year does the sun shine?
What is the average summer humidity percentage?
What is the altitude?
What is the average mph of wind velocity?
Are there thunderstorms and lightning strikes? Earthquakes? Tornadoes?
Hurricanes? Cyclones? Floods? Droughts? Volcanoes that are not extinct?

Many folks opt for other parts of the country. For valuable indicators to help in your search for the ideal place, see "Climatic Data for Leading American Cities."

Hiding from Humidity

Do consider what the humidity will be like. When there's a lot of moisture in the air, you feel like you're in a steam bath. Humidity saps your energy and leaves you perpetually damp and sticky. Creature comfort is hard to come by in the summer in places like Galveston, Texas; New Orleans, Louisiana; or Biloxi, Mississippi. At the other extreme are Las Vegas, Nevada, and Phoenix, Arizona—two of the driest places in the United States. While dry climates are healthful for some people, they too can have aggravating side effects. Dry, flaky skin is almost guaranteed for new migrants. Some people also suffer from tickling sore throats and nosebleeds in areas with very low humidity.

Cantankerous Considerations

Listening to the old sultry song, "Stormy Weather," is fun. Experiencing storms isn't. Blizzards are familiar visitors in snowy regions and put a damper on anyone's spirits. The majority of severe storms happen in the southern half of the nation. Thunder and lightning can provide a majestic spectacle . . . as long as they keep their distance. In many places

Climatic Data for Leading American Cities

State and City	Average Temperature (°F)		Sunny Days per Year	Humidity (%)	Precipitation		Average Wind (mph)	Elevation (feet)
	Winter	Summer			Rain (inches)	Snow (inches)		
Alabama (Montgomery)	55.1	76.0	233	71.80	47.10	0	1.5	183
Alaska (Juneau)	25.8	49.1	100	77.20	53.70	150.2	8.2	114
Arizona (Phoenix)	60.5	96.4	289	33.50	10.87	0	7.3	1,117
Arkansas (Little Rock)	41.3	82.1	212	69.30	43.08	4.0	6.0	257
California (Los Angeles)	60.6	72.5	293	63.30	6.54	0	7.8	270
California (San Francisco)	52.7	59.6	211	76.00	20.79	trace	9.3	52
Colorado (Denver)	36.3	63.5	210	55.00	16.87	83.2	8.7	5,280
Connecticut (Hartford)	33.7	64.0	165	71.00	64.55	58.2	8.5	169
Delaware (Wilmington)	41.1	76.1	181	69.50	48.13	9.5	9.1	74
Florida (Tampa)	66.5	79.8	233	75.25	42.18	0	8.7	19
Florida (Miami)	72.1	79.7	252	76.25	63.11	0	8.3	7

Source: U.S. Department of Commerce, National Oceanic and Atmospheric Administration. Based on standard 30-year period.

Climatic Data for Leading American Cities (continued)

State and City	Average Temperature (°F) Winter	Average Temperature (°F) Summer	Sunny Days per Year	Humidity (%)	Precipitation Rain (inches)	Precipitation Snow (inches)	Average Wind (mph)	Elevation (feet)
Florida (Orlando)	67.9	80.7	231	72.00	51.35	0	8.5	108
Georgia (Atlanta)	50.2	71.5	206	70.80	50.61	trace	9.2	1,010
Hawaii (Honolulu)	72.9	79.6	244	68.80	26.90	0	13.2	7
Idaho (Boise)	34.5	62.3	216	57.50	11.43	21.4	9.1	2,838
Illinois (Springfield)	35.3	67.8	176	74.30	32.03	26.2	11.2	588
Indiana (Indianapolis)	36.4	66.9	159	72.30	40.27	18.1	9.7	792
Iowa (Des Moines)	29.1	62.3	176	73.50	36.02	36.7	10.4	938
Kansas (Topeka)	37.7	68.4	180	69.80	31.21	26.1	9.9	877
Kentucky (Louisville)	42.4	69.5	177	69.00	49.38	10.4	9.0	477
Louisiana (New Orleans)	59.7	77.5	234	78.80	63.98	0	8.5	4
Maine (Portland)	28.6	58.1	178	74.80	48.62	123.7	9.6	43
Maryland (Baltimore)	41.8	67.7	186	69.00	52.33	13.0	8.8	148

Climatic Data for Leading American Cities (continued)

| State and City | Average Temperature (°F) | | Sunny Days per Year | Humidity (%) | Precipitation | | | Average Wind (mph) | Elevation (feet) |
	Winter	Summer			Rain (inches)	Snow (inches)			
Massachusetts (Boston)	36.5	64.3	175	68.30	53.11	40.7	11.4	15
Michigan (Detroit)	25.6	63.8	188	66.50	29.96	30.6	10.6	619
Minnesota (Duluth)	15.2	53.9	165	74.00	39.61	110.2	9.8	1,428
Mississippi (Jackson)	55.0	77.4	226	76.00	50.03	trace	7.4	310
Missouri (Kansas City)	38.7	70.6	194	66.80	27.75	15.9	10.3	1,014
Montana (Helena)	27.1	55.1	169	57.00	8.22	40.0	8.3	3,828
Nebraska (Omaha)	32.6	66.3	185	71.80	35.56	27.1	9.8	977
Nevada (Reno)	37.0	60.8	245	48.30	5.52	trace	8.4	4,404
Nevada (Las Vegas)	52.4	80.1	297	28.80	4.85	0.4	9.5	2,162
New Hampshire (Concord)	27.7	58.8	167	77.00	42.07	100.3	7.2	342
New Jersey (Trenton)	40.2	66.8	193	70.60	47.13	17.2	6.4	56
New Mexico (Albuquerque)	44.0	69.4	271	42.30	10.11	6.4	9.7	5,311

Climatic Data for Leading American Cities (continued)

State and City	Average Temperature (°F) Winter	Summer	Sunny Days per Year	Humidity (%)	Precipitation Rain (inches)	Snow (inches)	Average Wind (mph)	Elevation (feet)
New York (New York)	39.9	67.8	232	67.80	67.03	22.9	8.8	132
North Carolina (Raleigh)	47.8	69.1	201	70.50	51.74	4.0	8.6	434
North Dakota (Bismark)	19.9	58.8	171	67.00	15.16	45.6	9.6	1,647
Ohio (Columbus)	36.4	63.4	151	69.80	45.60	27.1	9.7	812
Oklahoma (Oklahoma City)	45.2	74.0	226	65.50	27.63	14.6	12.8	1,285
Oregon (Portland)	44.4	63.6	156	61.00	38.82	6.5	8.1	21
Pennsylvania (Harrisburg)	38.8	66.8	191	68.00	59.27	33.4	7.5	338
Rhode Island (Providence)	35.8	63.4	179	71.00	65.06	30.4	10.5	51
South Carolina (Charleston)	56.2	74.7	226	75.50	42.86	0	9.2	40
South Dakota (Rapid City)	28.5	59.6	202	64.30	17.19	23.1	11.1	3,162
Tennessee (Nashville)	47.4	71.8	198	71.80	54.41	2.5	9.1	590
Texas (Austin)	57.9	79.0	221	67.50	26.07	trace	9.0	597

Climatic Data for Leading American Cities (continued)

State and City	Average Temperature (°F)		Sunny Days per Year	Humidity (%)	Precipitation			Average Wind (mph)	Elevation (feet)
	Winter	Summer			Rain (inches)	Snow (inches)			
Utah (Salt Lake City)	37.5	67.2	211	51.30	15.74	76.8		9.5	4,220
Vermont (Burlington)	25.5	59.2	151	73.00	38.10	121.6		8.0	332
Virginia (Richmond)	45.9	66.8	188	73.50	59.34	14.3		7.4	164
Washington (Seattle)	42.9	69.4	151	72.50	48.36	22.2		8.6	400
West Virginia (Charleston)	42.9	66.1	128	71.30	51.15	26.5		6.1	939
Wisconsin (Madison)	25.2	60.8	163	75.50	30.96	50.2		10.0	858
Wyoming (Cheyenne)	31.8	57.6	204	53.30	12.04	48.6		13.5	6,126

they don't. Hurricanes, with their immense power, can last for days and cut a swath across hundreds of miles. Tornadoes concentrate their destruction and killing potential.

Volcanoes, though not officially storms, cause incredible destruction and death when they erupt—as those living near Mount St. Helens on May 18, 1980, can testify. Sixty people died before that catastrophe ended. The nearby community was devastated, and countless trees were flattened like matchsticks.

Earthquake-prone areas can be like a serial killer waiting to go on a rampage. A quake is the result of slippage or fractures of the earth's crust far below ground level. It occurs because of extreme stress. While California has the dubious distinction of being the earthquake capital, another part of the country may be even more volatile. We refer to the New Madrid Fault that runs along the eastern border of Tennessee.

In fact, an earthquake in the Mississippi Valley in 1812 measured even *higher* on the Richter scale than the devastating San Francisco earthquake. Some scientists fear a recurrence before the year 2000. Experts say it could register as high as 7.5 and affect states from Kansas east to Pennsylvania and from Illinois south to Louisiana. At the end of this discussion, we include maps to help you avoid these natural disasters if one or more of them hold special terror for you.

Comparative Data

The National Climatic Data Center publishes statistics for thousands of locations in this country. Their *Comparative Climatic Data for the United States* surveys 280 primary weather stations for long-term, monthly, and annual summaries. They include such particulars as normal daily maximum and minimum temperatures, average and maximum wind speed, percent of possible sunshine, rainfall, snowfall, plus morning and afternoon humidity readings. You can purchase it for $5 plus a $5 service charge from the National Climatic Data Center, 151 Patton Avenue, Asheville, NC 28801, 704-271-4800. They accept credit cards.

If the places you're considering don't have first-order weather stations, they may be one of the 2,000 locations with a cooperative station. That data is contained in *Climatography of the United States, Series 20*. It provides two-page publications for each location, which can be ordered for $2 per location plus a $5 shipping and handling charge, from the National Climatic Center.

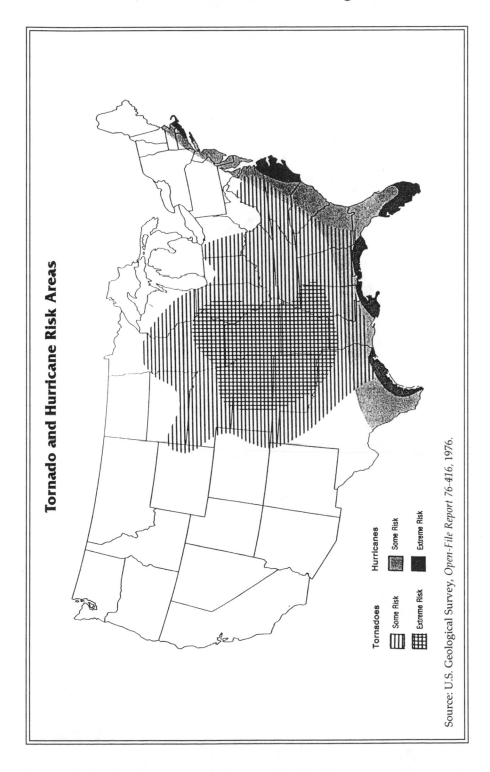

Tornado and Hurricane Risk Areas

Tornadoes
Some Risk
Extreme Risk

Hurricanes
Some Risk
Extreme Risk

Source: U.S. Geological Survey, *Open-File Report 76-416*, 1976.

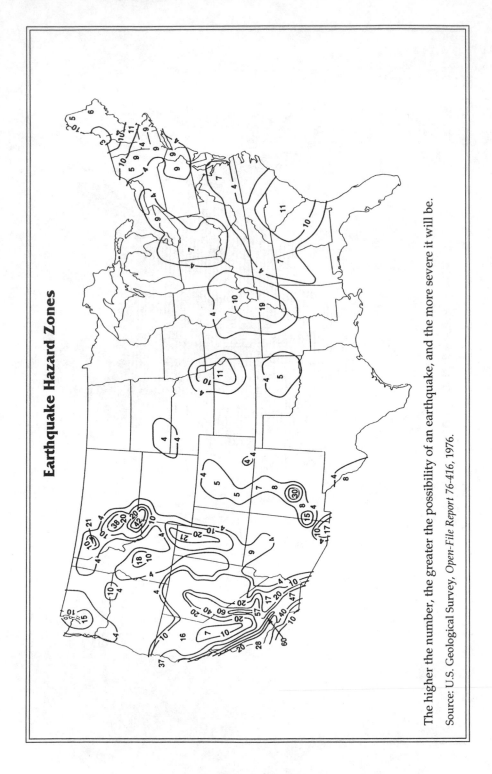

Earthquake Hazard Zones

The higher the number, the greater the possibility of an earthquake, and the more severe it will be.

Source: U.S. Geological Survey, *Open-File Report 76-416, 1976*.

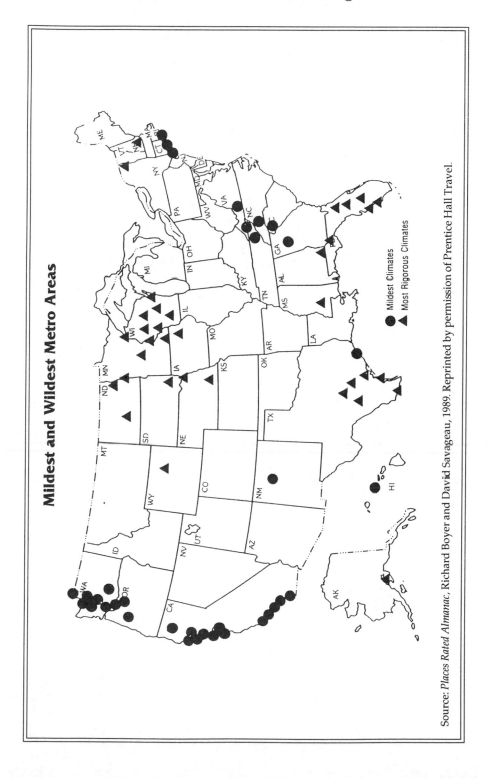

Mildest and Wildest Metro Areas

● Mildest Climates

▲ Most Rigorous Climates

Source: *Places Rated Almanac*, Richard Boyer and David Savageau, 1989. Reprinted by permission of Prentice Hall Travel.

Climatic Regions of the United States

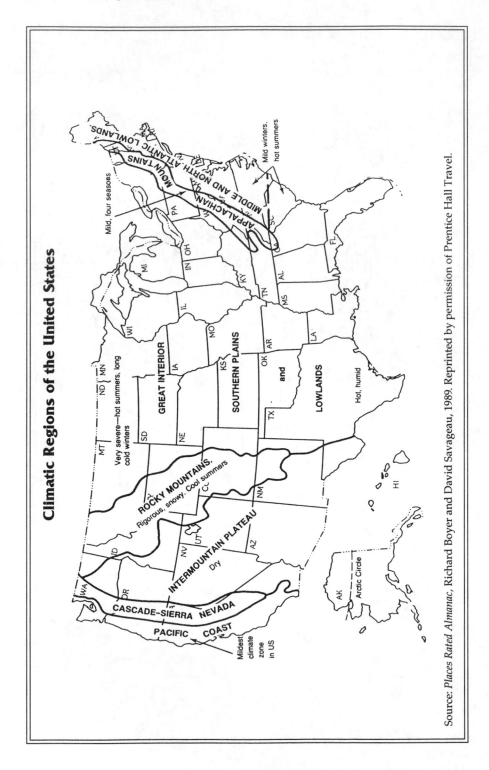

Source: *Places Rated Almanac*, Richard Boyer and David Savageau, 1989. Reprinted by permission of Prentice Hall Travel.

HEALTH AT THE CROSSROADS

Tension and anxiety are proven killers. An overwhelming three-quarters of Americans say they live with a notable amount of stress in their lives. Few would disagree the stress level of people residing in a rural setting is lower than it is for individuals trying to cope with today's urban madness. This is an enormous consideration when looking at overall health issues. Where you live affects more than just your sense of beauty and your wallet. It can also affect how long you live.

Psychology Today magazine did a study to determine cities with the lowest stress. Not surprisingly, they're smaller towns: (1) State College, Pennsylvania; (2) Grand Forks, North Dakota; (3) St. Cloud, Minnesota; (4) Rochester, Minnesota; (5) McAllen/Pharr, Texas; (6) Altoona, Pennsylvania; (7) Bloomington, Indiana; and (8) Provo/Orem, Utah.

In the coming years, more Americans will take their health into their own hands. We're already seeing more emphasis on *wellness*, an approach that reflects people striving for a balanced and preventive state of physical being. Middle-aged Americans will be doing fitness walking, biking, swimming, gentle exercise, and enjoying nature as they hike, camp, and bird-watch. The bottom-line motivation will be maintaining weight, keeping fit, holding stress down, and preserving healthy organs—rather than weight loss.

Evaluating Health Care

To evaluate health care in small towns, you'll want to look at the ratio of doctors per capita. In some rural areas they are as low as 53 per 100,000, compared with 163 per 100,000 in urban areas. How far is the hospital? Does it have 24-hour-a-day emergency coverage? If you need a specialist, how far must you travel? If sickness has been a frequent visitor, you may want to find out if a teaching hospital, medical school, or VA hospital is within reasonable commuting distance.

What are health care costs compared with what you're used to paying? How far is the dentist and optometrist? If you use chiropractic adjustment, be sure there's a chiropractor handy. And for some, a massage therapist or physical therapist is an important person. In other family situations, having a convalescent hospital, nursing home, or hospice nearby will be a consideration.

Health care is one area where most small towns take a back seat to big cities. Physicians cluster in metropolitan areas where they will be well paid for their services. State-of-the-art medical facilities, high-tech equipment, personnel trained to use them, plus fascinating new procedures are all more abundant in larger metropolitan areas.

Telemedicine, however, will change the face of health care delivery over the next couple of decades. It flashes as a beacon of hope for rural communities. To some, it means two-way interactive computer video transmissions between two doctors, a doctor and a patient, or a doctor and a hospital or clinic. To others it means a new delivery mechanism to electronically access or evaluate a patient's condition or records. Rural doctors will use it to consult with specialists in major cities.

As telecommunications and computer technology become more and more sophisticated, rural patients will benefit enormously. By the turn of the century, it is expected rural hospitals can let big-city medical experts examine CAT scans and other sophisticated tests via video hookups.

Federal Government Targets Some Answers

Federal health officials recently unveiled plans for a long-overdue national Medicare physician fee schedule designed to pay family and general practice doctors more, and specialists less. One of the goals of the fee schedule revisions is to correct imbalances in Medicare payments to rural physicians. It will also correct inequities between primary-care doctors, those most needed in small towns, and specialists such as surgeons. By raising Medicare fees for rural and primary physicians, the government hopes to encourage doctors to practice in these areas. Unfortunately, in practice, urban doctors and specialists are having their fees reduced.

The current system leads physicians away from rural areas and into higher-paying metropolitan locations. It also encourages doctors to specialize instead of opening family and general practices. General practitioners treat diseases and injuries, provide preventive care, and give routine checkups. They also perform some surgery, prescribe drugs, and refer patients to appropriate specialists if necessary.

Unfair government programs, such as Medicare, that fail to account for rural-urban differences, have contributed to the closure of many country hospitals. Medicare pays 35 to 40 percent less for a service in a rural hospital than it does for the same service in an urban hospital. While the cost of living often is lower in country settings, the cost of medical supplies sometimes is more, because smaller quantities are usually ordered. Consequently, rural hospitals and physicians are not fully reimbursed for treating Medicare patients. One physician computed his overhead per Medicare patient was $27 for a routine office visit. Yet Medicare paid him only $9.98. This is further compounded by the fact that the elderly comprise 12 percent of the total U.S. population, but account for 25.4 percent of the population in rural communities.

This, plus lower reimbursements from insurance companies and a high rate of patient nonpayment, makes it difficult to maintain essential services. Some full-scale hospitals have been downgraded to emergency centers, health clinics, or nursing facilities. Others have closed their doors.

Regional collaboration helps overcome some of the limitations of small size and limited scale. But it must be implemented in tandem with solving transportation needs. Other visionary planning ideas include granting scholarships to get doctors interested in the "outback," dispersing residency programs into rural areas, and introducing programs to help family physicians cover the costs of malpractice insurance or student loans. Many refuse to perform obstetric or gynecologic functions because the cost of liability insurance is enormous.

Another option is physician's assistants (PAs). We had two very capable PAs in First Try. While they were required to work under a doctor's supervision, the physician was there just one day a week. More than 22,000 PAs practice today in the United States.

Congress has finally become cognizant of the dire need for improved rural health care. A National Health Service Corps Revitalization bill, designed to encourage doctors to practice in rural areas, was recently passed.

Answers for Environmental Illness and Allergies

Thousands of people suffer from multiple chemical sensitivities or environmental illness (EI). They seek pristine surroundings free of toxic substances such as smog, molds, pollen, electromagnetic rays, industrial and agricultural poisons, and toxic waste dumps. The search is not easy. Many EI victims have relocated to Arizona, Idaho, and Washington to escape allergens. One ray of hope for people afflicted with EI is Gunnar Heuser, MD, a neurotoxicologist with UCLA.

Many more people endure troublesome allergies. Hay fever afflicts 35 million Americans. It's an allergic reaction to airborne particles brought on by pollen from seed-bearing trees, grasses, and weeds (especially ragweed), plus spores from certain molds. These proliferate in the middle regions where grasses and flowerless trees dominate. Yes, hay fever hunkers down and waits for victims in America's heartland. The Southwest deserts used to attract asthmatics and hay fever sufferers. But as they become more populated, landscaping and its accompanying problems multiply. Alaska and the southern half of Florida are still havens for hay fever sufferers. For more information, contact the American Academy of Allergy, Asthma and Immunology at 611 E. Wells Street, Milwaukee, WI 53202-3349 or call their Physicians' Referral and Information Line at 800-822-2762. There is also a newsletter called *The Wary Canary* for folks with allergies and environmental concerns. Contact them at P.O. Box 2204, Fort Collins, CO 80522, 970-493-8089.

Before we leave this subject, let's discuss health insurance for a moment. If you don't qualify for public assistance, have a health problem with large potential financial exposure, and can't afford typical insurance, where you live can be extremely important. Some states have more affordable insurance available to those with preexisting conditions. Check this out if the situation applies.

INVESTIGATING ENVIRONMENTAL CONCERNS

It's impossible to talk about health and not look at environmental problems. Many times, our health deteriorates as a direct result of self-created dangers—insidious substances too tiny for the eye to see, yet capable of rendering humankind extinct unless they are controlled.

About 20 years ago, we started hearing a lot about pollution, contaminants, additives, acid rain, asbestos, chemical spills, nuclear meltdowns, and other environmental hazards, as well as the importance of preserving our ecology, rain forests, and ecosystems. Before that, few of us realized what was happening. We had no idea our world was being systematically raped. Until then, we didn't know that unusually high rates of certain cancers had been linked directly to hazardous waste dumps, chemical spills, insecticides, industrial wastes, and other contaminants, or that multinational business interests were lobbying the government to keep needed, but restrictive, legislation at bay.

We ignored the clues, just as some of us ignore signs along the freeway warning of radar monitored speed checks; it wasn't until we saw the flashing red lights in our rearview mirrors that we realized the consequences of our apathy. Now the judge is in his chambers, and the ticket must be paid. We're now paying for molesting the balance God provided. Our children and grandchildren will pay an even greater price. Our great-grandchildren? Hopefully our belated actions will allow them to fare better. Air, earth, and water form the triangle upon which civilization rests. Without them, nothing else matters.

20th Century Environmental Tampering

While no part of the country is completely free of 20th century tampering, some have fared better than others. In its *Green Index Report,* the Institute for Southern Studies assesses the environmental health of all 50 states. They use 35 indicators in four general categories to draw conclusions. The results? New England, especially Vermont, is the most environmentally healthy part of the United States. The South, led by Alabama, has the worst score—seizing nine of the ten bottom spots.

If you want to really educate yourself, we'd suggest you get a copy of the *Green Index* by Bob Hall and Mary Lee Kerr. It's a state-by-state guide to the nation's environmental health and brims with tables, maps, and little known facts. Our focus must be on saving our species on the planet Earth.

For information on air-quality standards and any polluting source in areas you're considering, look in that locale's phone book for a local or state air pollution agency. Or call your regional branch of the Environmental Protection Agency (EPA); they maintain a hotline at 800-535-0202. They report on polluted lakes and beaches, toxic waste sites, and contaminated landfills. And they're a referral service for information on local pollution rates, the major chemical culprits, and other resources. This is an excellent information source for urban opt-outs.

Another aspect of air pollution is odor. In some parts of the country, taking a deep breath borders on being a masochistic act. Several towns vie for stench capital of the USA. So be sure *sniffing* is part of your relocation research! Clinton, Iowa, city administrator George Langmack explains, "Once you've experienced it, you can always refer to it as the dead animal odor from the rendering plant. When it's hot and humid and you get a direct shot, it will cause you to catch your breath in order to keep your supper."

Berlin, New Hampshire, has a nickname: "The city that paper built." The fumes from the paper plant used to be so foul, it made the paint peel from the houses. Today, getting a whiff makes your eyes water and your lungs ache. Devils Lake, North Dakota, also has the diSTINKtion of reeking like a sewer. Says city commission president Berta Soper of the fiberglass manufacturing plant, "It's an industrial odor." Residents of Chillicothe, Ohio, think their town has a stench like decomposed bodies. Not so, contends city personnel manager Robert Wakefield. He says it "smells like money." And little Red Bay, Alabama, stinks like putrid dog food. The reason for the pungent smell is just that: dog food cooking. The factory employs a lot of people in that town.

Let's face it: In some places the nose doesn't want to know! In others, the lure of sagebrush, eucalyptus, and pine are a welcome reprieve from big-city garbage stench.

The Life Blood of Water

Water, water everywhere—and not a safe drop to drink. That could be our lament if things continue as they are. Almost 17 percent of the population drinks water with excessive amounts of lead, a heavy metal that impairs children's IQs and attention spans and can cause high blood pressure and other health problems in adults. To get your questions answered about lead, call the EPA's safe drinking water hotline at 800-426-4791.

In the early summer, half the rivers and streams in America's Corn Belt are laced with unhealthy levels of pesticides. It's no secret that inept regulation, reckless land use, and irresponsible handling of chemicals are compromising the quality of the nation's drinking water. The EPA estimates that in 38 states, pesticides have already fouled the ground water used by half of all Americans as their main source of drinking water.

Four out of five of the most hazardous waste dumps are leaking toxins into the groundwater. People living in New Jersey, New England, and the western mountain states face an additional threat. Radon, a radioactive gas that permeates groundwater, is found in these regions.

When checking out a water supply, look for groundwater that runs deep so it isn't likely to be contaminated by fertilizers, pesticides, mine tailings, or microorganisms. Or there's another alternative: For several years, we took our water from a high mountain stream. It was pure snowmelt. There were no people or mining operations above us. But even using such natural water has risks. A few people have been known to ingest a microorganism called *giardia*, which causes diarrhea and headaches and can linger for months. Of course, filters offer more pure water and bottled water is an option.

Some people contend that pesticide residues on produce are even more dangerous than hazardous waste dumps or air pollution! The lean chicken may be poisoned with salmonella. And the fish we've opted for in place of a steak may have spent its life swimming in an alphabet soup of toxic nightmares. An evaluation of sport fish taken from the Great Lakes found that nine out of ten fish were tainted with levels of toxic chemicals. One in four contained levels regarded as harmful to humans.

Noise and big cities go together like salt and pepper. And noise pollution can also be unnerving and stressful. People in large cities learn to cope with ever-present clamor. But first-time visitors to Manhattan are amazed by the constant honking of taxi horns, blaring of sirens, and clattering of garbage trucks.

In the country, serenity is precious. Noise pollution isn't a factor. To be honest, when we go into major cities to speak, meet with clients, or do media tours, we have to steel ourselves to cope with the pandemonium. At busy restaurants, large social functions, or conventions we feel flogged by the noise—physically buffeted by an invisible negative vibration. Noise can make you weary in a hurry.

Before we leave the environment, there is one further point to address: nuclear power. Think about how you'd feel living near a nuclear power plant. (See "Commercial Nuclear Power Reactors in the United States" for their locations.) While Three Mile Island and Chernobyl are isolated cases, a catastrophic meltdown or low-level environmental contamination are legitimate concerns. At the end of 1988, 110 nuclear electric plants were licensed to operate in the United States. New England, as a region, has the most reactors, although Illinois has more than any other state. As electric energy needs soar, this power source may again become popular to meet the pending power crisis.

PUTTING LEISURE IN YOUR LIFE

Leisure, like the happy and sad masks of the theater, runs a wide gamut. There are the more sophisticated cultural pursuits, the arts. And there are recreational activities, entertainment, and nature's bounty. What's interesting is that the new breed of urban-to-rural migrants are as inclined to show up at a country fiddling contest or a community event as they are to attend the ballet or a chamber music performance.

A Dollop of Culture, My Dear?

Nowhere but New York City will you find 49 art museums, 34 professional theaters, 26 orchestras, 14 professional opera companies . . . and a partridge in a pear tree. But frankly, how many times do you par-

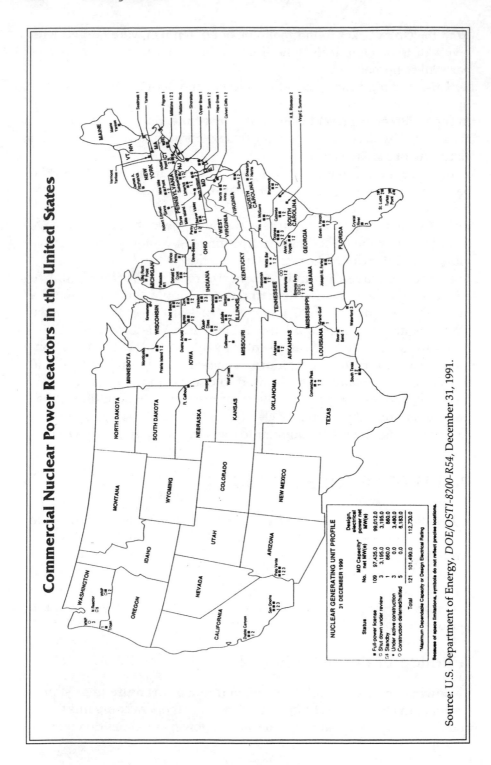

Commercial Nuclear Power Reactors in the United States

Source: U.S. Department of Energy, *DOE/OSTI-8200-R54*, December 31, 1991.

take of each in a year's time? Many of us find stimulation and enjoyment at the other end of the spectrum.

Small-town museums house works of considerably less value than metropolitan museums, but the docents are intimately familiar with the displays and infinitely more cordial. Art galleries? They're likely to be the walls of restaurants. (Sometimes the "finds" are astonishing.) Here in Buena Vista we have several art shows during the year. They feature all sorts of media and many works we'd be proud to have in our home. Last summer, the grassy lawn of a local restaurant was the setting of a Sunday brunch and outdoor jazz concert. And the area pubs don't need much of an excuse to bring in a band. As we write this, a touring ballet company is performing *The Nutcracker Suite* in the nearby town of Salida. Local churches bring in musicians and speakers.

In the summertime, festivals sprout like mushrooms in rural America. They celebrate everything from ethnic holidays and customs to harvest time and religious events. Small-town summer diversions also often center on bandstands, gazebos, or pavilions where local musical groups perform.

In case you're wondering what else there is to do in a small town, we just received the local chamber of commerce's event schedule for next year. Here are some highlights: Optimists Club Talent Show, Moonlight Ski Tours, Gun Club Gun Show, Snowmobile Rally, and the Trout Creek Pass Marathon Run. Then there's the opening of the Court House Art Gallery, performances of the Annual Melodrama, Collegiate Peaks Enduro Dirt Bike Race, and the Quilt Show—which overflows with exquisite handmade items each year. Next comes an Old Fashioned Fourth of July Celebration, Mountain Mania Annual Car Show, Collegiate Peaks Stampede Rodeo, and the Rock and Gem Show. In September the Autumn Color 5K and 20K Walk/Run beckons fitness buffs to enjoy the changing leaves. And this is all happening in a town of only 2,000 residents!

In our headlong rush to abandon the big city, must we also forsake artistic and intellectual fare? Not really. The Public Broadcasting Service is available in most areas. PBS can typically be accessed by way of cable. A flick of a switch brings the Bard, opera, symphony, programs on science and the universe, even engrossing children's shows. Programming has artistic, educational, and cultural merit. And we wake up to National Public Radio (NPR) each morning. The news is global, the interviews enlightening, the music delightful. And a direct satellite TV dish can bring in hundreds of TV offerings to your doorstep.

Another wonderful resource is the public library. Many loan every-thing from videos to CDs, books on tape to the latest best-sellers. Vir-tually all participate in interlibrary loan programs so they can usually get whatever you want. If you have youngsters, investigate the chil-dren's story hours. And if there isn't a Great Books or best-seller dis-cussion group, perhaps you could start one.

The Sporting Life

Entertainment, of course, needn't be highbrow. More people like sports than cultural activities. (Though futurists predict this will change by the turn of the century.) While you won't be in the stands rooting for the Dallas Cowboys, the Chicago Bulls, or the Los Angeles Dodgers from your rural Eden, there are other alternatives.

If you settle in a college town, some darn good football and basket-ball spectating may be in the offing. Collegiate sports are big crowd pleasers. And it needn't be just the most touted sports. You can watch tennis tournaments, swim meets, wrestling matches, and gymnastic competitions, not to mention track and field events. Rooting for the home team can also be fun at the high school level. Perhaps a minor league or semipro team plays in or near your new town. They're like margarine is to butter: Not the real thing, but a good imitation—and a lot cheaper. If you're a big baseball fan, consider relocating to Arizona or Florida. That's where the spring training camps are located for major league baseball teams.

Many of us want to actively participate in sports. While in the coun-try, you're not likely to find a posh private country club with a valet to park your car, but there's lots of good golf available. It isn't miles and miles away and you don't have to make reservations weeks in advance to get a good tee time. With over 25 million golfers, the demand for courses dictates that even most tiny towns have facilities.

Tennis, anyone? You bet! Not all courts are lit at night, however, and there may not be indoor facilities. You could also find yourself playing at the local high school during off hours when the students don't need the courts. Racquetball may also be a possibility.

Softball is big in many rural areas. Teams are sponsored by local merchants, and games are lively. This is a good way to get acquainted quickly with the other jocks in the community. Tournament competi-tion can be fierce and the winning team revered in the community. Of course, there are the usual teams for youngsters.

Bowling is another rural pastime. Towns from about 5,000 up usually have a tenpin bowling center. This is not only good family fun, but many adults join teams (another good way to get acquainted) and participate in tournaments. Once considered strictly a blue-collar sport, today doctors prescribe it for older adults and as therapy for many ailments.

Sporting enthusiasts will appreciate a survey conducted by *Outside* magazine. Out of the top ten sporting towns they picked, virtually all are small communities. Here they are in no particular order: Moab, Utah; Bend, Oregon; Talkeetna, Arkansas; Bozeman, Montana; Bishop, California; and Leavenworth, Washington.

Recreation and the Pursuit of Nature

There's lots to do besides sports. Going to the movies is as American as apple pie. If it is an amusement you expect to do a lot, be sure your proposed community has at least one movie theater. Many tiny towns don't. It isn't economical. When we lived in First Try, a family moonlighted from their day jobs and opened the movie each Friday and Saturday night.

Maybe you're among the one in ten people who enjoys going out to dinner at least once a week. Check out the cuisine scene. In Small Town USA it isn't always easy to find restaurants that combine the three ideals: quality food, good service, and a pleasant atmosphere. That isn't easy anywhere these days unless you're in a five-star eatery. Before you decide it's impossible, however, visit our Buffalo Bar & Grill and nearby, The Prospector in Leadville or the Country Bounty in Salida. You can find diners where the cook makes food as tasty as grandma does and serves portions fit for a lumberjack. You could even be as lucky as we are and find a waitress so conscientious she calls you when the daily special is your favorite.

Country recreation offers a wondrous kaleidoscope of options.

A body of water—and all the pleasures it can deliver—is usually close at hand. Water sports abound. In the summertime that may be swimming, fishing, waterskiing, jet skiing, or sailing and other kinds of boating. In cold climates, winter turns a pond into an ice-skating rink. And some folks love ice fishing. Of course, if there's snow that means both downhill and cross-country skiing, snowboarding, sledding, snowmobiling, sleigh rides, and rambunctious snowball fights.

The great outdoors has something for everyone. It ranges from the less strenuous (pleasure drives, sightseeing, photography, nature walks, picnicking, bird-watching, camping, and fishing) to the more active (hiking, backpacking, running, biking, mountain climbing, and white-water rafting).

We have the oldest national park system in the world. Its mission is to preserve irreplaceable geographic and historic treasures for public recreation. (See the adjacent map, "National Parks and Recreation Areas," if you want to locate near one.) State areas range from small day-use parks in wooded areas to beaches and to large rugged parks with hiking trails and developed campsites. Most state recreation areas offer older visitors reduced entrance fees.

If you want to view flora and fauna up close, head for a national wildlife refuge. There are 477 of them sprinkled around the country. This is a perfect place to observe and photograph birds, animals, and plants. And many of the refuges have visitor centers with fascinating displays about the inhabitants.

But you needn't depend on designated outdoors spots. In the country, the world is your oyster. Spending time with nature—from backyard gardening to wilderness trekking—helps us feel less stressed. Dr. Roger Ulrich, a professor of urban and regional planning at Texas A&M, conducted a study in which he showed students slides of trees, plants, water, and city scenes. The students reported the nature scenes, especially those containing water, made them feel more elated and relaxed. In contrast, the urban scenes tended to elicit sadness and fear. Further evidence was presented when electroencephalograph readings of the students' brain-wave activity showed significantly stronger relaxing alpha waves when viewing nature scenes.

Why is the Earth's bounty so soothing? It gives us a feeling of connectedness. There is an invitation to care for something other than ourselves. Exposure to other living things is deeply satisfying and pleasurable. And many of us associate nature with good times. Maybe we found a wild orchard and enjoyed the tasty pleasure of a harvest for which we had neither planned nor worked, or we visited a grandparent's or aunt and uncle's farm when we were kids. Memories of gathering eggs, riding a friendly old horse, shelling peas on the back porch, and perhaps trying to milk a cow, still warm our hearts.

We can give such memories to our children on a daily basis. For a small-town child, little things seem larger, more magnificent. The sun glistening on early morning dew that has been caught in a well-engineered spider web is a unique delight. So is a nest containing robin's eggs and the antics of the ensuing tiny birds. Crops planted, tended, and harvested are lessons in life. Excitement comes in different doses:

National Parks and Recreation Areas

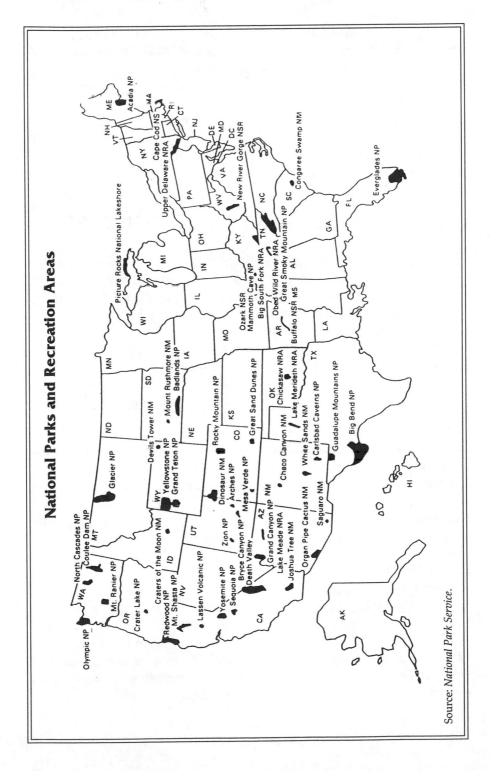

Source: *National Park Service.*

making a dam in the stream and cooling soda pop or watermelons for a summer snack; building a jump trail for dirt bikes; having deer look in your windows while you're eating dinner. These replace (or augment) excursions to zoos, aquariums, and expensive theme parks.

Think of your leisure as a block of marble waiting to be shaped and yourself as a sculptor. Will you mold it with culture and the arts? Recreation? Sports? Entertainment? Nature? We hope the country will enrich your life with new experiences and expectations, that it will allow you to shape a more satisfying destiny.

EVALUATING AN AREA'S INFRASTRUCTURE

This represents the underlying foundation or basic framework of a community. It embraces the demeanor of a town: whether it welcomes newcomers, is formal or laid back, conservative or liberal. Small towns can be either proud or decaying. Some are *Mayberry RFDs*, others more like *Peyton Places*. As you evaluate them, tune in to their attitudes toward planning and growth. In this discussion of infrastructure, we will also help you address the topics of education and transportation.

Population Trends and Planning Approaches

Few places remain the same for long. Either they progress or regress. Some grow quickly, some slowly. Others lose ground: Young people leave, businesses fail, storefronts are boarded up.

Especially if you intend to operate a business dependent on the area economy, you need to know a county's policy toward growth. Talk with the planning commissioners. Ask to review recent meeting minutes. Request a copy of any master plan. Do the planning kingpins demonstrate a willingness to support a high level of activity? Is this an area on the grow? Will its primary characteristics remain constant? (Or is it being repositioned, for instance, as a retirement haven?)

What's the work ethic like? Is this a thriving community with an eager workforce? Is local business and government leadership open to change? Is there an adequate phone system and are lines available? Without up-to-date switching equipment, you may encounter complications operating a fax machine, punching in extension numbers on long-distance phone calls, and using a modem.

In our nation, telephone service is, for the most part, a given. It tends to be one of the last concerns of a relocating Countrypreneur.

Tom: When we moved to First Try, we noticed our pristine ranch land didn't have phone lines. No problem: We set up a meeting with Mountain Bell to discuss our phone requirements. After an hour or so of adding machines clicking and computers humming, we were informed that Mountain Bell could install lines to meet our requirements for $60,000. Well it's a gross understatement to say Marilyn nearly fainted and I contracted severe heartburn!

But, being an engineer as well as an entrepreneurial spirit, I resolved to come up with something more feasible. A couple of weeks later, I devised an alternative to Ma Bell's scheme. And we decided to go ahead with our plans to buy the land, knowing that if my ideas didn't work, we could always pull lines from town for 60K.

After months of engineering analysis, trial, and error, we determined we could use the Motorola Pulsar 4 mobile telephone—given to us by a Good Samaritan—in conjunction with a high-gain antenna perched atop a 100-foot tower.

In theory, it worked; in practice, it worked 50 percent of the time—not good for a consulting service completely dependent on mail and telephone service. However, we got by. As adaptable beings, we tend to accept things after awhile. We were doing okay and we maintained a telephone in town for long conversations, conference calls, and critical communications.

Except for the fact that I was now spending approximately 50 percent of my time re-engineering—and repairing—our systems, life settled down to normal in unbelievably beautiful surroundings. From our window, we could look up Bear Creek nearly to the Continental Divide. It seemed you could see forever. The eagles swooped, soared, and played in a sky so blue it seemed the creation of an artist's mind. Well, it was—the greatest artistic mind of all!

For months, we went about our routine in a semi-orderly manner—until one day a Mountain Bell truck arrived at our front door. After asking us about how our service was performing and saying how much they appreciated our business—probably the largest monthly mobile telephone bills in recorded history!—the representative nonchalantly mentioned they were going to move the base antenna. "We don't really feel it will affect your reception much, but we'll keep in touch. We certainly want to make sure we maintain your service," he assured us.

A few days later, we got a call from another Ma Bell rep checking signal quality and clarity. After recording these he said, "Now we are going to switch antennas." That's the last word we ever heard over our mobile telephone link. And because our system was beyond the specified reception range to begin with, we had no recourse with the phone company. Silence fell. By this time our aforementioned folly of the historic hotel and restaurant had siphoned off the $60,000 needed to install lines. Now what? . . .

As we strolled down our country lane, like we had hundreds of times before, Marilyn confided concerns about continuing our present remote lifestyle. With what could have been a tear in the corner of my eye—or maybe it was due to the brisk breeze we were walking into—I murmured, "Honey, I guess it's time to leave."

So don't take things for granted. Check them out. We were so happy with real phone lines when we moved to Buena Vista that we overlooked the fact the lines were going through a complex conversion system to make them work on the pulse-modulated lines of today. This made fax use tricky and was very aggravating when trying to interface with the multitudes of current voice mail.

Fortunately this story has a happy ending. Now we're just like downtown Los Angeles—except for no smog, no traffic, and we have a clear view of the 14,000-foot peaks to the west. Oh well, we can't have everything. Thank heavens.

The ABCs of Education

If you have children, the quality of their education is probably a major concern. There's a lot to be said for small-town schools. The teacher-pupil ratio is usually smaller. Teachers get to really know their students and take into consideration personal situations. In a metropolitan setting, educators typically aren't aware if parents are divorcing, or if there is a grave illness in the family that might be affecting how Janie or Johnny is performing.

Computers and cable TV are also coming to the rescue of country schools that couldn't offer advanced, sophisticated training. Thanks to cable hookups, students can now take advanced courses in calculus or astronomy, for instance.

Rural doesn't have to mean rinky-dink. Take Harrison, Arkansas: With a population of 9,567 this mountain town is one of the lowest-spending school districts in the country. Yet their test scores are in the top 10 percent nationally and high school graduates go off to prestigious places such as Harvard, Princeton, Georgetown, and MIT. Furthermore, their band is so good it has been invited to Washington, DC, for presidential inaugurations. What's the secret? High expectations, parent involvement, teacher empowerment, site-based management, and community support.

Parents volunteer in their kids' classrooms. Honor Cards, good for discounts or free services at 52 local businesses, are presented for good grades. Parents and teachers collaborate to determine goals, then publish them via ads in the *Harrison Times*. Beginning in junior high, kids are encouraged to become comfortable taking college admission exams. By the time they're seniors, the SAT and ACT are old friends. This is a town where everyone works together to educate kids!

Another small-town success story revolves around the schoolhouse itself. It is the heart of the community in tiny Milford, New York. Besides the 40 classrooms used daily for students, it also houses the Boy Scouts, Girl Scouts, dance lessons, alumni basketball, the Rotary Club, and the theater group—but it almost didn't exist. The children were almost bused two hours a day to another school. A bond issue to pay for a new school failed miserably in 1984. That's understandable in a town where the typical household earns $14,780 annually and only about 30 percent of the homes have kids.

But school administrators and concerned citizens finally convinced voters that the town needed a school. The community pulled together and grew together and when the new school opened in September 1988, morale skyrocketed. The new school has advanced science labs and a theater that rivals off-Broadway facilities (pitched floors, upholstered seats, and a huge stage). Each classroom is wired for computers and cabled for video. Determination and cooperation won out. Today Milford students go off proudly to exclusive colleges like Yale and Cornell.

Are you looking for the ideal school? An Ohio company called SchoolMatch will use their database of nearly 16,000 public school districts and 14,000 accredited private schools to ferret out 15 school choices that come closest to meeting your needs. For this service, you pay $97.50. You can contact them at 800-992-5323 or check out their

Internet home page at http://www.schoolmatch.com. Company president William Bainbridge says the most important measure of a school district's success comes as a surprise to most people. Rather than the tax base or property values, it's the educational level of parents and the amount of money spent on library and media services.

The training of our youth is perhaps our greatest challenge. Nationally only three-fourths of ninth graders eventually graduate from high school. Because many public school districts are failing to educate their charges, private schools are a thriving alternative.

One out of nine school-aged children attends a private school. Private school applications have risen almost 33 percent from 1990. The vast majority of these schools are run by various religious groups. They dispense spiritual training along with rigorous education and are known for small classes and high SAT scores. Surprisingly enough, many small towns have good private schools. While the national average for tuition is $6,400 a year, rural offerings charge quite a bit less. In our town a small private church school charges $1,795 per year for grades 1–7.

Another alternative is home schooling. Religious reasons influence 85 percent of home schooling parents, notes the National Home Education Research Institute. Some parents are taking the education of their children into their own hands and turning out knowledgeable and self-reliant young people. If this appeals to you, check out the lively online newsgroup at misc.education.home-school.misc and the following magazines: *The Teaching Home, Home Education* magazine, and *Growing without Schooling*.

Transportation Tradeoffs

Getting to and from work is one of the greatest deterrents to living in the city. Commuting—which runs from approximately 7:00 to 9:00 in the mornings and 3:30 to 7:00 in the evenings—is a fact of life for millions of Americans. Commuting time increases with city size. Those needing to reach New York City spend an average of an hour and 21 minutes getting to and from work. That equals almost 39 eight-hour days each year!

Ribbons of interlacing freeways await others who wage a daily battle with gridlock. According to the Federal Highway Commission, congestion on the nation's freeways will be four times worse in 20 years. Those who drive in larger cities have their lives further complicated by parking tabs that sometimes top $400 per month. Millions of others climb aboard grimy cars to join the legions of subway straphangers. Big-city travel options include driving or taking a bus, subway, or commuter train.

Contrast this to country meanderings. The tension of competing with hundreds of thousands of other commuters is a thing of the past. Here, human legs are often the preferred means of travel. (This is a much more ecologically sound solution: pedestrians rely on food for fuel.) Some bicycle to work. A few even ride horses. And if you do drive, it typically takes less than five minutes from your doorstep to the portals of work.

A disadvantage of small towns is that some do not have any means of public transportation. Whereas buses and taxis are taken for granted in the city, they are not a given in Small Town USA. Especially for those who don't drive, it is important to determine that a shuttle service or some reliable method of local transportation exists. (For those seeking to establish a rural business, a void in this category may be an opportunity begging to be filled.)

Getting in and out of your rural paradise may be less than perfect. Most small towns are a distance from major airports. While many are served by feeder airlines, it can cost almost as much to get from your locale to the principal airport, as it does to fly across country. If you're a Lone Eagle and business travel plays an important part in your everyday life, bear this in mind when relocating.

Speaking of business concerns, proximity to interstate highways and airline facilities may also influence the cost of delivery of goods. Furthermore, with the merger of Greyhound and Trailways, bus service to remote places has been curtailed. The inescapable conclusion? Maximum mobility is diminished in rural locations. Many people feel the benefits outweigh this inconvenience.

Now that you've had an opportunity to gauge your move quotient by these seven criteria, let's move on to practical advice on how to turn the dream into reality.

4

---◆---

Turning the Dream
into Reality

Some people plan meticulously for a two-week vacation, yet don't educate themselves for making the decision of their lifetime. Read on, because knowing too much is far better than not knowing enough.

As you fashion a new future, remember that each of us wears a set of psychologically ground eyeglasses. The prescription includes our likes and dislikes, fears and joys, good and bad experiences—plus some truly distorted information. Being fair to yourself requires that you recognize your biases and correct any misinformation you've acquired.

CASHING OUT WITH YOUR URBAN EQUITY

You need capital to make your dream come true. There are more ways to generate cash than there are flavors of Baskin-Robbins ice cream. But for the person seeking to move to the booming backwaters and purchase or set up a rural business, some are more viable than others. We'll explore and exploit all those methods in Chapter 15, "Generating Capital to Launch Your Venture."

Here, we address the most natural avenue for funding your move: your urban real estate. Assuming you're a homeowner, the most obvious money source is to cash in on your home equity. You may well have four walls and a small fortune. If you own valuable real estate, you can apply 21st-century fiscal savvy by selling your expensive urban property and setting up shop in the country. Many of the people reading this book bought their homes several years ago. This real estate has appreciated at a mind-boggling rate. These windfall profits can be huge for property owners in most bigger cities.

The best way to turn paper profit into actual earnings is to sell and leave the city. By moving further afield, you'll gain a more substantial amount of money from your city property sale than you would have if you'd stayed in the city. The Coldwell Banker Media Center (http://www.coldwellbanker.com/media/index.html) provides a useful 1996 Home Price Comparison Index. The typical home profiled has approximately 2,200 square feet, four bedrooms, two-and-a-half baths, a family room (or equivalent), and a two-car garage. The home and neighborhood are typical for a corporate middle manager.

Going from Bergen County, New Jersey ($346,500) to Ft. Smith, Arkansas ($114,500) means you'd have an excess of $232,000. Take out what's owed on the old mortgage and other miscellaneous fees and chances are you'll still have a respectable nest egg for going into business. Who ever said "Be it ever so *humble*, there's no place like home"?

QUIT WORK AND LIVE OFF MY PROCEEDS?

In such high-profit cases, the "equity exiles" involved could have a mortgage-free home, invest their proceeds, stop working, and comfortably live off the interest. City-dwellers who sell their homes for big bucks sometimes try to get around the capital gains tax by sinking everything into what amounts to a palace in a smaller town. Instead it might be smarter to buy a comparable home, take the capital gains tax hit, and finance your future with the rest.

One family we know of sold their urban home for $475,000. Then they bought a house they liked even better in Eugene, Oregon, for $150,000. They paid the capital gains tax, then plunked the rest in government bonds. They have no mortgage payments and their treasury bonds provide them a secure income of more than $20,000 a year. (Do be aware, however, that your tax bill could actually go up slightly because you won't have as much to deduct on property taxes.) So you've discovered a windfall. Now keep reading to figure out how to spend it wisely.

While younger Americans who trade down to a cheaper house must pay tax on the profits, those over 55 may take up to $125,000 of home-sale profits tax-free. Of course, property tax bills and insurance bills ride like leeches on soaring real estate values. Trading down also shakes off many of these parasites. If you're not 55 yet, consider an installment sale for your home—which postpones or reduces the capital gains tax. Pick the brain of your accountant or tax attorney for guidance here.

Should selling your home be too drastic an initial step for you, consider using it for a line of credit. Home-equity loans are typically for 80 percent of the appraised value of the house—less the balance due on the mortgage, of course. Your house secures the debt. Interest rates are typically 1½ points over the prime rate and interest is fully deductible up to $100,000 of debt, no matter how you use the money. Some lending institutions charge up-front fees of around $300. About a fifth of all banks and credit unions, however, offer lines of credit with no closing costs. It pays to shop around.

PLACES, PATTERNS, AND PEOPLE

We were early urban opt-outs. Today, more and more people are swapping housing equity for lifestyle amenities. In southwest Colorado, for instance, homes priced at $250,000 are comparable to those carrying price tags of $1 million in southern California. Other top states attracting cash-rich Californians include Washington, Arizona, Oregon, Texas, Nevada, and Florida.

People are spreading out in random patterns that have no single focus. There are more dimensions to this out-migration than have been seen before. It's not a movement in the traditional sense. It has no center, no leaders, and no clear direction—other than one that leads *away* from the cities. John Herbers of the *New York Times* dubs it "the new heartland."

Based on the 1990 census, the Northeast is packed with people. Nearly 51 million individuals live in this most densely populated region. (Yet even here there are pockets of openness. Most of Maine is less populated, as are upper New York state and upper Pennsylvania.) Today, 78 percent of U.S. residents are jammed into metropolitan areas that claim only 17 percent of the land. The ten largest metropolitan areas are New York, Los Angeles, Chicago, San Francisco, Philadelphia, Detroit, Boston, Dallas/Fort Worth, Washington, and Houston.

Surprisingly, one-quarter of the area of the United States still meets the Census Bureau's definition of "frontier territory": two persons per square mile. Millions of us dream of mounting a horse, donning a cowboy hat, and riding into the western sunset. Louis L'Amour books offer readers a way to get back to their most cherished dreams and desires. Today, folks are turning this fantasy into reality.

Smaller towns in the Midwest are blossoming. People are fleeing cities on the east and west coasts and seeking sturdier soils in which to sink roots. They want traditional values, family ties, parks and blue skies, the smell of home-baked apple pie, uncrowded golf courses close to home, time for fathers to go shooting with their sons or snowmobiling with their daughters. There is a longing for the basics and living close to nature. *In* things now include: spirituality, sewing, nostalgia, and home cooking. It's not geography, but rather a state of mind.

Ethnic diversity also will shape our future. Many major cities now have a "minority-majority." *USA Today* reports that 57 percent of New Yorkers are minorities—due to the rapid growth of Black, Asian, and Hispanic communities. Houston tips the scales at 59 percent minorities, Memphis 56 percent, San Francisco 53 percent, Cleveland and Dallas are at 52 percent each. This increase in urban minorities is a result of the largest wave of immigrants since the early 1900s. The influx is mostly from Mexico, Central America, South America, Asia, and now Eastern Europe. Zooming Hispanic and Black birth rates further contribute. Demographers predict the state of California will have a minority-majority in about 20 years.

Other states with large Spanish-speaking populations include Florida, New York, New Jersey, Illinois, New Mexico, and Texas. Blacks are still overrepresented in southern states relative to their percentage in the national average. There are fewer Black people, however, in northern New England, the Rocky Mountains, and the upper Great Plains states. Here they make up less than 1 percent of the population . . . a terrific opportunity for a person of color wanting to capitalize on EEO-based hiring quotas.

Be aware that many small towns and rural areas are predominantly Caucasian. If you have youngsters, perhaps you don't want your children growing up in a clone-like society where everyone is of one race and ethnic background. Exposure to diverse languages, traditions, and thoughts can be enriching. Consider this when evaluating your relocation plans.

If you're a single person who hopes to find a mate, some states may be better than others. Ladies, you'll be interested to know Hawaii, Alaska, Nevada, and Wyoming have higher male populations. And for you gents, New York, Rhode Island, Massachusetts, and Florida offer greater pickings. A lot of people feel it's harder to find a fun date or a life mate in small towns. This isn't necessarily true. You're a big fish in a little pond. While there are fewer potentials to choose from, it's easier to get acquainted. One of our employees met her honey while browsing at the local rock shop. Three of the four single women we've hired from out of the area were in committed relationships a few months after arriving.

Because people are friendlier in small towns, it's just natural to strike up a conversation with someone who interests you. What may be perceived as "coming on" in swinging suburbia is accepted as being congenial in rural USA. Sure it's lonely sometimes. But you can be even lonelier in a city of one million. If you hope to find a country life partner, consider the age makeup of the residents when selecting your new hometown. If you're in your twenties or thirties, a retiree's haven would be a poor community to choose.

Country-bound singles might want to contact the Rural Network, Inc., at Rural Route 1, Box 129, Gays Mills, WI 54631. They help country-oriented singles provide support to each other. Their *Advocate* newsletter carries news, letters, pictures, and ads sent by people wanting to introduce themselves and share the adventure in their lives. While marriage is on the minds of some, others simply want to visit with like-minded individuals of either sex—and even sometimes open their homes to traveling singles.

There are other aspects to consider when selecting potential hometowns. Tempers flare more easily when people of different backgrounds, religions, and viewpoints get together. Some places are extremely difficult to break into. They have distinct biases. For instance, there are communities in the west that are almost exclusively Mormon. Unless you follow that faith, you'd probably be an outsider.

And many small towns are extremely intolerant. If you aren't second- or third-generation townsfolk, you'll have a difficult time being accepted. In Pottsville, Pennsylvania, for instance, 94 percent of the residents are natives of the state. On the other hand, Bullhead City–Lake Havasu City, Arizona, is extremely heterogenous. Only 16 percent of its population originally hails from Arizona. Towns with a broad mix of outsiders are typically a better choice. There are even strong pockets of political persuasion. Beware if you're a donkey lover and 90 percent of the area is elephant.

There is another important point to consider when selecting your utopia, one many people overlook. If you're moving to get away from the hustle and bustle—and you don't want to end up with the same thing again—avoid picking one of the most desirable places on the planet. If you don't, chances are you'll soon have lots of company. Bend, Oregon, is a classic example. Once a sleepy little town of about 8,000, it's been discovered. The population is now over 29,000.

When you've narrowed your list of possible towns, investigate the area's population trends. If they're on a fast growing curve, look out! Realize things will change. In such towns, septic tanks give way to sewer systems, fancier water treatment techniques are mandated, taxes for schools go up, and there will be more people. If you're seeking a slow-growth situation, don't pick a garden spot.

Also be cautious about locating in a one-industry town. If that industry fails, the ripple effect hits virtually every business and person in town. Living in a poverty pocket is no fun.

NARROWING THE FIELD

It's time to think through what you want. Are you looking to purchase a house in town? A farm or ranch? Perhaps a mobile home or a manufactured house on a small parcel of land is more within your budget. Do you want to buy an existing business? Unimproved land? A second or vacation home? Acreage for a future building site or to hold as an investment?

Some people are finding that a home in an intentional community— sort of a modern village where private residences are clustered near shared facilities fostering community and cooperation—is an answer for them. Faith Popcorn, the author of *Clicking*, believes "Cohousing will click in the decade and century ahead." For more information, contact the Cohousing Network at 510-526-6124 or visit their Web site at http://www.cohousing.org/.

Now that you've decided the type of property you want, how do you pare down the multitude of possibilities to three or four actual towns or counties to investigate? Think about areas that impressed you while vacationing or traveling on business. Has a colleague relocated to an area he or she keeps telling you is Camelot? Do you have friends or relatives in a charming little town? Has a certain state captured your heart?

Several helpful books provide area report cards. G. Scott Thomas' *The Rating Guide to Life in America's Small Cities* is a treasure. Coining them *Micro*politan areas, Thomas profiles 219 towns between metropolitan areas and country crossroads. To qualify, his cities must have a population of 15,000 to 50,000. He uses a statistical system to grade the quality of life in each place. Order it by calling 800-421-0351.

Another useful resource is *The 100 Best Small Towns in America* by Norman Crampton. It's a nationwide guide to the best in small town living from Culpeper, Virginia, to Elko, Nevada, to Red Wing, Minnesota.

If you're looking to buy property for a good return on your investment, we can't think of a more useful tool than the new book, *Boom Counties: Where Structural Change and an Ailing Economy Create Life-Shaping, Profitable Opportunities for Small Investors.* This is by real estate and urban development guru Jack Lessinger, PhD. A social theorist who really does his homework, Dr. Lessinger gives you a fail-safe strategy for long-run investment. The book includes more than 20 colored maps to help you target your most profitable options from the 586 counties profiled. If your home is in Los Angeles, San Francisco, Seattle, Miami, Atlanta, Houston, Chicago, Boston, or New York, you are riding a losing wave. The downward spiral will continue for decades according to Lessinger. Use this book to discover the rural counties that offer the greatest prospects for escalating property values. At $89 it's far from cheap, but his insider information can make you a lot of money. Order by calling 800-331-8355.

While not at all rural, another possibility is *Places Rated Almanac* by Richard Boyer and David Savageau. It looks at the best places to live in America. Perhaps it could serve as a compass to guide you to a favorable area, then you could locate a small town within proximity of the larger place it recommends. And for mature people seeking a change, there is *Retirement Places Rated.*

Another treasure trove is *The World Almanac and Book of Facts.* Here you'll discover information on the cost of living, environment, geographical data, record temperatures, humidity, altitude, latitude and longitude of cities, even climatological statistics. Refer to your previous list to refresh your memory about personal priorities.

If you plan on going into business, a survey by Dun & Bradstreet and *Entrepreneur* magazine—which appeared in their October 1996 issue—revealed five small cities as the nation's entrepreneurial hot spots. They are Reno, Nevada; Colorado Springs, Colorado; Madison, Wisconsin; Boulder/Longmont, Colorado; and Appleton/Oshkosh/Neenah, Wisconsin.

HITTING THE RESEARCH TRAIL

With three or four possible destinations in mind, it's time to visit your largest area library or do some online investigating. Don't rely just on printed material. Computer databases offer a wealth of up-to-the-minute facts and figures.

Two comprehensive resources at your fingertips are Web sites run by the government. A prime source for social, demographic, and economic information is the U.S. Census Bureau at http://www.census.gov. And we were impressed by the breadth of U.S. federal government agencies at http://www.lib.lsu.edu/gov/fedgov.html. Pay particular attention to the links going to Executive, Independent, Quasi-Official, and Other Indexes. Another hot spot is Scoop Cybersleuth at http://www.evansville.net/courier/scoop/. From these sites you can jump to hundreds of others.

One of the best ways to get a *feel* for a place is to read back issues of the local newspaper. Look in Editor & Publisher's *International Yearbook* to identify the daily newspaper. Write for subscription information, plus details on how to order a month's back issues. If the town is tiny, it may only have a weekly paper. If so, the nation's almost 7,000 semi-weekly and weekly newspapers are listed in *Gale's Directory of Publications*.

By carefully reading an area's papers you can mine tremendous knowledge. What are the lead stories? Do they reflect issues that are positive or negative? Read the letters to the editor to find out about area controversies. Are there stories about town spruce-up projects? An inordinate amount of crime? Special recreational or cultural activities? Planned tax increases? A recall election that flags local discontent? Scan the ads too. They help you get a sense of what retail outlets are available and the price levels. Don't overlook the classifieds. By studying real estate ads, you quickly get a sense of availability and the range of property values.

Next track down the addresses and phone numbers for the chambers of commerce and the state tourism offices (see Part Three). You can usually get local contact information from these state sources. You'll want to write the areas you're considering to request their newcomers packet or relocation kit. Identify yourself as a prospective new resident (and business owner, if applicable).

Also study the current year's *Statistical Abstract of the United States* and the most current *City and County Data Book*. Be sure and look at the dates on all charts, figures, graphs, and lists. Though it appears in a current reference work, much of this information may be three to five years old. You may also want to look at the *Digest of Education Statistics* and the *Occupational Outlook Handbook*.

Talk to people. Use your network to try and find *anyone* who has moved to an area that interests you. Contact these individuals and solicit their help and feedback.

To make your job simple, there is a real estate company that specializes in rural property. United National Real Estate has more than 300 affiliated offices in 40 states. They publish two catalogs a year. Talk about a wish book! Their one-of-a-kind catalog is jam-packed with tempting photographs and descriptions of rural hideaways: ranches, farms, country estates, homes in small towns, business opportunities, commercial properties, land, you name it. To order a copy (it's $4.95) call 800-999-1020, fax 816-231-5599, or write United National Real Estate, 1600 N. Corrington Avenue, Kansas City, MO 64120. Be sure to tell them the areas you're considering so regional offices can send you updates on any recent area listings that have come in since the catalog was printed.

Also get applicable copies of regional magazines—such as *Sunset, Yankee,* or *Southern Living*—and sift through the classified section for real estate ads. Ask local chambers of commerce for a list of area brokers to help you size up the market too.

By all means use the Internet in your search for nirvana. One interesting site we've uncovered for you is Home Scout, which lists over 300,000 homes from 122 different real estate Web sites in the U.S. and Canada. Begin your cyberspace real state adventure at http://www.homescout.com.

Although your chances of finding an ideal place are slim, there are less conventional ways of locating property. One is by writing to the Consumer Information Center, Pueblo, CO 81009, and asking for their *U.S. Real Property Sales List*. This is real estate no longer needed by the federal government. It varies widely in value and type and is acquired either by auction or sealed bid. While most properties are commercial or industrial, one list included a Victorian home in Dorchester, Massachusetts; a U.S. Postal Service facility in Rochester, New Hampshire; two working avocado farms in Miami, Florida; and a concrete building on 29 acres in Butler County, Ohio.

We located the church that now houses our offices through the Federal Deposit Insurance Corporation (FDIC), which has properties from failed banks. It took incredible tenacity. Each long-distance phone call led to another in a widening circle of confusion. But the result was worth it as we succeeded in purchasing the property for about half its market value. FDIC regional liquidation offices are listed in Part Three under "Government Sources." You can access their Web site at http:// www.FDIC.gov/. Click on "assets," then follow the bouncing ball.

You can order any phone directory published in this country by call- ing 800-848-8000. Prices range from $6 to $58. The mother lode you'll likely find will be well worth it. Sift through the Yellow Pages from cover to cover. You're looking to see if the health care providers you need are there, what kind of restaurant fare is available, what entertain- ment is offered, who your competition might be if you plan to open a business, what kind of educational facilities are available, etc.

Map reconnaissance is definitely in order. Trying to plan a move without maps is like attempting to repair an 18-wheeler with jeweler's tools. Several types will be helpful. Start with an atlas if you have one. It will help explain the physical geography and climatological zones. Contact DeLorme Mapping at P.O. Box 298, Freeport, ME 04032, 207- 865-4171. You can order a catalog of maps at no charge, then purchase individual maps or digital/CD formats.

These maps will be ideal for back-country exploring. So is a good odometer to measure distances on rural byways that aren't well marked. And don't overlook the everyday variety of maps you use when traveling. If you belong to an auto club, call and get appropriate state and city maps. Also ask your auto club for tour guide books of the area, pretrip packets of information, and routing details. Request back roads routing; you learn much more. Additionally, check with your travel agent for information.

A Web site you may find helpful is located at http://www.city.net. Go to "maps" and you'll discover an interactive map of the United States. You can zoom into certain areas, then print a copy for future reference.

As you begin looking at different maps, refer to the legend or key. It usually appears in the lower right or bottom margin. (By using a piece of string, you can measure the scale on the legend and quickly interpret distances.) It will explain the symbols and colors used to specify areas of importance or interest. Also, the scale of miles will be different on various maps, so be sure you're using relevant information versus details from other sources.

Topographic maps, which show the elevation and terrain, can save you a lot of time. Look in the Yellow Pages to find a local map store. Depending on how sophisticated you want to get, there are also soil, mining, hydrology (ground water), flood plain, and census maps—not to mention city master plans and zoning maps. Aerial photos also can be helpful in certain situations.

No doubt in your reading and research, you'll come across articles that hold particular interest for you. It's apparent the writer is an expert and you'd give next week's football tickets to be able to visit with him or her. There may be a way! Why not write and ask? Use the following "Form Letter for Research" as a model. There are three possible ways to locate the expert. One is to find the person's or company's name and geographic location in the article. Then call information for an area code. Next call information again at 1 (area code) 555-1212 and try to get a phone number.

Another sleuthing trick that works well if the person is of some note is to call the library and ask them to check "who's who" directories and other reference works for the individual's name and address. A third detective ploy is to write the person in care of the magazine or newspaper reporter and ask that the mail be forwarded.

Of course, when you receive the package from the chamber of commerce, this opens additional opportunities. There are real estate offices to contact, plus banks and economic development agencies to approach if you plan to go into business. Don't be discouraged if the chamber doesn't reply. Our hit ratio was less than 50 percent. Try calling and reminding them that it is a second request for relocation information.

PLANNING YOUR VISIT

You've pinpointed your places and done all the arm's-length research you can. Now it's time to plan your actual visit. A few words of caution: Coordinate your visitation time carefully. Avoid holidays and peak vacation times when everything will be so hectic you won't get a real feel for the place, or be able to get people's undivided attention. If time constraints dictate you must fly, be sure to arrange for a rental car (preferably a four-wheel drive vehicle) at the other end.

There are several ways to check out your dream destinations. The ideal is to take a sabbatical or leave of absence for several months while you really *experience* a place. This not only gives you plenty of time to make an informed choice but also assures you of ongoing income, should the test not be to your liking and you decide to return. Few of us live ideal lives, however.

Form Letter for Research

Date

Name
Address
City/State/Zip

Dear _____ :

I'm writing because of an article entitled _____ that I saw
in _____ . It was very exciting to read about what you're
doing.

I am in the early planning stages of _____ . The
knowledge and experience you've gathered on _____
would be tremendously helpful. Hopefully, you will be kind enough to
share some of it with me.

Thanks so much for your interest and cooperation! For your convenience,
I've enclosed a stamped, self-addressed envelope (or feel free to call me
collect if that is more practical—days: _____ , evenings and
weekends: _____). I'm eagerly looking forward to hearing
from you.

Sincerely,

Your Name

If you're not currently tied to a job, consider caretaking or house-
sitting in the vicinity you're considering. The *Caretaker Gazette* newsletter (2380 NE Ellis, Suite C-16RN, Pullman, WA 99163, 509-332-0806)
lists many provocative opportunities: free rent in an Ozark Foothills,
Arkansas, cabin; a possible partnership in a farming venture in Spen-
cer, Virginia; a primitive log cabin and board in exchange for caretaking 175 acres in Bristow, Indiana.

A more practical approach is to roam the countryside on weekends
and vacations. This way you can set up a network of real estate contacts
who know your needs and will contact you when something comes up.
And you can see the place at different times of year. This is crucial
information. A spot that's lovely in the fall may leave you wringing wet
from the summer humidity—or up to your elbows in mud when the

winter thaw hits in March. It's wise to sample the climate at its seasonal extremes.

Another good alternative is to do a vacation home swap. This economical idea allows you to be a temporary resident and quickly acquaints you with the true fabric of a community. You meet the neighbors (instead of the motel maid), absorb their culture, and get their perspective on everyday life. And you can check a wide array of local businesses—from grocery stores to hair salons, banks to service stations. Often a vehicle (and sometimes the family pet) is part of these hospitable deals. This approach lets you evaluate the new area at your own pace before selling your home and burning your bridges. The typical swap lasts two or three weeks and is especially attractive to retirees and families with small children.

Exchanges are not necessarily "your place for my place" arrangements. There are exchange clubs with dues of around $50 that produce directories of available properties. To learn about the various clubs and their specialties, not to mention many exchanging tips, we recommend you get a copy of John Kimbrough's *The Vacation Home Exchange and Hospitality Guide*. Of course, you could also run an ad in the local newspaper where you want to locate. Don't do this in a town of less than 1,000 people, however. It would label you as too unorthodox. One practical solution is to take your lodging with you—in the form of a trailer, motor home, camper, or tent. Tent camping, while taking up valuable time to make and break camp, affords a sense of adventure and is more realistic for bigger families.

Of course, any town over 500 population will have a motel or hotel. Some of them are clean, restful places run by delightful people. Others feature sagging mattresses, noisy air conditioners, and proprietors with the tact of Madonna. Be sure you check out the room thoroughly *before* you plunk down your cash. A good way to assure yourself of reasonable standards is to stay in a Best Western motel or hotel. To find their lodging options as you travel, or get a free directory, call 800-528-1234.

Don't overlook bunking with friends or relatives. Well . . . maybe you should overlook it. When you're seriously searching for a new place to live—a whole new lifestyle—why get sidetracked by social obligations and unsolicited opinions?

One creative businessman we know had his family join him for a convention held in a town about 50 miles from where they were considering relocating. While he attended convention sessions, his wife and daughter took their rented car and checked out the area. The company paid for his lodging, so his family stayed free and he was able to piggyback two additional days at the considerably reduced hotel convention rate.

Military retirees/officers can sometimes find economical accommodations on bases. Determine if there's a military base near your location and call their main number. Inquire if they have a guest house. Contact the guest house directly and ask for availability, costs, priorities, and the length of stay allowed. Check out any other rules concerning pets, children, food in rooms, etc. Or have them mail you a list of their regulations. Parameters vary widely, but it's well worth investigating. Base rates are cheaper than motels, and dining accommodations are usually close by.

Try to work in some fun activities, especially if you are taking children on the trip. Visiting a playground, park, museum, historical site, or other tourist attraction each day breaks the seriousness of the trip. It's a good idea to toss in some relaxing cassette tapes and a player too. And be sure to take comfortable shoes that allow for walking in all types of terrain. Other items might include sunscreen, insect repellent, a hat, backpack, and perhaps a walking stick if you plan to go really rural. If you have a hand-held cassette recorder, it is handy for recording your impressions or listing items for future follow-up. Short of that, take plenty of large pads, pens, and different colored Post-It Note pads so you can color code questions, different properties, etc.

Speaking of what to take, by all means include your camera—not to mention lots of film, extra batteries, flash attachment, plus zoom and telephoto lenses if you have them. Check the camera before you leave, especially if you don't use it regularly. Shoot and develop a roll of film to be sure everything is working. Take some flash shots, some in normal light, and some as close-ups. Remember not to shoot through a closed window or when the car is moving. Window glass plays havoc with auto-focus and a moving car often results in blurred pictures.

Finally, to check out the weather; you can do so anywhere in the United States for 95 cents a minute by calling 1-900-weather (932-8437). Then just enter "1" and the area code for the region you want to know about. Also be aware that even-numbered highways flow east and west; odd-numbered ones go north and south.

We hope we've given you the tools to find your way to your personal oasis. In the next chapter we'll explore doing a comprehensive on-site evaluation.

5

◆

Checking Out Rural Edens

People who want milk should not sit on a stool in the middle of a field in hopes a cow will back up to them. If you want to *know* a community, you'll need to be assertive, to cook up a strategy for relocation research. Whipping into town, looking at properties, and making an impulsive decision can lead to immense disappointment. (We know. That's what we did in First Try. We romanticized the place and were swayed by emotional urgings instead of sound logic.) Intuition should play a part—but only when leavened with analysis. That's what we help you do in this chapter: examine all the ingredients so you can create a life feast that will nourish you from now on. There are checklists and questionnaires culled from a combination of personal experiences and recommendations from others.

Probably the best place to head when you arrive in town is the chamber of commerce. We developed the following "Questions to Ask at the Chamber of Commerce" when relocating to Colorado. While you'll want to modify it somewhat, going over these questions with the chamber's executive director will quickly give you a solid handle on what the community is like. Be honest about the type of business you're planning. Consider, however, that one of the main aims of this person is to recruit new residents. Some are so good at it they could sell eggs to a chicken! The perfect spot is fictional. Different locations attract different people. Focus on your needs and preferences and realize you may get a slightly skewed—but understandably justified—picture from chamber directors.

Questions to Ask at the Chamber of Commerce

1. What is the population of the town? The surrounding area? Is it increasing or decreasing? Why? By what percentage?
2. What are the summer temperature highs and winter lows? How long is the growing season?
3. How far away is the closest university, college, junior college, or continuing education facility? Do you have a recent catalog of their classes?
4. What is the crime rate in comparison with other area towns? What's the most frequent problem in this area?
5. What are the hours of the local library? Does it encourage interlibrary loan? How in-depth is the reference section?
6. Is cable or satellite necessary for TV reception? Availability? Approximate costs?
7. What is the property tax rate? Sales tax base?
8. What recreational facilities or planned activities (festivals, special events, etc.) are available for fun?
9. What cultural opportunities are there?
10. How many grocery stores are there? Where do you shop for staples and sundries? How do prices compare with other towns in the area/state?
11. What is the availability of small houses or apartments to rent? Will most accept pets?
12. What is the water supply source? Is it chlorinated? Do people pay a flat monthly fee or is it metered?
13. What religions are represented? Is any one predominant?
14. Is there a good supply of nearby lots or acreage for building sites?
15. What social clubs and service organizations are established?
16. What is the cost of living compared to other area towns?
17. How do your utility and phone rates compare with other areas?
18. Is there any air pollution? Noise pollution?
19. What is the least desirable characteristic of this area? The most favorable?
20. What is the teacher-pupil ratio in the schools? How extensive is the athletic program? Is there a music and/or drama department? How sophisticated is the computer technology being used?
21. Are there recycling programs? How far is the dump? What is the fee?
22. Could I have a street map of the town and surrounding area?

Additional Business-Oriented Questions:

1. Are there any zoning restrictions on home businesses? Are there any restrictions about living in commercially zoned buildings?
2. What incentives do you offer a company to relocate to your area?
3. Is there an available workforce for my type of business?
4. What are typical monthly wages for secretaries?
5. What is the current unemployment rate? Is this rate rising or falling? Why? Is there a significant seasonal variance?
6. How well does the present telephone equipment work?
7. What role does the chamber play in helping new businesses?
8. How frequent are electrical power outages? What is the average duration?
9. What is the principal industry and/or agricultural emphasis?
10. Who are the primary employers? Are they stable?
11. Is there overnight mail, package delivery, and pick up? Does the post office have boxes available?
12. What businesses does the community really need? Are there any that would be *unwelcome*?
13. Is there an economic development office available and how can I contact them?

This session is almost guaranteed to leave the director bewildered; few people are so organized in their search for a new home as you have become. There will be several questions left unanswered. The following advice pinpoints more assistance.

FINDING MORE RESOURCES

Of course, real estate offices specialize in knowing the answers to newcomers' questions. Because their specialty is rural property, we'd suggest you contact the United National Real Estate office in the area you're considering and have a chat with the agent. (If you followed our earlier advice, you already know of several interesting listings you want to pursue.) Fill in the blanks left from your chamber of commerce discussion. Discuss the properties you want to view. Really get acquainted.

There are more sources who also will prove useful. Check with local or college librarians. Introduce yourself to the editor of the daily or weekly newspaper. If you didn't previously subscribe, spend some time in their archives going over back issues. Stories about proposed mines, new landfills, firms closing, planned recreational districts that will boost taxes (and offer more amenities), or news of barroom brawls and arrests all paint a vivid picture of the area's culture.

Pay a visit to the local banks and talk with the bank president or vice president. (Yes, you can get to the head man or woman in small towns.) Inquire about real estate repossessions you might consider. Determine if their hours are convenient.

If you plan to open a retail or mail order business, ask about the availability of merchant credit card status so you can accept VISA and MasterCard orders. In metropolitan areas, new mail order companies find it virtually impossible to secure this status. We had no problem getting it here in Buena Vista. As a businessperson, you might also want to negotiate with the bank president to drop service charges on your accounts.

Charged with the mission of rural revitalization, the county extension service is another good resource. The USDA operates extension programs in all 3,165 U.S. counties. The area agent can help you with agricultural, water, and soil questions—plus job skill issues, career decisions, and expanded business opportunities.

If you're going to open a business (or even purchase an existing one), government agencies and regional economic development authorities can tell you about counseling and government funds available for business start-ups, on-the-job training programs for new hires, and various incentive programs. And if you're considering purchasing an old building that needs repair, check with the local historical society about matching funds for preservation or special tax credits and incentives for restoration.

Migrating entrepreneurs will also want to talk with local business leaders, town council members, those who serve on the county board of supervisors, and other town boosters. (An abundance of additional business market researching tips are covered in Chapter 9, "Researching for the Right Opportunity.")

To simplify your investigation and be sure you don't overlook important considerations, use the adjacent "Ross Relocation Checklist."

Ross Relocation Checklist

(check if high priority or major concern)

Education
- ❏ Nursery school/Day care facilities
- ❏ Grade school
- ❏ Middle school
- ❏ High school
  - ❏ sports program
  - ❏ music
  - ❏ drama
  - ❏ computers
  - ❏ gifted/remedial programs
  - ❏ dropout rate
- ❏ Religious/private school
- ❏ Vocational/technical school
- ❏ Community/junior college
- ❏ College or university
- ❏ Continuing education
- ❏ Private tutors/teachers (piano, violin, guitar, etc.)
- ❏ Other _____

Community
- ❏ Churches
- ❏ Professional organizations
- ❏ Fraternal/sorority alumni groups
- ❏ Service clubs
- ❏ Senior citizen groups
- ❏ Youth groups
- ❏ Children's playground
- ❏ Youth team sports
- ❏ Veterans' clubs
- ❏ Shopping facilities
- ❏ Crime/fire protection
- ❏ Responsive local government
- ❏ Major industries
- ❏ Per capita income
- ❏ Unemployment rate
- ❏ General acceptance of outsiders

- ❏ Proximity to major metropolian area
- ❏ Handicapped access
- ❏ Other _____

Resources
- ❏ Water supply
  - ❏ availability
  - ❏ treatment
  - ❏ taste
  - ❏ smell
  - ❏ well permit
  - ❏ cost to drill a well
- ❏ Power supply
  - ❏ nuclear
  - ❏ electric
  - ❏ hydraulic
  - ❏ gas
  - ❏ propane
- ❏ Other _____

Taxes
- ❏ City and county sales
- ❏ State sales
- ❏ State income
- ❏ Inheritance
- ❏ Gasoline
- ❏ Other _____

Climate
- ❏ Rainfall
- ❏ Snowfall
- ❏ Humidity
- ❏ Winter lows
- ❏ Summer highs
- ❏ Average temperature
- ❏ High winds
- ❏ Percent of sunshine
- ❏ Elevation
- ❏ Other _____

Ross Relocation Checklist (continued)

Environment
- ❏ Parks/Green spaces
- ❏ Trees
- ❏ Water
  - ❏ ocean
  - ❏ lake
  - ❏ river
  - ❏ creeks
- ❏ Cleanliness
- ❏ Recycling facilities
- ❏ Odor-free
- ❏ Noise pollution
- ❏ Air pollution
- ❏ Other _____

Transportation
- ❏ Distance to:
  - ❏ airport
  - ❏ train station
  - ❏ bus terminal
- ❏ Public transportation system
- ❏ Taxis
- ❏ Handicapped assistance
- ❏ Commuting ease
- ❏ Bike routes
- ❏ Winter maintenance (snow plowing/sanding/salting)
- ❏ Other _____

Cost of Living
- ❏ Real estate
- ❏ Food
- ❏ Clothing
- ❏ Fuel
- ❏ Utilities
- ❏ Insurance
  - ❏ auto
  - ❏ fire
  - ❏ home
- ❏ Other _____

Culture/Entertainment
- ❏ Movies/theater
- ❏ Museum
- ❏ Library
- ❏ Bookstore
- ❏ Nightclub
- ❏ Restaurants
- ❏ Aerobics/Fitness or health center
- ❏ Other outdoor pursuits
  - ❏ golf course
  - ❏ tennis courts
  - ❏ swimming pool
  - ❏ softball field
  - ❏ racquetball courts
- ❏ Athletic activities
- ❏ Musical events
- ❏ National Public Radio reception
- ❏ Cable TV reception
- ❏ Other _____

Health Care
- ❏ Hospital
  - ❏ 24-hour emergency care
  - ❏ depth of facility
  - ❏ ambulance service
- ❏ Doctor
- ❏ Public health nurse
- ❏ Medical specialist
- ❏ Dentist
- ❏ Optometrist/optician
- ❏ Mental health care
- ❏ Clinic
- ❏ Chiropractor
- ❏ Massage therapist
- ❏ Emergency 911 number
- ❏ Special support groups
- ❏ Veterinarian
- ❏ Other _____

Ross Relocation Checklist (continued)

Possible Undesirable Conditions
- ❏ Environment
  - ❏ nuclear power plant
  - ❏ dangerous waste site
  - ❏ well water contamination
  - ❏ flood plain
  - ❏ radon
  - ❏ allergens
- ❏ Elements
  - ❏ hurricanes
  - ❏ earthquakes
  - ❏ tornadoes
  - ❏ avalanches
- ❏ Community
  - ❏ racial tension
  - ❏ violent crime rate
  - ❏ hate groups
  - ❏ gangs
  - ❏ high drug use
  - ❏ nearby prison
- ❏ Location
  - ❏ remote shipment
    - ❏ old fruits/vegetables
    - ❏ slow postal delivery service
  - ❏ limited shopping
  - ❏ inconvenient business hours
  - ❏ scant entertainment
  - ❏ lack of singles' activities
- ❏ Other _____

Considerations for the Mature
- ❏ Public transportation
- ❏ Health care
  - ❏ in-home assistance
  - ❏ elder care program
  - ❏ convalescent/nursing home
- ❏ Elevation

- ❏ Handicapped access
- ❏ AARP chapter
- ❏ Veterans' services officer
- ❏ Home-delivered meals
- ❏ Communal meals
- ❏ Weatherization/LEAP program
- ❏ Community center activities
- ❏ Other _____

Business Considerations
- ❏ Enterprise zone/Economic development
- ❏ FDIC property available
- ❏ County/local tax incentives
- ❏ Area labor pool
- ❏ Phone system sophistication
  - ❏ private lines available
  - ❏ call waiting
- ❏ Temporary help/On-call secretarial
- ❏ Services
  - ❏ attorney
  - ❏ CPA
  - ❏ overnight pickup/delivery
- ❏ Proximity to critical suppliers
- ❏ Access for pickup and delivery
- ❏ Power reliability
- ❏ Signage regulations
- ❏ Parking availability
- ❏ Chamber of commerce involvement
- ❏ Zoning for in-home enterprises
- ❏ Existing competition
- ❏ Computer user groups
- ❏ Corporate taxes
- ❏ Online service available
- ❏ Other _____

TACTICS FOR TESTING THE WATERS

Broaden your knowledge base by more firsthand explorations. But now instead of talking to various experts, you're getting to know the townsfolk. It's mingle time. You want to meet the natives on their own terms. So don't pull out a wad of bills or you label yourself a city sophisticate. On the other hand, ordering coffee at the local coffee shop and proclaiming, "What a great place to raise kids!" is sure to start up a dialogue.

To stimulate conversations, try using the "echo technique." This encourages people to expand on what they previously said and helps you pull out information not normally shared. Here's how it works: You simply repeat the last few words the other person has said. For instance, if Jane ends her comments with, " . . . and the heat is a problem." You pipe up with, "Problem . . . ?" She's likely to go on with something like, "Yes, the humidity gets so high in August we about die." Bingo! You've just gleaned data that may sway your whole decision.

Likewise if someone says, "Parker City is really an old-fashioned community," you come back with, "Old fashioned community . . . ?" And the other party will typically volunteer, "Oh, we have band concerts and parades for any occasion you can think of. And last summer everybody had a ball at the box lunch social." Here again you've uncovered valuable insight into the texture of this town's values. If traditional ways are important to you, this place might be a good match.

In the process of your informal interviews, also talk to recent migrants. What drew them here? Has the original attraction faded or bloomed? To what extent are they pleased with the move? Has the area improved or declined in meeting their needs? Just don't take everything you hear as gospel. Some people are as flaky as a good pie crust.

Successful relocation requires resourcefulness. Sometimes the most worthwhile information doesn't come to you directly, but rather through the conversations of others. Go to the restaurant where the most pickup trucks or sheriff's cars are parked. This is the local hangout. It's the place where you'll hear snatches of discussions about everything from the schools to local politics, farming to weather idiosyncracies, real news to plain gossip. Another place to conduct eavesdropping reconnaissance is at the local bar. Tavern-goers often get loose tongues.

Here are some additional hints: Strike up conversations with locals if you have a CB radio. Talk to vendors at roadside fruit, vegetable, or flower stands. Monitor throwaway newspapers or literature sitting on countertops around town. Read posters in merchants' windows to get a sense of a locale's activities. Take pictures of places and people who hold particular interest for you. Make a game of keeping your antenna attuned to everything and everybody.

But don't let yourself get bogged down with "analysis paralysis." After you've gathered the facts, it's how you *feel* about a place that counts. It may take two or three visits to establish a comfort level. That's fine. When all systems point to "go," move on as we discuss significant real estate purchasing pointers.

CHOOSING YOUR SPECIFIC DREAM HOME OR LAND

Getting a good real estate deal in the location of your choice is like throwing the one-two punch to score a knockout. We've shown you how to scope out the community; now let's progress to finding an ideal property—and total victory.

One person's fantasy is another's albatross. You might hanker to own 40 or so acres where you can raise animals and grow crops. The family down the street may prefer to trade their condo for a house just outside a small town, while the retirees next door prefer a little place right in the middle of town close to all services. The career-driven boomers a few streets over are looking for a second home in a recreational mecca where they can escape on long weekends. Each seeks a custom-made oasis.

People find their dreams take many shapes. Possibilities for shelter run the gamut. There are underground bermed homes, rustic cabins, grand Victorian ladies, sprawling ranch styles, peeled-log beauties, Swiss chalets, mountain A-frames, adobe haciendas, dome homes, and nondescript little houses. (By the way, we've discovered that a fair number of these exterior plain Janes sport stunning interiors. It's a country quirk that some folks spend a lot more on the inside than the outside.)

Detached houses continue to be the most appealing to both urban and rural residents. Condominiums have also gone country. This is an ideal way out of the rental market for young couples, and a solution for mature adults who don't want the responsibility of a big house and yard.

Mobile homes, once thought of as tin boxes, have come into their own in the past few years. When making a transition onto bare land they are a wonderful alternative for quick housing. A 14 × 70-foot mobile home offers nearly 1,000 square feet of living space. And some double-wides have all the luxuries of conventional houses, including hot tubs and whirlpool baths. Once in place, these babies become stationary when the wheels, axle, and towing tongue are removed. We offer a caution when buying older mobiles, though. It's sometimes impossible to get insurance if a unit is more than ten years old. So check with your insurance agent before investing in an older model. Also be sure the zoning laws allow mobiles where you plan to locate.

Manufactured (modular) homes are an even more popular alternative today. Add a pitched shake roof, a deck, some landscaping, and presto! Even the tax assessor may mistake one for a conventionally built house.

Let's talk briefly about subdivision lots. Disreputable real estate developers can make a tract of barren, parched earth or swampland look and sound like paradise. Each year they ring up billions of dollars in interstate land sales. *Always* visit property before you invest. Legislation enacted in 1984 offers some protection to buyers in larger subdivisions (over 100 lots and advertised in more than one state). But the byword is still *caveat emptor* (let the buyer beware).

It's also a good idea to verify any comments made by a real estate salesperson with the building department to check that zoning, electrical, and other criteria meet your needs. Sometimes a building must have considerable upgrading to be used for a different purpose.

One of the issues that quickly surfaces when contemplating making a move is whether you buy or sell first. It's a shame to find the perfect country getaway, only to be handcuffed because all your capital is still tied up in your city property. Conversely, what a pity to sell your city home . . . and not have a country retreat to go to. There is no foolproof solution. It seems wise to us, however, to put your house on the market once you've made the commitment to become an urban dropout and have narrowed your choices to a town or two. If you find the ideal place at the right price, then you'll have one leg up on being able to purchase it.

Unless you have the cash to carry two places temporarily, make your offer on the new real estate *contingent on* the successful sale of your old residence. If this doesn't work, you might try renting with an option to buy until your capital frees up.

Depending on what the economy is like, it may take time to unload your metropolitan property. In 1980, when we tried to sell our 2,400-square-foot home a couple of blocks from the beach, purchasers were as scarce as opera buffs at a Michael Jackson concert. We made the mistake of buying a second place before we sold the first. Finally, we accepted a ludicrous offer on our San Diego property to get much needed cash to make payments on the ranch.

Don't rule out a fixer-upper, especially if you or a family member enjoy working with your hands. You can also hire construction help cheaper in the country. Be sure, however, to have an engineer check for structural integrity and a building inspector determine what it will take to conform to local building codes.

If you anticipate building a custom home, it's a good idea to rent first or purchase an interim property. Then you'll have time to become acquainted with a qualified architect and builder.

WORKING THROUGH A BROKER

Especially when dealing with rural properties, it makes sense to work through a broker. Knowledge and familiarity with the area is vital. It isn't like suburban properties where it's easy to find comparable properties and know if you're getting a good value. Country property is spread out and more diverse in type and terrain. A competent real estate salesperson knows about problems unique to the area and which distressed owners need to bail out fast. He or she also knows better than to value country real estate through the eyes of suburbia.

By now you should have narrowed down those you'll work with to one or two. There's no need to deal with everyone. In most areas there are multiple listing services that catalog all real estate properties. Be sure to have detailed discussions with the real estate agents you choose so they know your individual likes and dislikes, wants and needs.

Owner financing has been a staple of country real estate markets for a half century. This is one of the advantages of buying rural property. Usually such loans can be arranged at rates below those quoted by banks and mortgage companies. Additionally, there are no points or loan fees, no detailed loan applications to complete, and no lengthy waits to see if you qualify. In fact, many owners financing their own properties never even check a buyer's credit, so someone cursed with a poor credit rating may be able to slip into a property.

If you're a veteran, consider a VA loan. Even if you've already used this benefit, it may be possible for you to get a restored loan entitlement. Their Web site promises to do away with red tape; go to http://www.on-point.com/vahomes/LoanInformation.htm and see for yourself.

What will you have to pay for rural real estate? By studying the United National Real Estate catalog, area newspapers, and subscribing to the *Rural Property Bulletin* (P.O. Box 37, Sparks, NE 69220, 402-376-2985) you can get a good sense of how area prices vary. Water is universally appealing—therefore a lake, river, stream, or pond automatically boosts the value. Trees are another drawing card. Property with a stand of timber will cost more than barren land. The closer to a large city, the higher the price.

Statistics divulged at a National Association of REALTORS® convention show the average house sells for 16 percent below the original listing price. If you take your time, you're more likely to find a bargain than if you rush into making a purchase.

In small towns off the beaten path you can sometimes buy a house for what a nice car costs today. Prices in the $30,000 range can still be found. And remember you need a lot less income if your monthly mortgage payments are based on a $20,000 loan (after a down payment), than if you're supporting a mortgage in excess of $150,000.

WHAT TO LOOK FOR IN A COUNTRY HOME

City slickers who don't educate themselves can really get hurt when they buy in the sticks. Choosing property before you're informed is the human equivalent of a dog exposing its belly in surrender. We know of two good books on the subject. *Finding & Buying Your Place in the Country,* by Les Scher & Carol Scher, tells you e-v-e-r-y-t-h-i-n-g: more than you would ever think to ask. (Order it by calling 800-621-9621, ext. 3650.) A faster read to help you avoid pitfalls is *Finding the Good Life in Rural America* by Bob Bone (800-331-8355). If you want to purchase a house or retail store rather than land, the following "Quickie Rural Home Evaluation Sheet" is helpful.

If you have any qualms about a piece of property, or are buying it directly from the owner, consider contacting a real estate agent in a neighboring town and hiring him or her to inspect it. You'll pay around $200. Also have them find out whether back taxes are paid and if the title is clear.

Quickie Rural Home Evaluation Sheet

Address: _____

Name of broker or owner: _____ Price: $ _____

Down: $ _____ Terms: _____ Annual taxes: $ _____

How long has it been on the market?_____ Size of lot/acreage: _____

Any other buildings on the property? _____

Total square footage: _____ One story or two? _____

Condition of neighborhood: _____ Landscaped?_____

Type of roof/condition: _____

Type of heating system/age: _____

Average monthly utility bill: $ _____

What is the water source?_____

Well permits? _____ Water rights?_____

Condition of plumbing: _____

Connected to sewer? _____ Septic tank? _____

How old? _____ Where located?_____

Condition of electrical system: _____

Telephone lines in/available? _____

Miles to town: _____ Does county maintain road?_____

Overall condition: _____

Special **good** features of property: _____

Special **bad** aspects of property: _____

There's more to a house than meets the eye. In mid-sized cities you can hire a home inspection service that will perform complete structural, wall, floor, ceiling, foundation, basement, and roof inspections. They'll also do a termite inspection; look at the plumbing, heating, and air-conditioning systems; check the septic tank; do a radon measurement; even examine built-in appliances. In many small towns, however, no such service exists. (Maybe this is a part-time business idea for you!)

You can personally do some checking by talking with the people in the county courthouse and at the assessor's office. They know more than you'd imagine. Also chat with the neighbors. You'll quickly find out such details as what the roads are like in the winter, if the creek ever overflows in the spring, and whether the school bus comes close by.

It's been said that neighborhoods have personalities—even in small towns. Be sure to look not only at homes, but also at the surrounding clues. The house may be perfect. But if you have toddlers or school-aged children, an absence of bikes and basketball hoops may give you a hint about this area. When you visit with the neighbors, ask open-ended questions. An older lady may complain about "all the kids in this neighborhood." If you have children, that's probably a plus. (Try to be around when the school bus arrives.) If you're a retired couple, you might choose to look elsewhere.

We knew a military family who tried this door-knocking technique. They thought they'd found the right house until they talked to a neighbor. "Now those people are military," the neighbor remarked, pointing across the street. "They'll only be here a year or two so we don't think it's worth the effort to get to know them. They're so transient, you know." Needless to say, the house hunters filed this information away.

Consider other clues as you survey areas. If you're a gardener, you'll certainly notice the yards around you. Do these neighbors share the same values about their grounds? It doesn't have to be a perfect match, but if something is likely to get on your nerves, admit it. You're the one who'll see it every day. When you've narrowed it down to one or two houses, drive by several different times during the day to "feel the pulse" of the neighborhood. And be sure to take lots of pictures; family and friends will all want to see where you're going.

While it's simpler to get a feel for the size of a lot in suburbia, understanding larger parcels of land is a more difficult challenge. Purchasing land is foreign to most city residents. Acreage is most often sold in parcels of 5-, 40-, 160- (a quarter section), 320- (a half section), and 640- (a full section) acre increments. The smaller the parcel, the higher the cost per acre. For instance, you may pay $3,000 for five acres but be able to buy a 40-acre parcel for $16,000. Acreage also can be deceiving. Part of it may run up the side of a hill and be unusable, yet you still pay for that by the acre.

Thousands of lovely farms with attractive buildings and good soil are for sale in regions that are not close to large metropolitan areas. They can be picked up at a fraction of their real value because the area is suffering from out-migration. If you want a bargain farm to play a large role in your future, check upstate New York, the Upper Peninsula of Michigan, and the Ozarks.

POINTERS FOR PICKING PARCELS OF UNIMPROVED PROPERTY

As you contemplate buying unimproved country property, there are many things to consider.

Number one is water.   Buying acreage without water rights is the equivalent of putting the fox in charge of the henhouse. And just because there is surface water on your land—a stream, river, lake, or pond—it does *not* necessarily mean you have the legal right to use it! Water rights are a commodity just like the acreage itself. One person can own the land, someone else can own the water rights. You need water not only for drinking and bathing, but also for animals and crops—so investigate this issue thoroughly.

In our county you can't get a well permit for outside water use unless you have 35 or more acres of land. If you want a lawn, a garden, or a place to wash your car, you're out of luck without the acreage. And consider whether the flow will lessen or disappear during the hot summer months. If there aren't adequate water rights, get bids for drilling a well *before* you make an offer on the land. Know how deep you'll likely have to go to hit water and if it will be potable (safe for drinking).

Look closely at zoning laws.   You can't always put a property to any use you want. There may be restrictions on whether a mobile home can serve as an interim residence, covenants in posh developments that restrict unsightly possessions or buildings, and limitations on using your home as an office (we discuss overcoming this in Chapter 12, "Home Suite Home"). And if you're serious about farming, be sure the place is zoned for agricultural use. Likewise, determine any zoning or deed restrictions that might prevent you from keeping certain types of animals.

Will you need a septic system?   If you can't connect to a municipal sewer system, be sure the soil will accommodate a septic tank. Check this out by having a percolation test done.

Investigate the soil.   Is it rich farm land? Tillable? Is there good drainage? What crops will grow best? Talk to the county extension agent about a soil analysis report to determine what kind of soil you have.

A rookie farmer or rancher might want to check with agricultural colleges such as those at Colorado State University or Texas A&M University. These and other universities hold a wealth of information and sometimes even have intern programs where junior, senior, or graduate students use their summers to work on farms. In this way you get the most up-to-date information available for very little cost. Room and board is necessary, and it's always thoughtful to include a little extra for spending money. The student will appreciate the experience and you've just gained a stronger footing in the agricultural industry.

What's the "lay of the land"?   Is there a suitable home site or will expensive grading be required? Don't get stuck on a flood plain. And if you plan to have a great view from a hilltop, check to be sure it doesn't catch traffic noises. Sound carries remarkably well in the country, especially at night. Your frontier fantasy will be quickly dashed if the sound of roaring trucks permeates the evening breeze. If you want to use solar power, is there a good southern exposure—or do mountains limit the hours of sun? Is there a driveable road or would the existing jeep trail challenge the most stalwart Baja racer? Putting in access roads is expensive when you factor in grading, gravel, shoulders, and culverts to prevent washouts.

Consider easements and encumbrances.   If the piece of land you want to buy doesn't have access to a public road, get an easement right to reach it without trespassing on your neighbor's land. And don't be surprised if the local utility company has an easement on your land giving them permission to run underground lines. Be sure to get a deed conveying clear title. If there is any question about encumbrances on the property, seek the counsel of an attorney. After all, you don't want a property dispute. What's a property dispute? *Ground beef,* of course!

What about mineral rights? It's wise to insist on getting the mineral rights to your property. Seem like an insignificant point? Not so. One poor soul—who had built his dream home and planted orchards and gardens—came home one day to find his house bulldozed and his mature orchard being uprooted. Turns out the company that owned the mineral rights found coal on his land and he had no legal recourse. Additionally, mineral rights sometimes can add up to huge sums for you. We know one man who got $800,000 for the minerals on his property. Besides, who knows what raw materials will be of value several decades from now?

Are there any natural hazards?   This might include excessive winds (terrific for generating windmill power, but difficult to live with), unstable soil and rock that could result in landslides, or steep terrain and thick brush that equal a fire hazard. Also consider any plans to develop nearby land. This could interfere greatly with your peace and quiet.

To simplify the selection process, use the "Rural Real Estate Checklist" (provided courtesy of Bob Bone). It is a list of questions the prospective purchaser should know the answers to before making a binding offer on country property. Because there are special considerations that relate to one kind of property to the exclusion of others, concerns that are particular to a certain area of the country—or even to the buyers themselves—this is not to be construed as being a complete list. The concerns addressed by these questions fit most properties, most of the time, and for most buyers.

Some states, such as California, require a broker by law to obtain a disclosure statement from the seller for *residential* property. A copy of this disclosure must be delivered to the buyer of the property. It is becoming common practice for more and more brokers to obtain such disclosures from sellers even if the law does not require it. United National Real Estate brokers follow this guideline during their transactions. Such disclosures will answer many of the questions posed in the "Rural Real Estate Checklist."

Rural Real Estate Checklist

Zoning, Building Codes, Covenants, Conditions, and Restrictions (CC&Rs)

1. Is the property in compliance with zoning and setback regulations?
2. Is the owner aware of any health, safety, or building code violations?
3. Are there any notices of abatement or citations against the property other than the mortgage?
4. Read CC&Rs if any. Are there any violations apparent?

Parcel

1. Is the property in a flood plain or special study zone?
2. Is there any indication or does the owner know of any drainage problem?
3. Is there any indication or does the owner know of any water accumulation in the basement or on the property?
4. Has the parcel been surveyed? Are the corners identified?
5. If there is a stream, river, or lake, does the property line run to the center?
6. Are there any legal limitations of the use of any stream, river, ditch, or lake on the property?

Road/Right-of-Ways

1. Is there deeded right-of-way to the property?
2. Is the road to the property public or private? Who maintains it? Who is responsible for snow removal?

Construction

1. Is the owner aware of any structural or foundation problems?
2. To the owner's knowledge, was any urea-formaldehyde or asbestos material used in the property's construction?
3. What type of roof does the property have? What is the age of the roof? Is there any apparent leaking? Has the attic been checked?
4. Has the property suffered damage from a fire or flood?

Systems/Appliances

1. Are the following items in working order?
   - ❑ Range ❑ Trash Compactor ❑ Air-Conditioning
   - ❑ Sprinklers ❑ Microwave ❑ Garbage Disposal
   - ❑ Garage Door Opener(s) ❑ Furnace ❑ Dishwasher
   - ❑ Water Softeners/Filters ❑ Refrigerator ❑ Water Pump
2. Is the owner aware of any problems affecting the plumbing, electrical, heating/cooling systems or the water heater?
3. What were the owner's heating and air-conditioning costs for the past 12 months?
4. Is the sewage system public? If not, is there a septic system? To the owner's knowledge are there any blockages or breaks in the lines?

Rural Real Estate Checklist (continued)

5. If there is a septic system, is the owner aware of any backup or over-flowing of the tank?
6. Do any problems exist with permits, operation, or system location?
7. What was the date the septic system was last pumped?
8. If the public sewage system is not hooked up, what would it cost to hook it up?
9. If there isn't a septic tank in, what would the total cost for a system be for your family size?

Water Source

1. Is the water source public? Who is the water company? What is the approximate monthly cost for water?
2. If the water isn't in, what would the cost be to hook it up?
3. If the water source is public, is there any problem with the main line?
4. Is there a well? Is it public or private? Is there a maintenance agreement between all parties?
5. How deep is the well? According to the owner, what is the gallons per minute? Size of casting? What size horsepower is the pump on the well?
6. Has the owner had any problems with the water pressure or has the well ever run dry?
7. Is the owner aware of any contamination or other reason the water would not be potable?
8. Is there irrigation water? If so, what is the source? What is the cost to obtain it?

Power

1. Is there power to the property? If not, how far is the property from power? What would the cost be to bring power to the property?

Services

1. Schools: What types are available? How far away are the schools? Does the bus pick children up?
2. Fire protection: How far away is the fire station? Are firefighters volunteers or are they paid?
3. Medical care: What is the distance to the nearest hospital? What about emergency care?
4. Mail: Is there mail delivery? If not, how do you obtain your mail?

Legal

1. Is there a homeowners association? If so, what are the dues per year?
2. Are there any disputes with neighbors regarding location or use of driveways, patios, fences, common walls, etc.?
3. Is the owner aware of any condition or situation that might result in an increase in assessment?

Reprinted from *Finding the Good Life in Rural America* by Bob Bone. To order, call 800-331-8355.

LIVING ON THE LAND

Some people dream of living *off* the land while they live *on* it. These homesteaders hope to generate enough income from vegetables, orchards, other crops, and meat they produce to make a living. It's tough. But it can be done—especially if you get enough capital from your city property to pay cash for your country spot.

Living simply, without electricity or a telephone, holds rewards for the hardy. Life can be rich: filled with your homegrown food, music, friends, and nature. Rather than an electric or gas range, you may use a cookstove fueled with firewood. Your refrigerator may be a cool natural spring.

Before our indoor plumbing was in place at the ranch, we rigged up a bathing arrangement that warmed the heart of every nonconformist. Imagine one five-gallon oil drum and kindling for a small fire. Start a fire under the oil drum. Add a bathtub, a gallon bucket, and one stream. Use the bucket to dip water from the stream and half fill the oil drum. Transfer the warm water into the bathtub. Bathe! Pull the plug and water the creek bank. What an experience to cleanse yourself smack-dab in the middle of nature—complete with birds chirping, a bubbling creek, and warm sunshine kissing your back.

However, some people (ourselves included) who have tried this "simple life" find it very difficult. You spend much of your time just surviving: chopping wood, stoking fires, boiling water, etc. You have to think and plan ahead. Nothing's immediate. You learn to organize yourself and your work in ways you never expected. It took us an hour's round-trip to get into town for the mail or groceries. Substantial shopping had to be done in a distant town. That round-trip consumed more than three hours.

Many others who have harbored the dream of self-sufficiency report the demands are too great. Fourteen-hour days, seven days a week, are not unusual if you're growing and preserving all your own food, making your clothes, plus providing for your own energy and heat.

Marilyn: Being a city girl, I proved myself in ways I wouldn't have dreamed of. It's funny the difference a pair of cowboy boots and work gloves make. Wearing those, I felt invincible (well, most of the time). I'll never forget the day Tom and our ranch hand had gone to an auction and I was alone. We had a mare ready to give birth. She had lost her foals the previous two years. When I went out to check her, one of the foal's legs was already exposed. Panic engulfed me. How could I help her? Which way should I pull? What if she kicked me?

An hour—and many prayers—later a gorgeous, spindly-legged colt stood nursing. And I sat there in awe, rejoicing in the wonder of God's creation.

There were other times I tested my mettle, other experiences that will always bring tears or a grin. I feel blessed to have had those opportunities to expand myself in fresh ways.

Because we used computers, we had a generator and a bank of batteries to supply power. Something was always going wrong. Fortunately, Tom used to earn his living as an electronics engineer, so he knows how to fix things. The typical city slicker would be lost trying to coexist with such obstinate systems. And that's just the tip of the iceberg. There are irrigation ditches to open (and close), tractors to get unstuck, animals to doctor, and much more. Trying to do all that—while maintaining two businesses—overwhelmed us. Though we have many cherished memories, the difficulties and inconveniences of home on the range just weren't worth it.

Although we miss the ranch and the animals, living in a small town with normal conveniences is much more realistic for us. So while we don't want to discourage those bent on being back-to-the-landers, in all honesty we must sound this solemn warning. Some people discover their dream of living in an isolated mountain cabin can become a nightmare. Sometimes it just doesn't mesh with their personalities, needs, and goals.

If you value your independence and still hanker for this rugged lifestyle, consider subscribing to *Mother Earth News, Harrowsmith Country Life, Backwoods Home Magazine,* and *Country Journal.*

Now that you know the ins and outs of purchasing rural property, let's investigate how you can fit in more easily once you relocate to your Shangri-la.

6

---◆---

Letting the Small Town
Viewpoint Work for You

How exciting it is to live your vision! As you move to the country, you have dreams and anticipations of what it will be like. Those dreams are important. They are the impetus that spurred you to move. At the same time, it's vital to remember nothing is exactly as we picture it will be. Many factors are beyond our control. If you look at this as an adventure—with open-ended possibilities rather than a list of expectations to check off—it will be much more fulfilling.

Just as you'd fasten your seat belt for a ride on the roller coaster, or take a deep breath before diving under water, prepare for relocating by looking forward to the unknown thrills ahead. Don't dwell on what you left behind. Above all, don't try to make your new surroundings a reflection of your past.

Remember *The Ugly American*? Although moving from the suburbs to the exurbs is different than visiting another country, the same principles apply. Too often people migrate, then radiate the feeling that locals are foreigners who should conform to the newcomer's ways. Be willing to change yourself. The countryside doesn't welcome transplants who insist on offering advice on how to live and do things, simply because that's the way the newcomer used to live and do things in the city. If it was so great, why did he leave?

Should your outlook differ from the local perspective, don't voice too many opinions. Sparks fly most easily when people of different backgrounds and viewpoints interact. Remember it was *their* town before it became yours. Be patient. It may take time to overcome their preconceived notions. Of course if you followed our advice, you didn't locate in an area hostile to newcomers. Having a good life is a lot like a boomerang: You have to toss it out before it comes back to you. National sales guru Zig Ziglar believes the best way to get what you want is to give others what they want.

DEVELOPING A MIND-SET FOR CHANGE

Let's be honest: The only person who really likes change is a wet baby. But if we want to adjust satisfactorily to a new community, we have to be willing to modify how we think and behave. The psychology of country living dictates that you must replace your urban mind-set with a rural one if you want to thrive. Rural people are more easygoing than city folk. If you come dashing in with brisk, rigid, sophisticated ways, you'll alienate your new neighbors.

We can manage our perspective as surely as we manage our time. When a closed mind re-opens, it's usually under new management. Moving means making adjustments. The difference in our reactions to new places, people, and customs depends on our expectations, awareness, and personality. If you're having trouble adjusting, reading *The Trauma of Moving* by psychotherapist Audrey T. McCollum might prove beneficial.

Moving is a profound opportunity for transformation. Realigning your thoughts can literally realign your life. Listen to your self-talk and identify any negative messages. (Research shows a whopping 87 percent of our thoughts are negative.) Replace these reflections with positive ones that tell you what's *good* instead of what's bad—what you *can* do, rather than what you can't.

Instead of wallowing in negativity, make a conscious decision to purify your thinking. Otherwise you'll be stuck in a down mood. When this happens, it's as contagious as chicken pox. Pretty soon the whole family or entire store or office becomes cloaked in gloom. Our beliefs wield tremendous power. Ziglar gives us another quote to live by: "It's your attitude, not your aptitude, that determines your altitude." Imagine yourself being successful, making friends, fitting in.

In a mathematics equation there are constants and there are variables. The constants of our lives—our family priorities, our faith, our values, our personal gifts—add stability wherever we go. The variables—our career choice, our homes, what we do with our free time, the friendships we develop—add spice and momentum. It's important to have a sense of what we can or cannot change and still retain a sense of who we are.

How adaptable are you? Because things move more slowly in the country, you'll likely feel you've been plunked down in some foreign experimental laboratory at first.

> Marilyn: When I moved from San Diego to First Try, it was major culture shock: a real socioquake! Everything was unfamiliar. All pretense was out. The old ground rules didn't apply. I flailed around like a fish out of water.
>
> It amazed me, for instance, when I learned we were perceived as a threat to the local weekly newspaper. Because it was known we did something with the written word, people jumped to the conclusion we might put this enterprise out of business. We were shocked: Who would want to be accused of trying to extinguish a family-run firm that has been faithfully serving the community for generations?

Habits are like cobwebs that turn into cables. Just because you've "always done it that way" doesn't mean you should continue in that fashion. *Flexibility* is the operative word here. Lifestyle changes pop up everywhere. Self-reliance is a big deal. Goods and services are not as immediately available as they were in the city. People are more informal. Real. Friendlier.

ATTITUDES: YOURS AND THEIRS

Certain values are different in the country. People are measured not so much by the size of their wallets, what they wear, or what work they do—but rather by personal qualities like honesty and resourcefulness. You can be yourself and be valued for that special self. There is less pressure to conform. Rural people are also more in touch with the earth. They count on animals, crops, and weather for their livelihood. Sunrises and sunsets are important events to them.

To get accepted may be as simple as a pleasant "howdy" when you meet. Asking residents for advice on local places or issues also is smart. It helps you get acclimated and it makes them feel important.

The Knight of Lightning Speed never made it to the boonies. Being impatient won't get you anything but heartburn. Sure you ordered lumber to build that add-on last week, and the delivery was supposed

to be here by noon today. Just because it's 4:00 PM and you've been killing time all day isn't going to change things. One of the sawyers may
have had a sick cow to doctor, or the delivery driver might have had to
plow his road before he could get out. Relax! Things happen in their
own good time in the country. No amount of prodding on your part
will alter that. The lumber will be there, albeit tardy.

Realize that population booms are threatening to small communities. On the other hand, orderly, planned growth that minimizes shock
to the infrastructure and current systems is welcome. Problems occur
when so many new people arrive that community services are stressed.
Street paving and repair must be accelerated, sewage and garbage controlled, utilities and water provided, houses built, schools enlarged.
This results in increased tax requirements and new stresses for the area.
Managed intelligently, growth is a positive process. A strong citizenry
contributes to a town, helping it expand and prosper.

SORTING IT OUT AND SETTLING IN

Continuity gives us a sense of belonging. Your home is an extension
of you, an expression of your self. It contains your individual imprint
and embodies your personal and family history. Displaying certain
mementos will give you, and other family members, comfort. These
artifacts can pull us from the past into the present.

Another way to speed your reconnection is through sensory signals,
smell in particular. Using the same kind of potpourri or cooking a family favorite meal with a tantalizing aroma signals "we're home!" People
have reported when spring came in their new locale, the fragrance of
lilacs blooming in a nearby garden gave them a sense that all was well.

Feeling at home speeds up when you know where to find things—
goods and services within the community. Something as simple as
learning how the aisles are arranged in a new supermarket is reassuring. It makes you feel you're more in control of your environment.
Knowing where to get your clothes cleaned, finding a good place for a
haircut, and discovering the best bakery in town are all reassuring
events.

OVERCOMING NEGATIVE FEELINGS TOWARD OUTSIDERS

Some small towns are intolerant. Rigid thinking makes them very establishment-oriented. They shun gays and lesbians, for instance, and look down on hippie or biker types. City slickers who come on too strong also meet a chilly reception.

Ironically, sometimes so do the very tourists who are much of the lifeblood of the community. Townspeople love the money they infuse into the local economy, yet comment privately they "can't wait 'til the season's over and the tourists leave!" Shouldn't we *rejoice* when they're here? Aren't they what pay our bills and allow us to live this existence?

Anywhere you go, you'll find good people and bad people, those you like and those you don't. There's a story of a fellow who moved to a small town. When he asked a native what kind of folks lived in the town, the man replied, "What kind of folks did you leave?"

"Oh, they were selfish and bigoted, small-minded and petty," came the reply.

"Well, I reckon you'll find the same kind here," the native mused.

Another newcomer came along and asked the native the same question. "What kind of folks live here?"

Again the native asked, "What kind of folks did you leave?" The second person flashed a warm smile. "Oh, they were wonderful. Warm and friendly, generous and fun. Real neighbors, they were."

The native grinned. "Yep. You'll find the folks here are much the same," he said.

Circumstances constantly live up to our expectations. We have an acquaintance who's so pessimistic he has one CB radio in his car—and a second one in his trunk, waiting to replace the stolen one. Another acquaintance assumes life is terrific. For her it is. She constantly opens the door to serendipity and in walks something even greater than what she anticipated. Life continually delights her.

LOSING YOUR ANONYMITY

You won't even have begun unloading the moving van before the word spreads like wildfire: The new family is here! Newcomers are a big deal in a small town. It's an event. People are just naturally curious. Remember the old game where you got in a circle and the leader whispered something into the ear of the next person, then it was repeated all around the circle? What happened at the end? It was a totally different message than what was originally stated, wasn't it? That's the way it is in Small Town USA. Situations get jumbled because people love to talk.

One of the hardest adjustments for us was getting used to the gossip mill. Someone once said gossip is news in a red satin dress. I'd liken it more to a pair of grubby overalls with many pockets for stuffing tidbits. Sid Ascher observed, "A small town is a place where everyone knows whose check is good and whose husband is not." In metropolitan areas most people don't have time to mind their neighbor's business; they don't even know their neighbors.

> Marilyn: In the boonies some tongues are malicious mischief makers. We encountered this in First Try. I've since learned, however, that gossip is a natural part of small town life, just like 4th of July picnics and summer band concerts. But to a city gal it was stifling at first when every move I made had an audience . . . and embellishment. This may be a difficult adjustment for you too.

The advice we'd offer is not to get caught up in gossip yourself. A good neighbor has two ears and one mouth—and uses them proportionately. Be a protector rather than a perpetrator. (Actually you may be protecting yourself as well as others.) The majority of people in a small town are related. It may be via a distant cousin, but they are *family*. Woe to the person who makes a snide remark about some other member of the clan. Give folks the benefit of the doubt. If you don't make disparaging remarks about people, you won't be on the outs with their in-laws.

You'll also find it harder to slip into the post office undetected to pick up the mail. When you're rushed and need to get back to work, it's inevitable you'll bump into several people you know. A hurried hello may offend them. Visiting for a few minutes is part of the price you pay for good neighbors when the chips are down.

Urban and rural are as different as playing old maid with your grandchild and bridge with your peers. Yet each has its attraction.

Tired of trendiness and materialism, Americans are rediscovering the joys of home life, basic values, and roots. They're rediscovering sentimental movies. Mixed-breed dogs. Pot roast. Family reunions. Erector sets. They enjoy modest pleasures and homier values. They're connecting with a Higher Power. They realize it's time to enjoy the little things, for one day we may realize they were the big things.

CHILD CARE IN THE BOONIES

The National Commission on Children reports that 81 percent of parents say they don't spend enough time with their kids. Concerned parents are trading the corporate culture for the family frontier in ever-increasing numbers.

Both parents often still work in a smaller town but child care is different. It's usually better. While there are fewer or no organized day care centers, informal home care providers offer several advantages. The adult-to-child ratio is normally lower. They are more willing to take a slightly ill child. The youngster is nurtured and allowed to form closer relationships. Meals are typically better as many substitute moms pride themselves on their cooking and baking skills. And if medications need to be given, they're not likely to be overlooked in the chaos of caring for countless numbers. In the winter, children are more likely allowed outdoors (it's easier to bundle and unbundle four little charges than 14). The overall environment is quieter; pleasures are simpler.

In the boondocks, a field trip may consist of watching cement being poured at a neighboring construction site or going down to Main Street to see the whole elementary school parade in their Halloween costumes. Kids also get to see the inner workings of another household. They're often taken along when the baby-sitter goes to decorate the church for an event, stops by the library to pick up books, or takes the car in for repairs. Such experiences enrich little lives more than remaining in a static environment.

In the city there is constant stimulation. It becomes a question of who can top whom. In a large nursery school, for instance, birthdays are frequent. So are clowns, elaborate cakes, and special treats. Parents try to outdo each other. Even show-and-tell becomes competitive.

With so much going on all day in nursery school, it's a letdown when the child comes home at night to parents drained from a hectic day. One friend tells of her three-year-old daughter begging for OshKosh brand clothing "with a little character" because the other kids had it. What a sad critique on our society when such tiny tykes are preoccupied with status symbols.

Nothing is perfect. There are drawbacks to country day care arrangements too. It's hard to find alternative care when the sitter goes on vacation or gets sick. And there aren't as many field trips to the zoo, planetarium, etc. Some parents don't find this a deterrent, however. They'd rather their kids didn't expect every day to be action-packed.

Continual activity warps youngsters and instills in them unrealistic anticipations about life.

MORE DIFFERENCES

Says Terry Barkett, a former member of the Chaffee County (Colorado) Commissioners, "You need to be a little more creative to live here. One difference I see in working in a rural area is you have to handle new ideas carefully, and over a long period of time. Change isn't accepted as readily as in a metro area."

Choices are also limited in rural areas. You won't necessarily find the color, model, or style you had in mind. (You may be lucky to find the item at all.) Specialty stores are nonexistent in tiny towns. Yet local merchants direly need your support. Buy locally whenever you can. When it isn't practical, make trips to the city count. Plan ahead. Buy in bulk.

Cynthia was used to shopping in malls. She wondered how she could get along without stores to browse. Then she discovered catalog shopping. About half of both men and women regularly buy products via direct mail. *The Catalog of Catalogs* is a wonderful resource listing more than 12,000 catalogs in 650 categories. Call 800-843-7323 to order it.

Even more exciting, electronic shopping will grow dramatically as consumers become impatient with checkout lines and inattentive sales clerks—or move to Small Town USA. You can shop 'til you drop via the Internet whether you live in New York City or Podunk. Catalog Mart boasts some 10,000 catalogs available free. Reach them at http://catalog.savvy.com. Or check out http://www.dreamshop.com for several other options. Another powerful online search opportunity is Buyer's Index. They have 3,500 mail order catalogs divided into 55 categories, plus World Wide Web shopping sites to help you find the goodies you need. They cover everything for business and professional people, hobbyists, plus virtually anything the average person would want. Reach them at http://www.buyersindex.com. Many catalogers have individual sites—such as Real Goods, which sells tools for sustainable living and can be found at http://www.realgoods.com/. So why wait *in* line when you can shop *on*line?

Fun in the hinterland takes a new slant. You might play a Mozart tape or CD in your car while taking a long, leisurely drive in the country. You'll more likely enjoy wildlife instead of a wild life. Making friends with God's creatures brings rich rewards. A squirrel, deer, or raccoon will never ace you out of a parking spot or cut you off on a crowded freeway.

Speaking of animals, to help you talk rural lingo, we've included a "Correct Country Animal Terms."

Correct Country Animal Terms						
Type	Horses	Cattle	Goats	Sheep	Swine (Pigs)	Poultry
Groups	Herd	Herd	Band	Flock	Drove	Flock
Newborn	Foal	Calf	Kid	Lamb	Pig	Chick
Young male	Colt	Bullock	Buck Kid	Ram Lamb	Shoat	Chick
Young female	Filly	Heifer	Doe Kid	Ewe Lamb	Gilt	Chick
Male of breeding age	Stud	Bull	Buck	Ram	Boar	Cock
Mature female	Mare	Cow	Doe	Ewe	Sow	Hen
Unsexed male	Gelding	Steer	Wether	Wether	Barrow	Capon

BEING A BIG FISH IN A LITTLE POND

"I always wanted to be somebody, but I should have been more specific," quips Lily Tomlin. It's a lot easier to be somebody in a small town than in the big city. If you interact in the community, you automatically become known. It's but a step further to become renowned. For some individuals, there is a certain thrill to being in the limelight. If you hanker for such prominence, celebrity status here you come! But even if you don't seek prominence, you'll be noticed. And you will get a reputation, for better or worse.

Sarah Hemingway explains that when she and husband Tom moved to Buena Vista they told their children, "In this town you're going to be a somebody. You can either be a good somebody or a bad somebody. But whatever you do, everyone will know about it." Life in a small town is life in a fishbowl. There are some positive aspects to that factor. It's a real incentive to live a worthy and good life. Another thing is when you're sick or hurting, small-town people tend to rally together like a family. Those are advantages to welcome.

"At the same time," Sarah elaborates, "it's critical that you learn to keep a zip on your lip. Information—good or bad—travels like lightning in small towns. By the time you've picked up brochures at the travel agency, someone is calling to find out when you're leaving on vacation. Learn the value of keeping confidence and you'll be miles ahead."

You'll also settle in quicker if you follow the tips in the next chapter. It addresses developing a satisfying life and making new friends.

7

Cultivating a Satisfying Social Life

In the city, people band together because they are white-collar workers, they make a similar salary, work in the same industry or company, went to the same college, or live in the same neighborhood. Rural residents mix it up more. The reason is simple. There aren't enough people in any one group to constitute a self-contained social world. Differences in lifestyle, social standing, and educational level are accepted. You see people because you *like them*.

And you entertain at home more. Things are casual, often spontaneous. Blue jeans replace cocktail attire most of the time. Bringing out the crystal and silver is an occasion, rather than what's expected. People live in a more relaxed atmosphere, visiting the city when they want stimulation—yet being protected from its everyday evils.

A move to Small Town USA is a move away from the hustle and bustle of city life. While many people understand this intellectually, they still find themselves wishing for the best of both worlds. Country workplaces can be every bit as busy and stimulating as those in the city, but the options for recreation and culture are much more limited. Country entertaining centers more on people and friendships than on happenings and events. There isn't a weekend edition of the newspaper offering new movies, musicals, exhibits, plays, and gourmet restaurants. More often the paper will tell of new babies, traffic violations, and school lunch menus. So perhaps it's time to take a personal inventory and look at your social needs.

WHAT'S YOUR F.Q. (FUN QUOTIENT)?

How do you go about deciding which leisure opportunities are best suited to you? Perhaps you feel like the mosquito that accidentally wandered into the nudist camp. He immediately recognized there was plenty to do—but *where* should he begin? The following "Fun Quotient Quiz" will help answer that question for you by probing your personal interests. We suggest you copy it so each family member can participate. The Fun Quotient Quiz was created with the help of Dr. James Conant, a psychologist on the staff of Fullerton State College, Fullerton, California.

It's not a test. There are no right or wrong answers. What excites one person will bore another. Just be *honest* with your responses. Wonderful new leisure doors will open if your responses are candid and thoughtful. Possible answers range from 4 (which means yes or almost always) to 1 (which means no or hardly ever). Now grab a pen and discover your F.Q.!

Fun Quotient Quiz		
KEY		
1 = *hardly ever or no*	2 = *sometimes*	
3 = *usually*	4 = *almost always or yes*	
1. Do you like to think about new ideas and concepts?		
2. Do you enjoy working with your hands?		
3. Do you consider yourself adventuresome?		
4. Do you like to guide others such as a teacher, speaker, manager, or presiding officer does?		
5. Do you spend much time enjoying nature?		
6. Is it easy for you to go to a party alone?		
7. Do you find it hard to make new friends?		
8. Do you enjoy collecting items like stamps, miniatures, bottles, antiques, etc.?		
9. Would you give time to a cause you feel strongly about?		

Fun Quotient Quiz (continued)

KEY

1 = *hardly ever or no*	**2** = *sometimes*
3 = *usually*	**4** = *almost always or yes*

10. Do you like quiet surroundings more than a bustling atmosphere?	
11. Are cultural events and fine arts pleasing to you?	
12. Do you like to invent things or systems?	
13. Do you feel it's more fun to do things on impulse rather than something you've planned?	
14. Are you skillful at getting people to do things?	
15. Do you consciously strive to have a stronger, healthier body?	
16. Are you more likely to be a participant rather than a spectator?	
17. Do you wish you were more open and free—less "uptight"?	
18. Would you prefer to deal with things rather than people?	
19. Do you enjoy helping others?	
20. Do you often get "roped into" things you'd rather not do?	
21. Do self-improvement pursuits stimulate you?	
22. Do you like to tinker and discover what makes objects tick?	
23. Do you get a thrill out of doing things that are considered risky?	
24. Do you have a lot of self-confidence?	
25. Would you rather be outdoors than inside?	
26. Are you active in one or more clubs?	
27. Do you prefer being alone the majority of the time?	
28. Does precise, detail-type work agree with you?	
29. Are you a good listener?	
30. Would you rather associate with people similar to you or those who are different?	
31. Do you consider yourself an active reader?	
32. Do you enjoy doing things around your home such as wallpapering, puttering, or gourmet cooking?	

Fun Quotient Quiz (continued)

KEY	
1 = *hardly ever or no*	**2** = *sometimes*
3 = *usually*	**4** = *almost always or yes*

33. Do you write poetry or keep a journal?	
34. Does it please you to influence others?	
35. Do you consider yourself to be an active person rather than sedentary?	
36. In your opinion, do most people like you?	
37. Do you dislike crowds?	
38. Are your possessions extremely important to you?	
39. Are you persistent when you take on a task?	
40. Does it bother you to be involved in several things at once?	
41. Do you like challenging, thought-provoking activities?	
42. Do you have a specific hobby area such as a workbench, sewing spot, special reading chair, etc.?	
43. Do you feel the need to do something creative such as painting a picture, arranging flowers, sculpting, or crocheting?	
44. Do you assume responsibility eagerly?	
45. Do you like animals, pets, or birds?	
46. Do you prefer being part of a team or group as opposed to solitary activity?	
47. Do others seem to think you're standoffish or unfriendly?	
48. Are you frequently let down by people?	
49. Do you like to teach others about something you do well?	
50. Do you prefer routine and continuity over frequent change?	
51. Are you happiest literally "doing nothing"?	
52. Do you feel you're a self-disciplined person?	
53. Do you like classical music?	
54. Are you interested in sports?	

Fun Quotient Quiz (continued)

KEY

1 = *hardly ever or no*	**2** = *sometimes*
3 = *usually*	**4** = *almost always or yes*

55. Do you enjoy competing with others?	
56. Do you enjoy traveling in foreign countries?	
57. Are you easily managed by other people?	
58. Do you get bored quickly?	
59. Does history interest you?	
60. Are family-oriented activities important to you?	

Total points and interest ranges in sets 1–6 (Total possible: 20)	High interest level: 20–15
	Medium interest level: 14–10
	Low interest level: 9–5

Set 1	Set 2	Set 3	Set 4	Set 5	Set 6
1 _____	5 _____	4 _____	6 _____	7 _____	2 _____
21 _____	10 _____	9 _____	16 _____	17 _____	12 _____
31 _____	25 _____	19 _____	26 _____	27 _____	32 _____
41 _____	45 _____	29 _____	36 _____	37 _____	33 _____
59 _____	60 _____	49 _____	49 _____	47 _____	43 _____
Total	Total	Total	Total	Total	Total

Total points and interest ranges in sets 7–9 (Total possible: 20)	Set 7	Set 8	Set 9
	4 _____	15 _____	11 _____
	14 _____	16 _____	31 _____
	24 _____	25 _____	43 _____
	34 _____	35 _____	53 _____
High interest level: 20–15	44 _____	54 _____	56 _____
Medium interest level: 14–10	Total	Total	Total
Low interest level: 9–5			

Fun Quotient Quiz (continued)

KEY

	Set 10	Set 11
	2 _____	3 _____
	8 _____	13 _____
	12 _____	16 _____
Total points and interest ranges in sets 10–11 (Total possible: 24)	18 _____	23 _____
	22 _____	53 _____
High interest level: 24–18	38 _____	
Medium interest level: 17–12	Total	Total
Low interest level: 11–6		

Interest Analysis

Set 1 characteristic: You tend to have intellectual interests.

Set 2 characteristic: You enjoy nature.

Set 3 characteristic: You enjoy helping others.

Set 4 characteristic: You tend to be an extroverted, people-oriented individual.

Set 5 characteristic: You tend to be an introverted, shy person.

Set 6 characteristic: You are creative, imaginative, and sensitive.

Set 7 characteristic: You have strong leadership abilities and interests.

Set 8 characteristic: You enjoy sports.

Set 9 characteristic: Cultural pursuits are important to you.

Set 10 characteristic: You prefer working more with things than with people.

Set 11 characteristic: You are an adventuresome person.

The Fun Quotient Quiz was designed to stimulate thinking and help people take a fresh look at themselves. It will assist in deciding what leisure activities are likely to provide you the most enjoyment.

Let's evaluate the patterns that emerge from your answers. Record the numbers you gave for each question in the corresponding blanks below the quiz. Total the scores for each set; then check them against the tables to determine your interest level. Now refer to the Interest Analysis to find what personal characteristics emerged.

Now let's take the Fun Quotient Quiz Interest Analysis a step further and do a little brainstorming. Suppose you tested high in set 5. For someone who's shy, taking up contesting and the wonderful world of sweepstake entries might be fun. The Internet is a perfect and safe place to meet new people and have fun. Or you could enjoy hobbies like crocheting or model railroading. The person with strong numbers in set 7 is a natural community leader. Why not get involved in politics on the local level, assume a key role in a volunteer activity, or become an officer in a service club?

An adventuresome individual (set 11) is a natural for kayaking or mountain climbing. If you test high in set 2, being surrounded by nature is a treat. Enjoy this new blessing. If you really shined in set 3, read on in this chapter where we talk about volunteering.

Looking at your answers to individual questions can also be revealing. Enjoy doing nothing (question 51)? Indulge yourself! Give yourself permission to lie back, watch the clouds, meditate, experience, just be lazy—without feeling guilty. And if question 59 tickled a dormant interest in history, why not trace your ancestors by studying genealogy, or get acquainted with local history buffs and learn the heritage of the area? There are many options.

RECREATION AND ENTERTAINMENT TIPS

So what, specifically, does one do for recreation and entertainment? Take a look around. What about your specific area is unique? If people come there for vacations, what attracts them? Also learn from those who have lived in your area awhile. What do they do for fun? Try it. You may like it. We've become avid river rafters since moving to Colorado.

This week our paper reports tryouts are going on for the production of *Annie*. What fun to go and watch the youngsters . . . and their "stage mothers." Of course, you could audition for a role yourself. Don't want to be part of the cast? Fine. Backstage workers are always in demand.

On a more athletic front, you might want to work out alone or with a companion. If you prefer the latter, look for an aerobics class or a dance class. Softball, small towns, and summer go together like Peter, Paul, and Mary. The competition is fierce and it's a good way for both men and women to get acquainted as there are usually coed teams. Of course it's free entertainment if you're on the spectator side. Our local horseshoe group has a tournament that goes all season; prizes for points accumulated range from a new rifle or shotgun to money, and everyone enjoys the big feed at the end. Billiards and bowling are popular, as is supporting high school sporting events.

In some areas a visit to the farmers' market is a weekly ritual. Not only will you find vine-ripened melons and fruit just in from the orchards, but also just-picked veggies and country-fresh eggs. And the proprietors are usually a talkative bunch who intersperse hawking their produce with local wisdom and friendly advice. There are more than 2,000 farmers' markets scattered around America. They come in all guises, from covered semipermanent stalls to farmers selling produce off the tailgates of their pickups. They're usually worth a detour.

LET THE INTERNET BROADEN YOUR HORIZONS

Want instant gratification? The World Wide Web (WWW) has opened incredible possibilities for recreation and contact with people all over the world. (Not to mention research if you want to chat with someone who currently *lives* in places you're considering!) For many, the WWW has replaced the corporate water cooler. Newsgroups, chat groups, bulletin boards, and listservs—terms frequently used interchangeably—cover every topic imaginable. *Boardwatch* magazine estimates there are more than 65,000 public bulletin boards and perhaps as many as 150,000 private boards nationwide. No matter what your interest—gardening, spelunking, dogs, literature, mushrooms, whatever—there are special interest groups (SIGs) of like-minded people online. Distressed parents are reassured by their computer compatriots, insomniacs have lively late-night discussions, Lone Eagles discover stimulating cyberspace companions. And those interested in various causes—such as ecology, politics, or peace—have discourses with other spirited converts.

This method of networking revives a safe and sane way of relating to strangers. It's like sitting on the porch in Grandma's rocking chair on a lovely moonlit evening and philosophizing with a kindred soul. It brings the world to your doorstep. In our increasingly fragmented society, community can be cyberspaced rather than place-based.

All it takes is a computer, modem, telephone line, telecommunications software, and a service provider. Want to locate more than 16,000 newsgroups and their "threads," which are specific subject discussions within a general topic? Go to http://www.reference.com and have a ball!

Even singles are being bitten by the love byte. Romance is blooming on computer screens via the Internet. Shy souls who hesitate to flirt face to face can visit anonymously with like-minded others.

When Faith Popcorn looks future forward, she also sees computers giving us other forms of entertainment. She predicts it won't be long before we have such fantasy adventures as mind-trips to Africa, the Brazilian rain forest, and the Himalayas. Or time-travel back to the French Revolution or the time our grandparents lived.

DEALING WITH THE FAMILY ISSUE

Severing family ties is never easy. One way to stay connected is to call more frequently. Plan to invest a little more in your phone bill during those first months. Many families are going online to stay connected. Once you're set up, e-mail is an inexpensive way to have lengthy visits with loved ones.

Another idea is to send videos of the new house, town, and surrounding area. Make the rest of the family a part of your new adventure. And consider launching a "continuing cassette program." This is where you add to an audiocassette snippets of intriguing tidbits and happenings as you think of them, toss in lots of love, then send it "home" every week or so. "Thinking of you" cards are another caring touch to ease the transition for those left behind.

It's also important *for your sake* to keep close contact with old friends and family during this time. They'll remind you of how special and loved you are on days you feel rejected or lonely. Absence doesn't always make the heart grow fonder. It can make it grow forgetful. Keep loved ones close in mind, spirit, and contact.

Yet sometimes it's good to get some space between you and your relatives (or your spouse's relatives). Then grandma or auntie can't routinely badger poor junior or discipline the other kids in inappropriate ways. Nor do you have to listen to unsolicited advice about how to live your life.

Visits will come in bigger chunks, otherwise known as vacations. (*Theirs*, not yours.) If this area was captivating enough to entice you away from the city, it must have many redeeming qualities. Before too long, those left behind will probably journey to your new environs. In fact, branches of the family tree you didn't even know existed could show up to check out your new digs.

So will your friends. When you move to the country, everybody wants to visit: some, once to satisfy their curiosity; others, frequently to escape their own lifestyles. Establish some rules. Nobody just shows up. They must call and arrange a suitable time first. And if you're a busy homesteader with animals and crops to tend, you may want to make it clear they will *participate*. Handled properly, having friends and loved ones come for short visits is a wonderful way to keep in touch and enrich everyone's life.

MAKING NEW FRIENDS

Take time and choose your friends carefully. Those who are anti-outsiders probably won't change. Why waste time on them? You'll find plenty of other folks to laugh with and enjoy. Just don't be in a hurry to please everyone.

Because a vibrant social life will not likely come knocking at your door, it's up to you to make things happen. When Bill Seavey and his wife moved to Bend, Oregon, they decided to sponsor their own party to get to know their neighbors quickly. The potluck "worked wonders," Bill reports. When you find people you think you'd like to know better, invite them over for Sunday brunch or dinner. Prepare one of your specialties or something unique to the area you came from. Don't be discouraged if every attempt doesn't pan out.

One of the lessons we learned is how important it is to *respond* when someone does reach out. When we initially moved to First Try, there simply weren't enough hours in the day to run three businesses and have any social life. So the first couple of party invitations we received were declined. Rejecting those offers of friendship proved to be a social blunder. The invitations came to an abrupt halt. Though it was never our intention, the locals decided we didn't want to mix with them. Once such word gets around, your fate is sealed.

It's tough to be outgoing and vivacious, to mobilize energies already sapped by the other tasks of moving. Yet those early weeks are so important. It's worth reaching down in your personal reserves to muster the time and energy to respond, to be available. People who do welcome you warmly expect their gestures to be met with reciprocity. But many of us are anxious and afraid of being rebuffed. We miss our old comfortable relationships. That's only natural. Yet making the right contacts now can relieve loneliness and establish contact with a kindred soul. Try to extend yourself.

Clubs and classes are fertile friendship fields. These spontaneous joinings bring together people with common interests.

Marilyn: I met two of my best friends in San Diego through a writing class. Similar concerns and goals were the glue that cemented our relationships. If there is a Newcomers' Club in your new area, by all means attend. While some people shun such groups because they want to penetrate the "in crowd" of long-time residents, attending newcomer functions is an excellent non-threatening introductory step. Often there are subgroups, such as those interested in gourmet cooking, bicycle riding, or crafts. If no such club exists, you might consider starting one. Or at least investigate enrichment classes like music appreciation, quilting, woodworking, painting, literature, etc.

Once you're settled in, one way to find special friends is to become a fate-shaper. A fate-shaper gives destiny a nudge. One imaginative widow who had sold her big home and wanted to move to a smaller town set out to rent a *way of life* instead of an address. Finding a suitable looking apartment complex, Gladys asked about the make-up of the residents. The manager explained there were six widows among the 30 tenants. Her next action was to call on each of the widows and ask candidly if they were interested in playing bridge, having morning coffee, or going for a Dutch-treat dinner occasionally. Four of the women were elated that somebody was moving in who could be a companion.

Lauri devised a clever way to encourage others to get acquainted with her. Whenever she and her sons went to the park, she always took along fate-shaping *props:* a tiny chess set, a cribbage board, and a current best-seller. She never read the book, however. It laid on the blanket in full view of anyone who wanted to use it as a peg on which to hang an introductory conversation. The chess set and cribbage board were also unspoken invitations.

Another way to attract others is to become an expert. Then when someone wants information or help in your field, you're the natural resource. This is an ideal entry for teaching at the local community college where you'll meet other adults interested in your field.

Robert Fulghum says in *It Was on Fire When I Lay Down on It,* "The grass is not, in fact, always greener on the other side of the fence. No, not at all. Fences have nothing to do with it. The grass is greenest where it is watered." To have a friend, you must first be one.

Giving of our time and self promotes lasting goodwill. Stopping by to see a friend in the hospital (even though her jaw is wired shut) is an act of love. So is leaving a football game to help a buddy tow his car home or volunteering to watch a couple's puppy when they go away for the weekend. These are acts of love. So is starting a plant from a slip of your prize-winning fuchsia. Or clipping an article you know your friend would love to read. Such are the unselfish acts of true fellowship. Wonderful, intimate companionship awaits you in your new town. Just give it a little time, a gentle nudge, and you're sure to find people with whom you have an affinity.

THE VIRTUES OF VOLUNTEERING

Over the past decade volunteerism has been gussied up—hair done, nails polished, and jewelry in place—to catch a beau. No longer does she offer only routine tasks like filing and envelope-stuffing. And her suitors are no slouches either. They come with ties on straight, socks matching, and flowers in hand.

This romance between community needs and willing individuals will blossom even more as the century turns. People feel a need to contribute. They're hungry to nurture our world and the people in it. Some even see it as a calling.

Today's volunteers serve in myriad ways. They present guided tours at museums, write publicity releases, tutor a needy child, plan gala charity events, or serve on town councils and advisory committees. Others counsel prison inmates, coordinate fund-raising campaigns, coach sports teams, plant trees, do outdoor community beautification, even perform musical extravaganzas for the elderly.

Finding the right service niche is very personal. We each have some things we do better than others, special inborn qualities and talents. So the first step toward courting the lovely lady of volunteerism is a self-inventory.

Once you have some idea of what you are most qualified for, and what you want to do, it's just a case of wedding you to the right volunteer opportunity. Some places you might check are the school, hospital, nursing home, and the Cooperative Extension Service. Of course your pastor, priest, or rabbi will leap at a question of how you might help. Any political candidate or party will find you an assignment as quickly as a comet streaks across the heavens. Health and welfare agencies, plus service and civic clubs are also likely candidates.

Volunteering is an ideal atmosphere for making new friends and feeling the joy that comes from knowing you enhanced the life of another. It gives an opportunity to refurbish skills grown rusty from lack of use, or master new ones. It puts purpose in life. Invest yourself. The dividends may exceed your wildest dreams.

INGENIOUS WAYS TO ENRICH YOUR LIFE

The challenge is to stay rooted and not rutted.

We find nourishing ourselves spiritually is important. Just as our bodies need food, so do our minds and souls. By reading spiritual materials—or listening to uplifting tapes—we submerge our subconscious in positive ideas and constructive action. When you feed your spirit wholesome fare, your entire being feasts.

In rural settings, one of the foremost centers of activity and fun is a local church. In our town one church sponsors potlucks, interesting speakers, open gym nights, activities for teens and young children, and musical entertainment. They even have Christmas decorating parties—complete with rooms full of pine boughs, staple guns, baby's breath, glue guns, and plaid ribbon.

For many, the backyard is replacing the boardroom. Eastern ex-apartment dwellers, who never had a plot of ground of their own, are enchanted with gardening. They cultivate tomatoes and squash as enthusiastically as they used to cultivate mentors and bosses. Outdoor barbecues supplant cocktail parties.

Just because you live in the country, however, don't think you have to find everything right there. If you've enjoyed symphonies, ballets, theater, and museums before, continue to enjoy them. You have a city within a couple hours' drive. Check out their fine arts options and make an investment—in both time and money—for occasional tickets. Take a mini-vacation. A long weekend every two months or so does wonders for the soul. Salve your financial conscience by doing your city errands on the same trip. The break in your routine and surroundings will be welcome, and you'll find yourself refreshed and eager to head back to "the sticks."

You can also turn your computer into a classroom and get your BA, BS, or MBA by enrolling in an electronic degree program. Geared for working adults, each class usually takes five to six weeks to complete. For more information on one resource, contact the Online Program at the University of Phoenix at 100 Spear Street, Suite 110, San Francisco, CA 94105; or call 800-742-4742. You can also check out their Web site at http://www.uophx.edu/online.

We know one local family who entertains fascinating guests from all over the world. They are a host home for SERVAS, an organization that encourages international travelers to visit briefly in private homes across the globe. Says one older couple who can't travel themselves, "SERVAS brings the world into our living room through the visits of friendly, enthusiastic people from every continent." For more information, contact them at 212-267-0252.

Think of your relocation as an adventure. Slow down. Enjoy every minute. Take time to fantasize about how much happier you're going to be and how positive change can be. Understand you're weaving new threads into the fabric of your life while old ones ravel and fray. Sure you face an unknown future. So did our ancestors. Yet with vision and courage they accomplished remarkable feats. So can you. Let your spirit soar!

And if you want your income to soar along with your spirit, really tune into Part Two. Next comes proven advice on how to successfully go into business for yourself, telecommute with your present employer, or find a new job in Small Town USA.

PART TWO

◆

Business Aspects

8

◆

Evaluating Your Entrepreneurial Options

Being self-employed can make you feel a little like Christopher Columbus sailing off into the unknown. It's both exciting and scary. Those with an entrepreneurial spirit have their heads above the crowd. They're risk takers who see economic freedom. Statistics show that more than one out of every four people would start their own business if they won a million dollars. You can do so for a whole lot less. But starting a business is only the beginning. Keeping it going year after year is no small feat.

The startling fact is that 65 percent of all new businesses fail within five years. They are either undercapitalized, in a poor location, or the owners lack marketing acumen—and the realization that gaining and keeping customers must be a constant, ongoing pursuit. That's the bad news.

The good news is that many are extremely successful, especially when they're led by people like you who *educate themselves before taking the plunge.* That education is the focus of Part Two of *Country Bound!* So if you want to BYOB (be your own boss) rather than being in occupational limbo, read on! It has been said the best way to predict the future is to invent it.

We'll explore what personal characteristics it takes to run a company well. (Not everyone has them.) And we'll be your brainstorming partners, helping you become a master at foreseeing your ideal future and initiating positive change. Here you'll uncover how to determine windows of opportunity, turn a hobby into a living, and create your ideal "cashing out" career. We're off on a journey to discover a brave new entrepreneurial world!

DETERMINING IF YOU HAVE SELF-EMPLOYMENT POTENTIAL

Jane Applegate, champion of small business and a syndicated columnist, says the growth of small businesses is fueled by two factors: (1) affordable technology and (2) reluctant entrepreneurs who are the victims of downsizings and layoffs. Corporations continue to lay off enormous numbers of people each year.

Striking out on your own takes equal amounts of moxie and motivation. If one or both of your parents were in business for themselves, you're already a step ahead. Studies show those who come from such families have a greater tendency to be successful. Some feel having a close relative who was an entrepreneur is the single most telling indicator. You benefit from having these role models. All that shop talk over the dinner table wears off. You may have been in an apprenticeship program and didn't even realize it!

Take a look at the following "Characteristics of an Entrepreneur." If you don't have most of these qualities, it could be wise to jump ahead to Chapter 18: "Finding a Rural Job: Gutsy Strategies Mother Never Told You."

Go-getters typically start early in life. They have newspaper routes, set up lemonade or vegetable stands, do babysitting, help with haying, mow lawns, etc. They like to earn their own money.

> Tom: After working on the family farm six days a week (the draft horses had to rest—not so the humans), I rode the range on Sundays "cowboying" for nearby ranchers. I made $5 a day counting cattle, herding, branding, and bronco riding to break horses when I was 14 years old. That's how I earned the money for my first full-size saddle.

> Marilyn: I began earning money regularly when I was nine years old. I had a loom and wove potholders, then sold them door-to-door around the neighborhood. I soon discovered this "product line" was too limited, however. So I also bought and re-sold kitchen gadgets, small gift items, and boxes of greeting cards.

Characteristics of an Entrepreneur

- ❏ Self-directed with a strong internal focus of control
- ❏ Highly independent
- ❏ Lots of energy
- ❏ A futuristic outlook
- ❏ Often got poor grades and was rowdy in school
- ❏ Careful about money
- ❏ Persistent to the point of being obsessive
- ❏ Creative, supports experimentation
- ❏ Earned own money at an early age
- ❏ Has vision, intellectual creativity
- ❏ As an employee, arrived on the job early and often left late
- ❏ Street smart
- ❏ A high tolerance for ambiguity
- ❏ Willing to take risks
- ❏ Competed in sports, debate, etc., in school
- ❏ Little need for peer approval
- ❏ A low tolerance for frustration, little patience
- ❏ Enjoys having power
- ❏ A sales personality, good communication skills
- ❏ Anxious to take on responsibility
- ❏ Focused, strong ability to concentrate well
- ❏ Devotes more time to work than hobbies
- ❏ Dissatisfaction with bureaucracy and "the system"
- ❏ A decisive self-starter
- ❏ Intuitive, willing to go with hunches
- ❏ Not afraid of change

Why do people go into business for themselves? Money is usually secondary. Freedom—having command over their own destiny—is the major reason given by those who have shunned employee status. A MasterCard BusinessCard Small Business Survey polled 405 owners of small businesses. Eighty percent had left jobs at other companies. The main reason for 35 percent of them was to be their own boss and have more control over their work and lives. Surprisingly, only 24 percent of them did it for the money.

"When you become your own boss, the only orders you take are for more business," remarked one individual who recently left a large company. Another quipped, "I'm recovering from major surgery. I just had the boss removed from my back."

For many small business owners, control over their lives also means less leisure time. Fifty-eight percent of those polled above said they have less free time now. You really only have to work half a day though. And it makes no difference which half: It can be either the first 12 hours or the last 12 hours. (Just had to toss that in.) Entrepreneurs are a hard-working bunch, but they're basically content with their lot.

In discussing this book with Jeanne, a REALTOR® who specializes in selling rural property, she observed that often what people would *like* to do is vastly different from what they're *equipped* to do. Many want to play, not work, at a new business. The very times they need to be there are when they want to be gone. For example, the guy who loves fishing buys a tackle shop, then resents having to open it on weekends when *he* wants to be out fishing. (One alternative to this predicament is to go into business with another person or couple.)

Most people who start their own small businesses are technical experts. They know their product or service intimately and can design, create, and perform at a high level of proficiency. While many have college degrees and some sport MBAs, education doesn't seem to be the critical factor. A survey by the National Federation of Independent Business found that 40 percent of those studied had no college training. Eight percent were even high school dropouts. The vital factor was the knowledge they sought before going into business. The seed for success is self-education. This is what develops the pioneers of small business, the true heroes of the American economy.

It was once unusual for people over 50 to launch a new business. Today this mid-life adventure is played out in every state in the union. The Roper Organization forecasts the next major wave of entrepreneurs will include an unusually high proportion of older Americans. Many of these people have been forced out of jobs by early retirement. Close to 20 percent of start-ups are begun by men and women age 50 or over. Folks in their sixties and seventies are retiring from one career, then starting in an entirely new field—finally doing what they've dreamed of all their lives.

Age often works for them. They're less impetuous, have wisdom gleaned from years in the workforce, and know themselves better than their younger counterparts do. And when it comes to international trade, maturity is respected abroad—especially in Japan. It is imperative, however, that older entrepreneurs take precautions to do everything right. If the business turns sour, it's infinitely more difficult to start over at 55 or 65 than it is at 25 or 35.

No doubt about it—whatever your age—you'll encounter physical, emotional, and financial strains when you start a new business. Here are seven penetrating questions. Answer them honestly.

1. Are you aware that running your own business may require you to work 12 to 16 hours a day, six days a week?
2. Are you prepared to work even Sundays and holidays if necessary?
3. Do you have the physical stamina and energy to handle such a workload?
4. What about emotional strength? Can you withstand the strain?
5. Are you prepared, if needed, to temporarily lower your standard of living until your business gets firmly established? (This may be especially relevant if you refuse to work such long hours.)
6. What about your family? Are they willing to go along with the strains they too must bear?
7. Have you faced the fact that you could lose your investment?

Some people join the ranks of entrepreneurship for the wrong (or at least questionable) reason: Lose job—start business. As we've tried to show, not everyone is suited to being his or her own boss, either by temperament, background, or discipline. People who've always had their work lined out for them—and a supervisor or manager telling them what, when, and how to proceed—may be overwhelmed with all the added responsibility. A few naïve souls even think starting their own business will be *easier* than job hunting!

EXPLORING THE ALTERNATIVES

Perhaps what you're now doing can be accomplished from anywhere. If you relocate an established business to a rural area, you and your company inject capital into the economy. You're then bringing something to the table. If you already have a going concern, the question then becomes: Is your business relocatable? That depends on the business and the new site you choose. It's certainly easier to pick up where you left off than to start anew. Some enterprises can be run from anywhere.

In *The Third Wave,* futurist Alvin Toffler envisioned "electronic cottagers"—people who would work from home in a computerized information age. That is now reality. Lone Eagles have nested in every state.

A 1995 study by Washington State University researchers found that three-fifths of self-employed Lone Eagles own service industry businesses. They specialize in engineering, accounting, management, advertising, sales, etc. They don't see themselves as being servants but as being of service. They are older, better educated, and have higher incomes than the norm.

But let's suppose you're a massage therapist contemplating moving to a town of 4,000 where no one currently offers this service. A visit with the local chiropractor and physician shows they are receptive to referring certain patients to you. Bingo! You have a transportable skill.

Or imagine you have an accounting firm. Maybe you don't want to move too far away and can set up a mobile van to service your existing clients from your new, more remote location.

To be successful, offer products or services your prospective new town would really love to have available. Ask key townsfolk, "What do you *need* here?" Also find out what businesses have come and gone in the past five years and why. Such information can be quite revealing.

What kinds of enterprises are most likely to make it in the country? According to David Birch of Cognetics, Inc.—who wrote an excellent book called *Job Creation in America*—"Remote start-ups and success stories (tend) to be a little different from the mix found in metropolitan America. Generally," he says, "they fall into four groups: (1) satisfy fundamental needs, (2) revolve around natural resources, (3) are needed because of an area's remoteness, or (4) would be practical no matter how remotely situated."

Perhaps the last group is the most viable. These consist of mail-order firms, specialty manufacturing, and others not dependent on the local economy for their well-being. Our two consulting firms—one specializing in publishing and marketing books for professionals with specialized knowledge to share, the other in publicizing and marketing small businesses and professional practices—serve clients from coast to coast. While we occasionally assist a local, that's a rarity. Yet we infuse the area with tax dollars and provide jobs and paychecks that further enrich the local economy.

As Ralph Waldo Emerson observed, "If a man can write a better book, preach a better sermon, or make a better mouse trap than his neighbor, though he builds his house in the woods, the world will make a beaten path to his door." Where you are isn't as important as *who* and *what* you are.

Too often, people open new storefronts that directly compete with existing establishments. That's not a good way to win friends or stay financially healthy. Small towns can only support a given number of like establishments. While the owners of two different flower shops may be making a living, for instance, if a third opens and siphons off part of the trade, everybody is in trouble.

There's a higher degree of risk if you open a new competing retail outlet than if you purchase an existing one. If you've always wanted to operate a gift shop, talk to local real estate brokers and the owners of current gift shops in town. It's doubly difficult to tackle a new environment and a new venture at the same time. Maybe you'd be more comfortable studying Chapter 10, "Buying an Existing Business or Professional Practice."

Another entrance to career change is moonlighting. It also provides a buffer against the unemployment that results from corporate roulette. With companies merging and purging employees as fast as they do databases, moonlighting offers a safety net.

The ideal time to position yourself to launch a business is while you're still on the payroll. Sure this means working extra evenings and on weekends. Many ambitious moonlighters also use vacation days, sick leave, and lunch hours to pursue their second job.

Starting a business while you still have a regular paycheck allows you to test your business plan, line up clients, and establish cash flow—all without taking any risks. You can build relationships in your industry and go the extra mile with people in your field. It also gives you time for training, both in your field and as a new businessperson. *Gradually* testing your entrepreneurial skills is like learning to ride a bike with training wheels. Once the wheels are removed, you have the experience and confidence to zip right along.

Downsizing continues to plague workers in corporate America. According to the Summer of 1996 issue of *The Accidental Entrepreneur,* layoff announcements rose 97 percent to 30,810 in April 1996 over the 15,678 in April of 1995. The bonfire of corporate layoffs that began in 1991 has turned into a rampaging wildfire. AT&T is considering laying off 4,000 people. This will continue to turn up the heat on middle managers. And with the collapse of the savings and loan industry, major bank mergers, plus trouble in telecommunications, defense, and computer firms, hundreds of thousands of jobs are still in jeopardy. (You didn't realize when they told you you'd be on the cutting edge of the company, they meant your *head* would be on the chopping block, did you?)

But then you may have already decided the fast track is the wrong track for you. As baby boomers reach middle management, there are signs they are rejecting corporate cultures that suck them dry. One authority recently observed in the *New York Times* that the "me" generation is turning into the "flee" generation as executives watch the best years of their lives slip into the corporate black hole. One woman we know decided to stop deferring real living, downsized herself voluntarily, and now lives inexpensively yet without feeling poor.

According to figures from the National Federation of Independent Business, 43 percent of people get their business ideas from their prior jobs. And many of these people nab their previous employer for their first client as corporations increasingly outsource jobs previously handled in-house.

One corporate escapee warns that life on the "outside" is very different, however. "It's easy to become mesmerized at a large company and lose any idea of what life is like on the outside," reports engineering consultant David Hudson. A helpful book on surviving and thriving the ups and downs of being your own boss is *Making It on Your Own* by Sarah and Paul Edwards.

These days, developing a business that appeals to the more mature market is like betting on a sure thing. It's the age of opportunity. By the year 2000, there will be an astonishing 61,700,000 individuals between the ages of 45 and 64. Not only are these numbers impressive, so are the ones in their bank accounts. This segment of the population controls approximately 75 percent of the financial assets in America.

What does that mean to you? Think about what graying baby boomers will want and need. Real estate, recreational equipment and clothing, entertainment, personal services, and health care lead the pack. Entrepreneurs who know how to catch this age wave will prosper far beyond the norm. Thousands of new products will be invented to make these people more comfortable as they age.

Service opportunities sprout like wildflowers after a spring rain. Jeff Ostroff, business consultant and author of *An Aging Market: How Businesses Can Prosper*, pinpoints seven kinds of businesses that stand to benefit most from our aging population. These are endeavors oriented to the home, health care, leisure, counseling, education, managing finances, and slowing the aging process.

Migrating retirees are revitalizing dozens of small towns. Between Social Security, pensions, and investment incomes, a "mailbox economy" is emerging as unprecedented numbers of mature Americans head for the hills. They need real estate, home cleaning services, transportation and delivery services, bookkeeping help, financial planning, travel agencies, and auto repair—to toss out a few possibilities. And restaurants smart enough to develop inviting menus with smaller servings at reduced prices will get out of the starting gate fast.

Those pushing 70 in the year 2000 aren't like our grandparents. Today's mature people are much more active and energetic. They like to travel and be involved, to look and feel good. Cater to these needs and you'll be as fortunate as Cinderella when the prince discovered the glass slipper fit her foot.

Many businesses in the boonies are often shared by husband and wife. Entrepreneurial couples run bed-and-breakfast inns, motels, restaurants, home-based enterprises, and a wide variety of shops. Sharing work and life can be both a blessing and a curse. You'd better have a strong marriage. There's no doubt being in business together will add stress to the relationship. It's ideal if you possess complementary skills. Both of you having similar abilities and being responsible for the same area is likely to be as volatile as two male cats wooing the same feline female. On the other hand, if you love being around each other, it affords great opportunity for togetherness. There's also a special bonding when both of you pull together for a common work goal.

Remember that in Small Town USA you aren't just selling resources, you're also selling relationships. People go out of their way to trade with folks they like. That doesn't preclude the fact, however, that for retail stores location is often everything. Many shops depend on foot traffic for survival. Parking is also a big consideration. Potential customers will become frustrated and take their business elsewhere if they encounter a hassle finding a parking spot. For planning purposes, also factor in seasonal variances. If you relocate to a tourist town, for instance, 60 percent of your business may be done during the three summer months.

Locally dependent businesses are limited, however. While they usually provide adequate incomes, a broader base is necessary to make it big. The kind of expansion typical in the city—opening additional branches—isn't practical. More creative ways of blossoming are needed. A printer, for instance, might also carry office or art supplies. We'll discuss more about how you can diversify to multiply later.

Most self-employed people we interviewed are satisfied with the performance of their firms. They wouldn't consider working for someone else for a higher salary. These proprietors experience yin and yang harmony between their lifestyles and their careers.

BRAINSTORMING TO BREAK YOUR BARRIERS

How do you get from the itch to the idea? It's one thing to want to move to the country, quite another to support yourself once there.

One of the best ways to generate a whole host of possibilities is to invite a group of people to help you think of ideas for a business opportunity. Set an initial time period, maybe two or three hours, and explain that brainstorming is a time to be creative, not judgmental. Set a positive tone. You might start out by reminding everyone that "No one of us is as powerful as all of us."

In a brainstorming session, each participant generates as many options as possible. All ideas are welcome, even if they sound kooky, impractical, or wild. The point of this exercise is to explore a range of possibilities, not to sell any one perspective. Brainstorming stretches the imagination and produces acres of ideas from which you can harvest the best.

It isn't necessary to have a room full of people to accomplish wondrous acts though. You can take other approaches by yourself with lined pad or computer keyboard. One method is called "freewriting." Sit down for 15 minutes and write anything and everything that comes into your head. No fair stopping or crossing out words. And don't worry about spelling or punctuation. The object is to lose control, to reach your intense inner thoughts so you can harness that energy.

Another dynamite doorway to your mind is called "clustering." This is a magic key for getting in touch with your secret reserves of imaginative power. Clustering is a nonlinear personal brainstorming process similar to free association. It's like writing a map of ideas, beginning with a core word or statement, then branching out with associated ideas in many directions.

Starting with a main idea in the center, give your mind free rein and radiate thoughts and images out from this nucleus. Write new ideas in circles—which, in turn—are connected by lines to other circles. Ideas spill out with lightning-fast speed. They form associations that allow patterns and solutions to emerge. Chaos becomes order as ideas surface in a gradual map that accesses our interior landscape of thoughts. There's no right or wrong place to start; nothing is forced. While this is an excellent solo exercise, it can also be effective done in a group setting.

When searching for a new idea, look from all angles. Successful businesses are often simply a different application of an existing concept. Can you reverse something? (Look at the huge new industry of fragrances for men. Twenty years ago, guys wouldn't touch perfume.) When using "reverse psychology," think about not only the opposite sex, but young to old, indoors to outside, etc.

Minimizing or maximizing may hold the key to your entrepreneurial triumph. The computer field gives us a perfect example of how minimizing has led to new profit centers. From PCs that sat on our desks, they went down to portables, then to laptops. Small is beautiful. So is big. Our aging population, for instance, will increase demand for large-print books in the years to come. Can you capitalize on less or more?

Combining two or more things may be your cure-all. For instance, a clever person put clocks together with radios several years ago and developed a whole new line of merchandise. In the service arena, some upscale beauty salons are now converting into mini-spas where a woman can be pampered from head to toe for a day.

Many successful new ventures offer only a slight variation on a proven market leader—just enough to establish an identity and a profitable market niche. Look how PC compatibles and clones quickly nipped at the heels of the IBM PC, and how overnight delivery services flourished once Federal Express proved it was possible.

When inventing your own business, try to improve on something for which there is already an established market, rather than beginning from scratch. Reverse it. Minimize it. Maximize it. Combine it. Examine the possibilities from every perspective.

OCCUPATIONAL VARIETY TO ADD SPICE TO YOUR LIFE

Is the advice business for you? Consulting is a promising field for rural entrepreneurs. It's no secret that the information explosion is upon us. We started as hunters/gatherers, went to farming, then became factory workers—now we're in the knowledge age. Are you sometimes overwhelmed by the increasing number of things you know less and less about? Join the crowd. Yet most of us are an *expert* at something. Find that something and capitalize on it!

As corporate downsizing continues, it bolsters the demand for subcontractors. Often these are former employees. Hiring consultants is less expensive for the company than maintaining an employee full time and paying fringe benefits. Often the work can be done from a remote location. Enter you. It's entirely possible you can serve your current or previous employer as an outside consultant—doing much the same tasks you did while on payroll. This may be just the pad needed to launch a consulting practice.

Consultants should like people. You have to be able to sell yourself and your abilities, then interface with organization personnel. You must be capable of putting together a compelling proposal, not to mention meeting deadlines. In addition to the marketing strategies needed to launch any business, it's important you price your services properly. An excellent book on this subject is *How to Set Your Fees and Get Them* by Kate Kelly. If this idea appeals to you, also get a copy of Brian Smith's *The Country Consultant*.

Running a country inn appeals to many city dwellers. Bed and breakfasts (B&Bs) have boomed in the last decade. Today there are more than 7,000 licensed commercial B&Bs. It's estimated one in seven of them is on the market at any given time, so there are many to choose from. Prices range from $20,000 to $100,000 per guest room and figures from a recent survey report that those with 11 to 20 rooms are more profitable than smaller establishments. The hot spot for starting an inn is the Midwest, while the Sunbelt runs a close second, according to the American Bed and Breakfast Association. Having a B&B is a lot of fun if you enjoy people and making them comfortable. Guests become friends who return year after year, becoming almost extended family. Innkeeping is also a lot of work.

Because the field is extremely competitive, you may want to offer something extra, such as catering to families with small children. In this case you'd have cribs and high chairs available, provide a space for preparing formula, have toys on hand, and childproof the house. Of course, being able to arrange baby-sitting is an added benefit for traveling parents.

The recipe for innkeeping success is one part personal touch, one part lovingly restored antiques, one part delicious food, and seven parts location. Guests also want their country atmosphere mixed with a generous dollop of luxury. Ambiance is everything. To test-drive this business idea, stay at several inns yourself. Talk to the proprietors. Once they understand you're seriously considering buying, most will gladly share their joys and woes. Also check your local library or bookstore. There are several good books on the subject.

The restaurant business is the denim dream of a lot of people. Beware of this industry. People often romanticize the experience of owning a restaurant. In truth, it's an enormous amount of work. But of more concern, the failure rate is phenomenal. Even experienced restaurateurs are going under.

On the other hand, recreation and entertainment-oriented businesses flourish in tourist areas. These also can be fun. If you love whitewater rafting, horseback riding, or dune buggying, for instance, perhaps you can buttress your bliss into a business. Active recreation runs the gamut from fishing to hunting, water sports to snow skiing, desert diversions to mountain activities. A golf enthusiast might open a miniature golf course, a surfing buff a surf shop complete with lessons. Bait and tackle shops, taxidermy work, sporting goods stores, boat sales and storage—the list of potentials goes on and on.

Concocting gift baskets is another intriguing alternative. This can be both creative and lucrative. They retail for between $35 and $70 and contain food, wine, tea, gourmet coffees, snacks, gift items, useful articles, fun prankster objects, you name it. Style sells. Because the presentation is very important, this vocation taps your artistic abilities. You buy in bulk and enhance your baskets with ribbons, greenery, natural-looking reeds, and theme balloons.

Why would anyone buy a gift basket? For birthdays, anniversaries, showers, thank-yous, get-wells, new homes, retirement, thinking-of-yous, grand openings, corporate promotions, nostalgia, virtually any occasion—or for no occasion. Naturally, these gorgeous delights are popular for holidays like Christmas, Valentine's Day, and Mother's Day. You can even develop masculine themes such as baskets for handymen, gardeners, fishermen, and sports fanatics. And think about selling your baskets in bulk to companies. They make wonderful employee benefits.

A charming alternative to traditional floral bouquets, gift baskets have lasting value. Some clever gift basket creators even have bridal registries and mail all across the country; thus they're not dependent on the local economy. Of course that doesn't rule out making local deliveries as well. If this area interests you, we suggest you subscribe to *Gift Basket Review*, c/o Festivities Publications, Inc., 815 Hanies Street, Jacksonville, FL 32206, 904-634-1902.

The list of manufacturing possibilities is almost endless. We know of one rural area that is trying to recruit sporting goods manufacturing, medical and dental equipment manufacturing, plus geothermal users such as greenhouses and fish farms. Another manufacturing likelihood is clothing. Small towns like clean industries that won't pollute their environment. If you're considering making a product, be sure there is a suitable local labor pool.

Then there are bowling alleys, secondhand stores, camera shops, campgrounds and RV parks, bakeries, craft shops, car washes, Laundromats, and taverns. What about well drilling and septic tank sales? Construction companies and subcontractors, concrete, carpet sales, and real estate agencies are more prospects. Look in the Yellow Pages if you need to spark your imagination.

And for some, back to the land is their call of the wild. They go into tree farming, or raise berries, grapes, or other crops. Some develop a massive garden and become truck farmers. Of course, there are chickens, turkeys, hogs, cattle, horses, sheep, and goats to raise—not to mention exotics like alligators, ostriches, and llamas.

Marilyn: We tried our hand at this while living at the ranch. We weren't big-time farmers or ranchers—but we had some frustrating, funny, and humbling experiences. We raised our own meat: a few cattle and a pair of hogs. I'll never forget the time Tom came home with two new pigs. These little critters had been raised indoors on a concrete floor. When they came out of the horse trailer and hit the dirt, they froze. Pigs are smart. They just knew this pebbly stuff underfoot meant no good. We convinced them to move around and their fear soon vanished.

But by the next day, they had another problem. These were pure white pigs that had never seen the light of day before. Their little white bodies had turned a rosy red. They were sunburned! (Porky and Petunia got even with us when we were trying to catch them for butchering. They led me on the chase of my life! And they weren't even greased.)

Another time I was helping Tom catch a young bull that needed doctoring. Tom had him roped and the rope was attached to a sturdy tree. Being the epitome of a naïve city girl, I made the mistake of getting between the bull and the tree. The beast made a few fast turns and pinned me against that tree faster than cowboys rope steers. Feeling a rope cutting into your body as it tightens makes you wish for suburbia in a hurry. Fortunately, Tom intervened and we finally got me rescued; the bull was doctored and turned loose.

Only slightly less adventuresome was teaching a calf to drink from a bucket. (For you citified folk, you do this when you're milking the mother cow. The calf gets fed via bucket; you get the rest to drink, make butter, etc.) You straddle the calf, or back him into a corner, so you can get his head in the bucket of warm milk. Knowing this is totally unnatural, he fights you with the strength of a gorilla. Usually he wins. The bucket of milk dumps all over you and you get to start again.

Once you have him settled down a little, the easiest way is to use your finger to simulate the mother's teat and get him to suck. If you've never felt the rough tongue of a calf, you've really missed something.

After doing this twice a day for a week or so, your back has a semi-permanent kink. The reward? The calf greets you with bawling anticipation when he sees you approaching with a pail. You still need to hang onto your wits—and perhaps a fence—however. Once the pail is empty, he's likely to root it right out of your hands looking for more.

Another thing baffled me in my early country days: People referred to mealtimes by odd names. They would say "dinner" and I'd think of the evening meal and be all set. But they meant lunch. Why didn't they just say "lunch"? I reasoned, relying on my southern California upbringing. To further complicate the issue, "supper" was served in the evening. What ever happened to *lunch* boxes?

While the ranch turned out to be the wrong road to the right destination, it gave us wonderful memories. But enough of our escapades. A useful and folksy reference for those who want to go back to the land is the *Small Farmer's Journal*. Get information on this quarterly magazine by writing P.O. Box 1627, Sisters, OR 97759, or call 541-549-2064.

If you're in the businesses of inventing things and currently in the research and development phase, there's a governmental program that presents cash awards to qualified applicants. For information, contact the Office of Innovation, Research and Technology, U.S. Small Business Administration at 409 3rd St. SW, Washington, DC 20416, 202-205-6450. Request their guidelines for submitting a proposal. And there is a quick and cheap way to protect your invention for two years: Get a disclosure document for $10. Call the Patent and Trademark Office at 703-308-0900 for particulars.

Grants are also available from the Department of Energy and the National Institute of Science and Technology. To receive program information, write The Energy Related Inventions Program, National Institute of Standards and Technology, Building 820, Room 264, 820 W. Diamond Avenue, Gaithersburg, MD 20899, or call 301-975-5500.

Mail order is an ideal boonies business. Properly approached, it can thrive regardless of what happens locally. Ads in various national magazines and newspapers put dollars in your mailbox. Or you can rent mailing lists of prospects interested in your product. What do you sell? The options are infinite: crafts you make, items you purchase for resale, books you publish.

Speaking of publishing, many country folks make a nice living writing and selling books, booklets, special reports, and newsletters. For everything you need to know to write, publish, promote, and sell your own book, get a copy of our *Complete Guide to Self-Publishing* by calling 800-331-8355. We also offer free guidelines to help new writers get started. For a copy send a self-addressed stamped envelope to Writer's Guidelines, Box 1500-CB, Buena Vista, CO 81211.

Personal services are popular with Countrypreneurs. Perhaps the town you're considering needs a taxi, limo, or shuttle service. With a fleet of one vehicle, you can keep busy all day. In some states, dental hygienists can work from their homes, as can beauticians. And as people live longer, elder care for their parents is becoming a big concern for many baby boomers. With the cost of convalescent homes and private duty nurses skyrocketing, the market for senior day care centers is excellent. Perhaps you would feel personally fulfilled creating a supervised setting for senior adults.

Businesses need service providers too. Ever thought of offering a professional billing service? With the right software, knowledge, and marketing, you can be serving small businesses all over the county. And this could lead to doing other accounting and tax work.

Many small towns could benefit from having temporary secretarial and word processing help available. If your skills fall in this area, consider offering vacation relief, coverage during illness, and aid with overload projects. And you can probably pick up work from fledgling firms that can't yet afford a regular secretary, but need help a few hours a week. Develop a core of loyal customers and they will provide you with an ever-increasing stream of profits.

One man we know has a mobile washing service. Using his power washing equipment, he's cleaned driveways, parking lots, restaurant freezers, telephone booths, boats, signs, shopping carts, dumpsters, awnings, even airplanes. His motto? "We wash anything, anywhere, anytime."

If you want help advertising, publicizing, or maximizing your service business, get a copy of our *Big Ideas for Small Service Businesses*. It contains 229 ideas to make your life easier and your business more profitable. Order by calling 800-331-8355.

TURNING AVOCATIONAL PASTIMES INTO REGULAR PAYDAYS

By looking at what gives you pleasure—your hobbies and personal interests—you may find a wonderful career opportunity waiting in the wings. This is the second largest source for business ideas. Eighteen percent of people use a hobby to get a handle on the world of work. They grease the slide for change in a multitude of ways.

A computer buff begins to repair computers, gives training, serves as a consultant, or writes software programs. A man who's enthusiastic about using his video camera brushes up his skills and "angles" jobs videotaping weddings, graduations, and special events. A homemaker who recovered her sofa and love seat turns commercial and begins earning money reupholstering furniture for others.

Many skills used to run a home can be translated into paying professions. Do you win raves for your cooking and baking? Joann Roth always had a dream of being a caterer. Her business began when she catered a series of small dinner parties from her clients' kitchens. You might prepare a luxurious breakfast in bed for 2, elegant gourmet dinners for 20, or traditional wedding suppers for 300. Maybe your forte will be special occasion cakes.

Or nutritious home-cooked meals for busy working couples. You line up 10 or 12 couples who purchase your service two or three times a week, prepare that evening's dinner in bulk, then deliver it on beautifully presented trays. We'd wager in a town of any size, there are many overloaded entrepreneurs who would happily pay for such a healthy convenience.

Or how about becoming an event planner? Even in small towns, some people are too busy to plan their own social or corporate activities. With research, organizational insight, and chutzpah you're set to coordinate weddings, anniversary bashes, mini-conventions, meetings, reunions, bar mitzvahs, charity events, and gala parties.

For a lot of people, a rut is a grave with the ends kicked out. Ron Fuller became very disillusioned with his corporate rut. Although he was in upper management in a Michigan furniture company, he had all kinds of responsibility—but no authority. So he left the corporate world in the dust.

"I always liked to work on cars," reminisces Fuller. "I've got several friends who race and I have pitted for them . . . changed tires, worked on engines, a little bit of everything." All this came in handy when he accepted a job managing Mountain View Motor Sports Park in Mead,

Colorado. The 1.7-mile racetrack accommodates everything from in-line skates to Indy cars. He does everything around the track: maintenance, cutting the grass, fixing wires and speakers, doing phone work, greeting folks, and performing safety inspections. "There are two things that I like about this job," says Ron. "One is being outside and two is the people." Ron used his avocational interests to escape the corporate rut.

So did Phil Albin. Tired of being a securities broker in Houston, he turned to his hobby of fixing things. He knew how hard it was to get competent repairs done, so Albin launched The House Doctor as a maintenance and repair service targeted primarily at absentee owners.

His first job was weeding a flower bed for $3.75 an hour. The owner kept asking him, "Are you sure you're a gardener?" Today, The House Doctor has a gross annual income of $150,000—divided between Albin, one part-time helper, and occasional subcontractors.

Margaret Day of Watch Hill, Rhode Island, is a musician. Initially she only played her harp for family, friends, and at occasional weddings. Then she began playing professionally. Business is booming and has developed into a full-time career for her.

Irene Burrows' work has been saluted around the world. She spends part of every day making flags for domestic and international customers. Her creations have gone to the U.S. Department of Education, the Securities and Exchange Commission, AT&T, the Netherlands Air Force, the Cotton Bowl, and the NCAA basketball tournament. Leaving a job with J.C. Penney, she eventually formed the Independence Flag and Banner Company to capitalize on her seamstress skills. "I just love it," says Burrows.

Jackieanne Shepherd is a former fine arts teacher who left the classroom for wheat weavings, dough ornaments, corn dolls, and canvas rabbits dubbed Wild Hares. "You can't rely on a local market or even the summer tourist market if you expect to make a business of crafts," she counsels. "Much of my exposure comes through shows in Denver, Colorado Springs, Grand Junction, and New Mexico." She feels it is critical to keep ahead of the trends and on top of whatever is the latest in crafts.

Donna Harmon designs wreaths for a living. Not just evergreen holiday wreaths, but also ones for all seasons. A big challenge is coming up with innovative designs. To trim costs, Harmon grows many of the materials she uses in her wreaths, such as miniature pumpkins, baby's breath, and wheat. In addition to local outlets, she displays at shows to generate more orders.

Cheri and Curt Welty also turned their hobbies into a business. "It's nice to be able to make a living doing what you love," says Cheri. Their enterprise includes Curt's stained-glass windows, lamp shades, and wall hangings, plus mugs he creates with designs for skiers and rafters. Cheri's contribution includes weavings and classes. Additionally, she has introduced a line of high-quality yarns.

One gentleman was responsible for commercializing his wife's lifelong hobby of fine-needle, baroque textile embellishment—an astoundingly beautiful amalgam of embroidery and needlepoint crafts. He started by getting several locals to pay for textile decorating lessons taught by his wife. The pair also developed a mail-order business offering supplies, patterns, and instructions for this craft.

Getting known and established is perhaps the most difficult part of making a living from one's art. Though the work is good, it's tough to get going until you've developed a reputation. And it's hard to know the best way to merchandise your wares. Options include direct sales, craft shops, galleries, mail-order craft catalogs, home parties, craft cooperatives, and through sales representatives.

Of course pricing is another challenge. Figuring out what the traffic will bear sometimes requires a crystal ball. Short of that, we'd suggest you pick up a copy of Barbara Brabec's new *Handmade for Profit—Hundreds of Secrets to Success in Selling Arts and Crafts*. It's a unique crafts marketing idea book.

WHAT'S YOUR PASSION?

"Those whose work and play are one, are fortune's favorite children," said Winston Churchill. For some of us a nagging displeasure with work begins to consume us, a stoic acceptance numbs our senses and reduces our productivity. When that happens, it's time to leave. Maybe you're asking yourself all over again: *What do I want to be when I grow up?* Because we spend more of our adult lives working than doing just about anything else, that work experience should yield a major return on our investment. If you're experiencing a negative emotional cash flow, get liberated!

God has given each of us a gift. Some people term it a *calling*. We experience great joy when we let this light shine, when we give to life on earth something no one else can contribute in quite the same way. Yet finding your mission in life, what you're most enthusiastic about, isn't always easy.

If you're having trouble identifying your passion, scheduling a few sessions with a career counselor knowledgeable in entrepreneurial topics makes sense. These individuals have personal insight and professional experience in guiding people into satisfying livelihoods. Their unbiased individualized assessment can prove extremely helpful. You'll find them in the Yellow Pages under "Career and Vocational Counseling." Small Business Development Centers, which we discuss later, can also offer invaluable guidance. This may also prove a wise strategy for relocating spouses unsure of which way to turn in the new town. And if this description fits you, be sure to read the upcoming chapter, "Finding a Rural Job: Gutsy Strategies Mother Never Told You."

You'll probably be encouraged to take an aptitude test. This gives you an inward view, yielding an objective profile of your natural abilities. In many jobs we end up denying a part of ourselves. When we do this, we get antsy and antagonistic. Aptitude testing confirms the enormous variety of human talent. Though somewhat expensive, it may be the price of admission to a happy and rewarding new life.

In the end *you* will be the cornerstone of your business. So know thyself. It's your interest, fervor, energy, skill, time, and effort that make a new enterprise happen. Before you make decisions, take a personal inventory.

What are your skills? Literally submit a résumé to yourself. And don't be shy. List all work experience. Note any areas of competency that relate to a business. Write down your volunteer work, hobbies, and other activities. Look at your education, both formal and informal. Have you taken special courses or attended useful seminars?

Now inventory your likes. What would you do for free? If there were no financial requirements or other constraints, how would your days go? How do you spend your time off? Do you enjoy gardening? Computers? Tinkering with your car? Making handicrafts? Writing? Helping people? Go back and look at your Fun Quotient Quiz.

Next look over your two lists and make a third one of your strongest skills and greatest likes. This final tabulation provides a good basis for helping to decide the type of business to start. Of course, there must be a marriage between what you want to do and what people are willing to pay you for.

Another valuable measurement is to get input from 20 friends, relatives, or colleagues. Ask each to tell you *one* thing you do well. You might be amazed at the results. They may see your abilities differently than you do. After trying this exercise, one man who planned to open an advertising agency reported, "I've got a great list. But there's one funny thing. No one I spoke with mentioned advertising as one of my strengths!" What revealing feedback. This could open wonderful new horizons—or save you from making a horrible mistake.

Don't become so enamored with *your* likes, however, that you fail to measure them against reality. We're reminded of a Michigan couple who enjoyed fine wine and good food so much they opened a gourmet wine and food shop in Flint. Only after they lost their $60,000 investment did they realize most of Flint's wine drinkers patronized the one-stop-shopping supermarkets where they bought their libations along with their groceries. When you're considering opening a new business dependent on the local economy, a good question to ask is "Why doesn't this town already have such a place?" The answers are often penetratingly revealing.

If no one else is offering what you have in mind, why not? Perhaps you've hit on a brilliant idea. Or maybe others have already tried it and failed. Ask around. Don't be surprised if your ideas change. Welcome these modifications; they often lead to the ideal solution. Give this input serious consideration. You may find starting a certain kind of business in the country makes about as much sense as opening a tanning salon in a desert.

As you further refine your business options, creating a personal balance sheet might make sense. Let's suppose you and your spouse are considering purchasing a specific restaurant. You might list your assets and liabilities as follows:

Assets	*Liabilities*
Gloria's a wonderful cook.	We don't know the restaurant
Cliff does a great job of baking.	business.
Both of us are in our forties.	We're used to 40-hour weeks.
We're high-energy people.	We're unaccustomed to
Cliff's handy and can fix plumbing, etc.	performing these tasks.
Cliff can do initial remodeling carpentry.	The restaurant has been closed a year.
Gloria is excellent with people.	Decor needs to be jazzed up.
Gloria is experienced with ads/ promotion.	
Gloria knows how to keep books.	
We have adequate down payment.	

Want a foolproof way to check out a business before you plunk down your dollars? Volunteer to work there for free! Or if this seems too blatant, offer your services gratis to a similar business in another town, perhaps where you're currently living. Although this won't give you the local flavor, it will provide heaps of insider information about buying strategies, customer service, vendors, industry policies, etc.

Chris Meyer traded Los Angeles for tiny Scottsville, Virginia. She also wanted to trade a career in video production for one in drama therapy. Working the phones from California, Meyer landed an unpaid internship with Jan Goodrich, a pioneer in the field. By donating her time she will quickly learn if this field is really for her. We cover many more sophisticated methods for researching an industry and a geographic area in the next chapter.

"Either we're prisoners of change or we'll use it to our competitive advantage," states futurist and technology forecaster Daniel Burrus. But how do we "use change"? And how does the smart budding entrepreneur struggle through an endless sea of information to discover the innovation that will launch a cutting-edge business? One way is to get Burrus' exciting book, *TechnoTrends,* which details 24 technologies that will revolutionize our lives. Fortune 500 companies hire Burrus to tell them how to integrate the discoveries outlined in this book into their corporate plans. Now you too can tap into the wisdom of this futuristic problem-solver to go beyond your competition.

Also investigate Chapter 12, "Home Suite Home: The Information Age Option" and Chapter 13, "Telecommuting: Bringing Your Job Home." Both address using technology to your advantage.

The following "Occupational Satisfaction Scale" was adapted from a model in *How to Uncover and Create Business Opportunities* by Dr. Dale Rusnell and Bill Gibson. This is an excellent book for generating start-up ideas. The following scale will serve as a barometer to help clarify your personal needs and determine whether you desire to work indoors or out.

So you've pinpointed your passion. Now it's time to focus on accomplishing it. There are several useful techniques. One is to visualize yourself in your new career actually performing the tasks involved. Close your eyes. See and feel your dream. Smell the hay if that's what you want to raise. Feel the fabric in the garments if it's a clothing store you yearn to own. Hear the music if teaching piano is your vision. Apply all the senses to your dream. Go through the daily process in your mind's eye. By repeatedly seeing ourselves doing what we want, we condition our subconscious mind to accept this as reality.

Another proven route to success is to affirm what you want. Write out a statement about your new career. Phrase it in the present tense, as though you already have what you want. Rather than saying you're

Occupational Satisfaction Scale		
Type of Activity	**Satisfaction Level** **(1 = not satisfying** **10 = extremely satisfying)**	**Type of Activity**
Indoor	1 2 3 4 5 6 7 8 9 10	Outdoor
At home	1 2 3 4 5 6 7 8 9 10	In office/Store
Physical	1 2 3 4 5 6 7 8 9 10	Mental
With others	1 2 3 4 5 6 7 8 9 10	Alone
High travel	1 2 3 4 5 6 7 8 9 10	Stationary
Fixed schedule	1 2 3 4 5 6 7 8 9 10	Flexible schedule
Routine activities	1 2 3 4 5 6 7 8 9 10	Diverse activities

"going to do" such and such, state it as if you already own the store or do the thing you aspire to. Write this affirmation several times each morning and evening. It's also a good idea to repeat it aloud. When we truly *believe* something, it is ours.

Look at the big picture. A new business in a small town is an event. Sometimes projects rise or fall due to the personalities of the people in charge and what they intend to do. How might the community perceive your venture? List any groups, businesses, or individuals your enterprise might antagonize. How would it harm them? Can these effects be offset? List key people who could oppose you. Why would they do so? How can you shape what you have in mind to get their support, or at least keep them neutral?

Now think of groups, businesses, or people who might receive special benefits. What resources, effort, or support might they give you? This kind of perception forecasting can be invaluable. It allows you to get into the heads of people and figure out how to fashion win-win liaisons in advance.

MAKING THE MOST OF YOUR MONEY

Severance pay, lump sums from retirement plans, and golden parachutes are allowing thousands of Fortune 1,000 executives to pull the rip cord on corporate life and launch careers of their own. If you're laid off, get as much of a cushion as you can. Some companies offer "reduc-tion-in-force" policies about once a year. Be patient and maneuver until you qualify for such a plan. Most planned layoffs give you several weeks of severance, medical coverage, and insurance.

When someone starting a business has a lot of money, however, it can be a deterrent, according to Paul Hawken, author of *Growing a Business*. "Most small businesses fail due to lack of imagination rather than capital," he says. The temptation to *buy* solutions is overwhelming. Yet ideas don't come with check stubs attached to them. "Necessity nur-tures invention," contends Hawken. (If you suffer from the opposite dilemma—no capital—take heart. We devoted Chapter 15 to "Generat-ing Capital to Launch Your Venture.")

"Many professionals are equity rich," says David Savageau, author of *Places Rated Almanac* and *Retirement Places Rated*. "Now they want to split and look for a nice countrified place. Lots are coming out of south-ern California. They are individuals who have capital and are willing to take the risk. Quality of life is their prime consideration." Savageau advises a business should require less than $150,000 to start or buy and should operate with fewer than four employees. He points out that be-ginning a small manufacturing firm may appeal to engineers who want to make a part or a circuit.

It's not unusual for fledgling firms to be undercapitalized. The basic money rule is to have enough to get the doors open and keep the busi-ness going for at least 90 days—with absolutely no cash income. And don't count on credit from your suppliers to stock your inventory. It's ideal to have a reserve above this amount, or a prospective partner who can be brought in if the business turns out to be a late-bloomer.

Few first-time entrepreneurs are prepared for clients or customers who pay their bills late—or not at all. Meanwhile the company must meet its financial obligations and may not have enough cash to pur-chase goods or services to satisfy new orders or cover payroll. If possi-ble, structure your payment schedule so at least half the amount owed is paid *before* the goods or services are delivered.

Speaking of money, one of the severest blows comes when you find out what health insurance costs. When contemplating self-employ-ment, be sure to take this into consideration. (And try to extend your in-surance coverage when leaving an employer.)

A couple of other cautions: don't lock yourself into a long lease ini-tially. We just had dinner with a couple who lamented having to keep a dying business in operation until they could escape a five-year lease.

And be careful of putting a lot of money into remodeling right away. You may need that extra cash to tide you over during slow times.

Also allow for "shrinkage." If you're in the restaurant business, that may mean a cook who takes a side of beef or slips butter out the back door. In a retail store, it is the merchandise that's stolen by innocent-looking customers. In a bar, it's the liquor the bartender or servers tote home. Of course cash registers can come up short too. Even in manufacturing environments this goes on. Quantities of either raw materials or the finished product disappear.

DIVERSIFY TO MULTIPLY

Synergy—the combined effect of two or more things working to-gether—may be what allows you to make a living in the country. Rural folk often wear almost as many hats as Imelda has shoes. They have to. There simply isn't a large enough population base to support just one endeavor. Besides it's more fun when you have your fingers in several pies.

A barber we know uses the extra space in his three-chair shop to sell potted plants. His customers feel as if they're getting their hair cut in a garden. They tell their wives, who come in and buy plants at attractive prices. In turn, the ladies often bring the kids back for a haircut.

Laundromats have really capitalized on this idea. They are now operated in conjunction with bars, restaurants, exercise rooms, tanning salons, video game arcades, video rentals, you name it. Some even offer dry cleaning and tailoring.

We know of one funeral home that doubles as a wedding chapel. "We want to be part of more than just the final event in a person's life. Whether it's a wedding, a seminar, or just a get-together, we want to provide a warm, friendly place for people to meet," says a company spokesperson. Their Abundant Living Center serves the community and brings in extra revenue for the company.

One smart motel operator located near a ski and rafting area put together a deal that keeps her "no vacancy" sign on most of the time. She works with nearby resort and recreation operators to create getaway packages for both winter and summer. A family campground stimulated more business by buying a few horses and offering riding (at no less than $60 a day), pack trips, hay rides, and an evening steak dinner ride via horseback.

When we owned the hotel in First Try, we scrambled to think of practical add-on money makers. Because it was a historic hotel, in keeping with the period, we didn't have phones in the rooms. But we did discover we could keep half the revenue from an on-premise pay telephone. That proved profitable. We also installed some video games in a part of the lobby. They brought in a sizeable chunk of change each month.

The list of options goes on and on: A music store owner sells recorded music, sheet music, strings, reeds, and can special order larger instruments. To be different, he also tunes pianos. A bookstore promotes several sidelines: church supplies, audiotapes, and greeting cards. A real estate office carries maps and regional guidebooks. A maid service offers plant care, pet care, and house-watching for their traveling customers—while a hardware store is also the local bus depot and serves as the UPS pick-up point.

Diversification of business equals multiplication of dollars. You might start a new sideline business that relates to your original company, calls for similar skills and know-how, attracts the same customer or client base, or utilizes similar facilities. For instance, combining child care and elder care might make an excellent merger.

Farmers and ranchers always look for ways to augment their primary income. They have many irons in a crowded fire. Some set up fruit, vegetable, or flower stands; offer breeding services; raise earthworms; fix fences for their neighbors; or lease grazing rights for part of their land.

In some states, they also make money off hunting rights, charging $300 to $500 per person for hunters to have permission to come on their property to hunt deer, ducks, geese, etc. In most farm households, canning is as common as quilts. Pickles, relishes, chutneys, chili sauce, and preserves are sold at flea markets or given as gifts.

Those into horses often break others' animals, shoe them, or offer riding lessons. They also sometimes serve as guides and outfitters, taking out groups of hunters unfamiliar with the territory. Some even butcher the meat and do taxidermy work. Many farmers with fruit or vegetable crops set up popular "pick-your-own" operations where area residents pay a fee to garner all the produce they can personally pick.

Fee fishing is also an alternative for those with ponds. Farmers stock their ponds, then allow the public to indulge themselves for a flat fee, or pay for the fish they catch. This is a painless way to expand your income. Of course equipment also can be rented or leased, or the owner can perform services himself—such as snow removal, welding, or custom haying. We had a backhoe we planned to use for jobs beyond our own needs, but it didn't work out quite that way.

Tom: In First Try, a couple of our ranch hands had broken down the transaxle on our backhoe to repair it one summer, then got pulled away on an emergency job and never returned to the backhoe task. Fall came and went, then winter descended. As you might guess, we suddenly needed the backhoe.

I set up shop in the old stable behind the hotel. Wind whistled through the cracks, but a kerosene heater kept my fingers from freezing. After much thinking and trying to figure out the configuration, I finally got the transaxle together, hoping everything was right. I really had no reference because I hadn't taken it apart.

Then one bitter cold January day Marilyn and I went out to install the transaxle in the backhoe and finish the job. Wouldn't you know the rest of the parts had been left strewn all over the ground? No big deal in summer. BIG deal in winter—with a foot of snow to paw through. We lit a fire in a five-gallon oil drum to thaw our frozen hands and proceeded with the job. It was a long, miserable day crawling around in the snow trying to find minute nuts, bolts, and other parts.

But we finally got the transaxle and beast back together, gave each other a conquering smile, and lit 'er off. I climbed up on the driver's seat and shifted into gear. The backhoe lunged . . . in the wrong direction. I had installed the ring and pinion backwards! The backhoe now had ten reverse gears and two forward ones! Needless to say, we never rented it out. (We only share this story with you because you can't see our red faces.)

We sometimes think our son, Steve, is the champion of diversification derby days. He runs a multiplicity of small businesses. While his main emphasis is selling tires, he also retails auto supplies; does auto repair; gathers, cuts, and hauls firewood; buys and resells an occasional vehicle; rents out himself and his backhoe and homemade crane; and carries hunting supplies during hunting season. And, now that the local hardware store went under, he also carries a line of hardware and lumber.

With the emphasis on *multi-function*, in the future, related services will be clustered. Instead of traipsing to the dry cleaner's, then to the shoemaker's, and finally to the tailor's—these functions will be brought together for one-stop shopping. Already in Seattle there is Espresso Dental. It's a combination dentist's office, espresso bar, and legitimate massage parlor. Leisure time and dental hygiene are collapsed into one time slot. Any service that saves time, money, or aggravation will have a lot going for it.

Some businesses are considered seasonal income producers, or year-round ventures that are only part-time. In that case you'd darn well better combine two or more ideas or you'll starve (look how popular cranapple juice is). We know of one operation, the Pool and Yule Shop, that blends swimming pool maintenance and supplies in the summer with a Christmas shop in the winter. Someone adept at helping people with their taxes might be a ski instructor in the off-season. Get creative. There are many complementary pursuits that go together like biscuits and gravy.

Lastly we'd like to introduce you to something we've dubbed Link-Think. In this concept, you get together with other businesses and set up a cooperative approach to encourage the customer to purchase a chain of items. For instance, when a real estate agent sells a home, there are several other businesses he or she might alert to this prospect. They could include an interior decorator, a carpet and drapery salesperson, an insurance agent, and a landscape architect or gardener. If the new residents have children, the list might also include a diaper service, day care facility, private school, etc.

For this to be a win-win situation, the referred business could pay a small fee to the real estate agent. Get the idea? With LinkThink entrepreneurs can forge strong chains of prosperity with each other.

Now let's move ahead and scrutinize ways to thoroughly examine the industry and geographic area you contemplate joining. Knowledge is power. Get set for some mighty astute maneuvers to arm yourself with lots of both.

9

♦

Researching for the Right Opportunity

Depending on hearsay to evaluate what business you should be in makes about as much sense as using a yardstick to measure temperature. You'll need to do your research systematically and intelligently. Yet *research* is a scary term. It sounds intimidating. Expensive. Boring. It needn't be any of these. In fact, it can be as exciting as going on a treasure hunt—a hunt for nuggets of information to help you establish a solid enterprise.

You'll want to map out your strategy for gathering facts. Use tools that are economical and effective. Explore the market intelligently. Our aim is to illuminate innovative ways you can accomplish this so someone else doesn't mine the gold while you get the shaft. The information here is of primary value to those who want to have their own business, but job hunters will also find it worthwhile. In this chapter you'll learn two things: ingenious ways to discover inside intelligence about an industry, and methods to shadow potential companies and competitors. We'll show you how to extract a quarry of vital information.

For some people, research involves priorities: Do we decide *where* to live, then figure out how to earn a livelihood? Or do we take the opposite approach and look for a place that *needs* what we have to offer? David Savageau—coauthor of *Places Rated Almanac* and owner of Pre-LOCATION, a personal relocation consulting firm—advises to identify the business first, the location second. If you have a specialized skill, we agree finding the place is probably the wisest choice. But perhaps you're like many folks who don't have a definite career path. Then what?

TAKING THE FIRST EASY STEP

To show you just how simple market research can be, let's create a hypothetical case. Suppose you're an avid fisherman and the idea of opening your own tackle and equipment store makes your pulse race almost as fast as hooking a five-pound trout. First you need to know how many other tackle shops are in the area. How stiff is the competition? To find out, it's back to the trusty Yellow Pages. Congratulations, you've taken the first step in research. (No, it won't always be that easy. For more sophisticated businesses, the investigation is naturally more complex.)

Now you might visit the competition as a customer. In this role, you can determine such details as whether the location seems ideal, how complete the inventory is, and what prices are like. You can also gauge how accommodating and knowledgeable the proprietor is. This is of particular importance in a small town.

Don't be surprised to find yourself at the chamber of commerce next. There you'll glean particulars on the number of residents within the town's trading area, their average income, and their age level. What an encouraging sign, for example, if there are many retirees or pre-retirees. These people have plenty of time to fish. You can also find out tourist figures—a primary consideration for your type of business. If you choose to reveal your plans, you can also ask if anyone else is talking about opening a similar business, or how progressive the existing competition is. (Remember how fast word travels in rural places, however. If you don't want it known you're contemplating opening a certain kind of business, talk in generalities. You would be looking at entering the "recreation industry.")

Research comes in two varieties: primary and secondary. Primary research is the snooping you do yourself. It often takes the form of surveys or interviews. Secondary research depends on material already available. In it, you analyze existing information. That might include databases, corporate reports, government documents, magazine and newspaper stories, Internet Web sites, etc.

When our fisherman embarks on secondary research, a logical place to contact is the trade association to which other similar entrepreneurs belong. There is an association for virtually every interest or endeavor. They can be located in two ways: Contact the American Society of Association Executives, 1575 Eye Street NW, Washington, DC 20005, 202-626-2723. An even more complete list can be found at your local library (as can many of the reference works we mention in this chapter) in the three-volume *Encyclopedia of Associations*. Start in Part Three with the name and keyword index. When we look under "fish," there are many options. Reading the names of the associations quickly narrows the field of candidates, however. Then go to the proper number in Parts One and Two to learn more about the mission of each association and how to reach it.

What can associations do for you? Lots! They conduct surveys about salaries and revenue generated, and can put you in touch with suppliers, for starters. In addition, they publish newsletters, journals, or magazines with useful how-to articles. Ask to speak with both the membership coordinator and the public information director. Explain that you're considering joining the industry and ask how they can help.

To see how well a business might do in a particular geographic area, check the *U.S. Census of Retail Trade* for the average number of inhabitants per type of store. Let's say you want to open a women's clothing shop. According to this publication, such a business takes 5,000 residents. A bookstore, on the other hand, needs 26,000 inhabitants to support it. Next, determine the population and number of similar retail operations in the area you're considering. If the enterprise you're interested in starting would be under the recommended ratio of people to type of retail store, be cautious. But don't let this undermine your plans entirely. Many businesses are successful in spite of ratios far under the desired ones.

TRACKING THE TRENDS

It may behoove you to get into a cutting-edge business rather than doing something traditional. Here are some ideas to help you predict the future.

If you're looking to pinpoint trends before they're common knowledge, *American Demographics* may become your best online buddy. This magazine covers consumer trends primarily for advertising types. It offers just the kind of reconnaissance you need. Find them on the Internet at http://www.marketingtools.com.

The Department of Commerce publishes the *U.S. Industrial Outlook* annually. It traces the growth of 200 industries and provides five-year forecasts for each. Another potentially helpful publication is the *U.S. Statistical Abstract*. It's a compilation of data, reports, and charts from various federal agencies. The government is constantly conducting studies on industries, new technology, and social trends. These and many other helpful publications are on sale from the Superintendent of Documents, U.S. Government Printing Office, Washington, DC 20402. Write for a free catalog.

The Rochester Institute of Technology released a list of 12 fields it describes as "hot career choices for the remainder of the 1990s and the start of the next century." They are: information technology, environmental management, imaging science, microelectronic engineering, packaging science, telecommunications, food marketing and distribution, biotechnology, travel management, allied health sciences, electronic still photography, and biomedical photographic communications. In the November 1995 issue of *Home Office Computing,* an article on spotting trends stated the best businesses for the year 2000 fell into four categories: personal services, job services, security services (there's that "S" word again!), and technology.

Attending trade shows is a further way to stay informed. In the midseventies a lady by the name of Mable Hoffman did just that. She noticed several manufacturers' exhibits were introducing a small appliance called a Crock-Pot. She reasoned consumers would need new recipes and guidance on how to use their new cookware. This trend-conscious lady went home and wrote a book called *Crockery Cookery.* The last time we checked, it had sold over 3 million copies!

Be sure, however, you are tuning into trends, not fads. A fad is here today and gone tomorrow, like the hula hoop. Ignore these transient crazes. Don't let a turkey gobble your time and capital. Look for trends that have staying power. Before we started writing *Country Bound!,* we tracked the fact that several major magazines carried cover stories about Americans' desire to escape big cities.

Reading Your Way to the Hot Careers

Following are books, magazines, newsletters, and newspapers to help you stay abreast of trends and create exciting new business opportunities:

- *Clicking,* by Faith Popcorn and Lys Marigold, shows you how to position yourself for the way things will be. It covers 16 trends to future-fit your life, your work, and your business.
- *The Popcorn Report,* also by Faith Popcorn, not only pinpoints consumer moods but is just plain fascinating reading.

- *Powershift*, by Alvin Toffler, is both entertaining and profound as it serves up insights we need to survive in the future.
- *TechnoTrends*, by Daniel Burrus and Roger Gittines, shows you 24 ways to use technology to go beyond your competition.
- *Trend Tracking: The System to Profit from Today's Trends*, by Gerald Celente with Tom Milton, offers a formula for trend analysis that people can apply independently for business survival and growth.
- *The Trends Journal*, edited by Gerald Celente, is a quarterly publication that focuses on business trends and how to manage them.
- *Advertising Age* and *Ad Weekly* magazines help you get a feel for what new products, consumer interest trends, and ad agency advance plans are on the horizon.
- *American Demographics* magazine forecasts consumer trends for business leaders. Back issues on specific topics are also useful.
- The *Wall Street Journal* gives an excellent overview of breaking business news.
- *The Futurist* is a fascinating journal of forecasts, trends, and ideas about the future. Global in scope, it's available only through membership in the World Future Society.
- *John Naisbitt's Trend Letter* offers cutting-edge news on a variety of topics twice monthly.

Note: Several of these publications are available online.

SLEUTHING AS YOU SCHMOOZE

Once you've determined the industry you're going to enter, it's time to interview others in that same business. Naturally you'll pick someone in another town who is not a direct competitor. Schmoozing is a real door-opener. People love to talk about themselves, so you should have little trouble finding folks to visit with, especially if you play your cards right. Intelligence is like money—if you don't let on how little you've got, people will treat you as though you have a lot. Start with general questions, then move gradually to more specific inquiries.

Go armed with a fistful of well-constructed questions designed to ferret out answers to the tough inquiries. You want to know what has been their biggest stumbling block. Would they do it all again? How much money did it take? Would it be more today? What's the biggest mistake people just entering this business make? Don't go for yes-or-no answers. If your aim is to loosen lips, keep the conversation open-ended so people will elaborate.

Many other individuals can contribute to your information arsenal. Think about sales and support personnel from companies with complementary services. What about chatting with past employees or alumni from competitors? Talk to distributors, dealers, and franchisees serving your potential customer or client base. Get in touch with the county extension agent. These individuals are wonderful repositories of area business knowledge.

How about key vendors? Most industries have major suppliers who know about the industry they serve and the companies within that field because of repercussions to their own business. Cooperative vendors can provide you with timely and valuable research and development details. They know who is in financial trouble, which company has management problems, who is planning to expand, etc.

Don't overlook the local newspaper. The managing editor is usually a repository of knowledge. Place a phone call, stop in to converse briefly, or even extend an invitation for lunch. (Be sensitive to deadlines, however. If the paper comes out on Thursday, Tuesday and Wednesday are frantic times.) Also check the paper's archives for articles about competitors or industry-related stories. Then contact the reporter who did the piece. He or she probably has additional background information that could shield you from making a mistake. While you're at the paper, also monitor classified advertisements to see hiring patterns.

Another resource is your local economic development group. This is an umbrella organization and clearinghouse for area business information. Request a list of all companies who recently relocated to the area. You want the *whole list,* not select names. Then you can pick entrepreneurs at random to interview. This gives a more balanced view than if you are provided just the names of known town boosters.

Also ask about any proposed interstate highway changes or plans to add or alter other major thoroughfares. Many downtown sections became ghost towns when the freeway bypassed them. You don't want to relocate to an undesirable location. Is the business you plan to open currently missing from the local scene? Inquire why. There may be a valid reason your type of business has been unsuccessful in this locale.

Talk to people. Any people. All people. This informal research is sure to uncover some interesting prejudices and beneficial advice. Big corporations conduct "focus groups" where they pick people's brains.

You're taking a less formal and less costly route to the same destination.

DETECTION METHODS WORTH A FINE RANSOM

Shortly, we'll show you ingenious ways to track your quarry through the paperwork maze. But nothing is so revealing as reality immersion—being there yourself. If you've ever participated in a police "ride-along" program, for example, you know what an eye-opener it is to spend a night on the beat with a cop.

Try to find a way to get direct experience in the business opportunity you're exploring. Beyond being a customer, consider taking a job in the industry for a short time. Or volunteer to work for nothing for a few days to get a feel for things. If you're determined to own a restaurant, find a sales representative for a food wholesaler who will let you tag along as he or she makes calls. You'll have a whole new respect for restaurateurs—not to mention traveling sales representatives—at the end of a week.

Cushion your entry into a new business with knowledge. Study the competition intensely. "Most people don't do enough of this type of homework," says William Dunkelberg, dean of the School of Business at Temple University in Philadelphia. "If others are doing something similar to what you plan to do, go watch them—even if they're in another town."

Reading trade journals devoted to your proposed field is another way to hit the information jackpot. You probably received a copy when you contacted the association related to your interest. Study it carefully, not only from an editorial perspective but also by looking at the advertising. You can learn a lot by reading the ads. Additionally, ask about any special issues. These highlight developments, trends, and leaders in the industry. *Inc.* magazine does an annual special issue called "The Inc. 100," in which the fastest growing businesses in the U.S. are featured. Also go to a major library and ask about the various periodical indexes. They will lead you to more written bonanzas.

Books, though not as timely as newspapers or magazines, also contain a wealth of information. So if you're looking for who knows what on a specific topic, we'd suggest you visit the world's largest bookstore at http://www.Amazon.com. This is an incredible site where you can enter key words and it will search out the titles you need.

It's been said those who want advice the most, like it the least. Yet expert advice when launching a new business is an invaluable aid. There are many places to find individual experts. Federal Information Centers are one such source. You can unearth a free government expert on any topic. To locate data from the Federal Information Center, call 800-688-9889.

Penn State publishes a media expert guide of selected faculty and staff contacts. They have individuals proficient in the areas of farm management, self-employment, construction management, nutrition education, fiber optics and lasers, mushrooms, employing older workers, you name it. To find out about these experts, call their office of public information at 814-865-7517.

There's even a *Yearbook of Experts, Authorities and Spokespersons*. This encyclopedia of sources lists individuals, associations, and clearinghouses for myriad topics. Look for it online at http://www.yearbook.com or at your local library.

Can you guess one final intriguing place for locating a guru on a specific topic? Doctoral dissertations! University Microfilms International (800-521-0600) offers a free catalog of selected dissertations by subject area available for purchase. Prices range from $36 to $70 depending on academic or nonacademic status and if you want a softbound or hardbound copy.

It may be even more useful to contact the creator of the dissertation to get your questions answered. We can tell you from personal experience that an author has a lot more research and knowledge at his or her fingertips than ever reaches a manuscript page. What appears there is often only the tip of the iceberg. Hiring the author of a work as a consultant might be an extremely shrewd move.

Another checkpoint of interest to some entrepreneurs is your local office of the Environmental Protection Agency. In larger towns they provide information on proposed new plant and office construction, environmental impact, size, production, capacities, employees, and financing. For details, contact the Public Information Reference Unit, Environmental Protection Agency, 401 M Street SW, Washington, DC 20460, 202-260-7751.

The county courthouse holds as many secrets as a locked diary. Yet you can legally pick that lock and gain access to many court records. In most jurisdictions, the clerk of the court keeps chronological indexes that record charges or complaints. They also include the names of the defendants and plaintiffs, the date of filing, a case number, and disposition, if resolved. Armed with the case number, you can track down and look at these files. Often proprietary information—details not normally released to the public—are contained within. Some firms even reveal their annual sales figures, other private financial data, or research and development (R&D) plans during a court battle.

FLUSHING OUT SOPHISTICATED FACTS

To follow a more conventional paper trail, one place to look is the state corporation office. If a company is incorporated, the state will have details on the nature of the business, names of directors and officers, location, and capitalization.

Local, state, and federal government agencies can be a mother lode of information. To unveil competitor activities, backtrack by asking yourself what you have to fill out to be in business and meet the requirements of various agencies. Then seek copies of identical kinds of paperwork for your competitors.

When you start doing heavy-duty researching, you're likely to run into two acronyms: SIC and DOT. SIC stands for Standard Industrial Classifications, which are contained in—you guessed it—the *Standard Industrial Classifications Manual*. It contains detailed listings of all industries, their codes, and their definitions—which will take a reference librarian to interpret for you. The SIC system facilitates the analysis of data on all industries in the U.S. by individual establishment. If you look in the alphabetical index in the back, for example, you'll find a shoe repair shop is 7251, while shoe stores, retail, is 5661. Once you've mastered using this, it's a noble brainstorming partner.

The *Dictionary of Occupational Titles* (DOT) is a catalog of almost 13,000 occupations known to exist in this country at present. It's also a horror to work with. Richard Nelson Bolles, in his wonderful *What Color Is Your Parachute?*, suggests you first go to the *Dictionary of Holland Occupational Codes: A Comprehensive Cross-Index of Holland's RIASEC Codes with 12,000 DOT Occupations*. Whew! "It gives a comprehensive list of occupations which your 'code' suggests," explains Bolles, "plus the DOT number for each of the 12,860 occupations, thus enabling you to go to the *Dictionary of Occupational Titles* and look up more detailed information on each occupation that's of interest." If you're at a loss for what career route to take, cuddling up with this monster for a few hours could prove extremely beneficial.

Want more details about individual counties you're considering starting a business in? Coming right up. Let's scrutinize a series of publications from the U.S. Department of Commerce called *County Business Patterns 1993*. (This is the most current data available as we go to press.) There is a separate report for each state. The particulars contained here can be extremely useful for making basic economic studies of small areas. Order from the Government Printing Office at 202-212-1800.

Under Colorado, we looked up Chaffee County where we live. Let's say you're interested in moving your general building contractor business. You'll find there are 14 existing "general contractors and operative builders" in Chaffee Country. Most of them are small: ten have four or fewer employees, two have five to nine on the payroll, and two have ten to 19 employees. You'll also find such statistics as the total number of workers in that industry, plus the overall annual payroll. Maybe you want to open a service station. There are already 16 of them in this county and they divide among them an annual payroll of $839,000. Hanker to buy a motel, hotel, or other lodging place? You'll be competing with 28 other establishments who hire a total of 220 employees.

Want even more definitive information? Have we got a gem for you: *The Sourcebook of ZIP Code Demographics*. Volume One is the *Census Edition* with engrossing recaps of the 1990 figures. It weighs no less than *seven pounds* and is a most current and specific reference covering the latest demographic and marketing information. Here you'll discover facts on population, housing, and household data—plus income estimates. Zip codes are each profiled by more than 80 variables. With zips you can get even more exact than with counties. Now we can look at the two primary towns in Chaffee County—Salida and Buena Vista—separately.

Household and family income projections can be decisive in deciding where to locate your business, especially if your product or service depends on discretionary income. Here you have at your fingertips these figures for every zip code in America. Age distribution tables cover five-year increments. If your enterprise caters to a certain age group—perhaps teenagers or the mature market—here are dynamite statistics to guide you. You'll find the percentage of households with children and those with single people. Ethnic mix is also addressed. Race percentages are shown for Whites, Blacks, Native Americans, Asians, and those of Hispanic origin.

Under the housing category, you'll learn the dollar value of specified owner-occupied units. If you're debating between several locations, this will be helpful information. So might the vacancy percentage. And the percentage of those whose primary home is elsewhere draws a picture of how many residents live there year-round. There's even a state-by-state comparison for each of these categories in the back of the book.

Today the grandaddy of research awaits you on the Internet. You can become a cyberslueth in no time at all with the multitude of search engines waiting to help you locate specific information. Many people will recognize the names of Yahoo!, Alta Vista, and Lycos. But what you probably don't know is that there is one-stop-shopping waiting at http://www.search.com. Here you can access more than 250 Web and usenet search engines from a central Web page! Instead of searching each engine individually, Search.com's "slave driver" engine organizes search engines both by category and alphabetically. It even eliminates duplicates. What a tremendous time-saver for you. Have fun.

If you need really complicated reconnaissance and are willing to pay the price, there are several more traditional options. For nationwide survey results on a variety of topics, contact the Gallup Organization at 47 Hulfish Street, 2nd Floor, Princeton, NJ 08542. Or call 609-924-4600 and ask for the research library. For the individual and business, charges for survey results vary.

Outside firms that do secondary research are listed in *Burwell's Directory of Fee-Based Information Services*. This directory describes hundreds of information brokers in the U.S. and abroad.

Findex, the Directory of Market Research Reports, Studies and Surveys contains both industry and company reports. Studies by think tanks and social research organizations complement those from Wall Street and research firms around the world. Prices vary widely.

The American Association for Public Opinion Research is a trade association for individuals interested in public opinion. They hold annual conferences, publish a directory of their members, and offer free of charge a "Blue Book," which lists companies that produce surveys, what category of information they provide, and names and contact information. For more information or to receive a copy contact AAPOR at P.O. Box 1248, Ann Arbor, MI 48106, or call 313-764-1555.

Of course once your information is gathered, it must be processed, analyzed, and interpreted in a systematic and objective way. Try not to let your emotions overrule your logic. Being in the right business in the right rural location can be a lucrative, exciting adventure—or a life sentence. Do your homework and research carefully. The future belongs to those who are prepared.

Perhaps you are an established corporation considering a move to Small Town USA—what some call Penturbia. If so, then consider "A Checklist for CEOs."

A Checklist for CEOs

Despite the benefits, penturban living is not for every company. What's your firm's small-town index? Here are ten questions CEOs should consider if they are contemplating a move to the new corporate frontier:

1. Will relocating to a small town enhance your firm's survival, growth, and profitability? What is the likely impact to the bottom line?
2. Can you distance yourself from the rest of your industry and not be penalized? Will your key customers react favorably to your new address?
3. Can telecommunications adequately replace face-to-face contact in your business? If so, are you prepared to make a major investment in state-of-the-art technology?
4. Are you willing to spend possibly large amounts of time traveling to and from your small-town headquarters? Are your customers, suppliers, bankers, and other resource people willing to entertain a similar increase in travel? Are you willing to purchase corporate aircraft?
5. How much pruning can be done at corporate, regional, and divisional headquarters? Do you really have your heart in a mini-headquarters, or do you need strength in numbers at your side?
6. Are you prepared to adopt a decentralized philosophy that a smallish head office in penturbia requires? Do the corporate culture and your own management style encourage delegation and discourage hands-on involvement in day-to-day operations? How talented are your operating company personnel? Are they up to the task of managing with limited guidance?
7. Are you willing to trade off the anonymity of urban living for the fishbowl environment of a small town? Does your management team share this view?
8. Can future generations of top-notch talent in your industry be attracted to a frontier locale?
9. Would your small-town destination accommodate the two-career couples among your management? Are you prepared to assist with spousal employment? How will women, Blacks, Hispanics, and other groups be received?
10. Most important, do you and your top executives really want to live and work in the penturbs? Are these values shared by all their family members?

If you answered "yes" to these questions, penturban living may be for you. If not, stay put!

Source: The New Corporate Frontier: The Big Move to Small Town USA, by David A. Heenan. Copyright © 1991 by McGraw-Hill, Inc. Reproduced with permission of McGraw-Hill, Inc.

What if you're a budding entrepreneur, but not prepared to start from scratch? You want to buy a business or professional practice that's already up and running—a proven success. Then keep reading, because that is the subject of the next chapter. (Or skip ahead if you've already decided on your business approach.)

10

◆

Buying an Existing Business or Professional Practice

Purchasing an existing retail store, service business, or professional practice removes much of the risk. It's like taking an ocean voyage on a seaworthy vessel as opposed to launching your excursion in an untested dinghy. Current establishments already have a following—a customer or client base on which you can build. Locals are in the habit of doing business in particular places. When you buy that place, you also probably gain their loyalty—to a degree. (We'll discuss how to solidify—and boost—that loyalty later.) Naturally, some cash flow is also guaranteed.

FINDING A SUITABLE BUSINESS

While virtually every hamlet has a general store, gas station, bar, and restaurant, few of us want to go that remote. A greater population base brings more diversity. There are likely to be beauty shops, a lumberyard, antique shops, cleaners/Laundromat, flower shop, hobby/craft store, real estate offices, bookstore, recreational facilities, travel agency, various retail stores, plus some light manufacturing. This is in addition to health practitioners, attorneys, CPAs, and various consultants. The options run a wide gamut.

Think about what you want to do—and what you abhor.

You may have been a middle manager used to delegating routine jobs. If you buy a country business, chances are *you* will be the one doing those jobs—plus cleaning the john and shoveling snow off the sidewalk—at least at first. Are the trade-offs worth it to you? Does hefting 50-pound sacks of feed or concrete bother you? If so, stay away from businesses that require those activities. If you contemplate purchasing a bakery, are you willing to get up at 3 AM to start the ovens?

Does the idea of cleaning guest rooms turn you off? Then don't buy a B&B, motel, or hotel. We guarantee that the time will come when you're the only one available to change the linens and tidy the rooms. On the other hand, if you enjoy playing host or hostess, this occasional downside is a small price to pay for having a livelihood you love. Resist the urge to start a restaurant if you know nothing about this industry. Statistics show this profession has the highest rate of failure.

Boy, can we vouch for that! When we began operating the hotel and restaurant we bought in First Try, it seemed so simple: just hire a qualified staff, serve good food, and get the word out. "Qualified staff" are the operative words here. Reliable cooks are as hard to come by as a cool breeze in Death Valley.

You recall the adage, "If you want something done right, do it yourself" don't you? We modified that to "If you want it done at all, do it yourself!" Tom took his turn at cooking while Marilyn acted as both hostess and waitress. But his patience quickly evaporated. "This is not why I came to the country!" he announced, giving notice that his last day was coming soon.

> Marilyn: So I also became the cook. The first time I had to prepare a banquet I really agonized. We had reservations for 46. I'd done dinner parties before, but this was ridiculous! How in the world did one judge how much to prepare? Well I wasn't about to dish up 43 servings, 44 servings, 45 servings . . . and then run out. So I made plenty. Did I ever—we ate beef stroganoff for weeks afterwards!
>
> And in the process of being rural restaurant keepers, we learned several tricks—not the least of which was how to slam-dunk eggs. Many restaurants fail because all their profits go out the back door in waste. Offer a sparse, pared down menu. Create interesting daily specials that recycle leftovers. Keep your steaks frozen until you get an order (no spoilage that way). Audit the bus trays to see what's coming back; that's a clear signal people don't like something. Find a way to become known for something special.

We began a special Sunday brunch. People traveled up to 100 miles to partake of our historic ambiance, friendly service, and tasty food. One of the menu items we featured was quiche. I'll never forget the day a gentleman studied the menu, then ordered a "quickie." Little did I know when we left San Diego, that one day I would own a hotel and restaurant and become known for my "quickies."

Some businesses are almost recession-proof. No matter how bad the economy gets, people still have to eat, so grocery stores are good possibilities. And during tough times folks fix things rather than buying new ones. Thus auto mechanics, shoemakers, and appliance repair people will be in demand. And the worse things get, the more taverns flourish.

There are some firms that specialize in rural properties. United National Real Estate has commercial as well as residential offerings. Their semiannual catalog tells of farms, ranches, business opportunities, and commercial properties from coast to coast. To receive a copy, call 800-999-1020. Once you provide them with your specific needs, they offer a free search among their thousands of properties. Strout Realty also specializes in the country scene. Look for them in your Yellow Pages.

Another possibility is *Investor's Business Daily*. Reach them at P.O. Box 661750, Los Angeles, CA 90066, 800-831-2525. Then there's *Business Opportunities Journal* at Box 60762, San Diego, CA 92106, 619-223-5661.

While usually lean or nonexistent, the "Business Opportunities" or "Investments" classifieds in the local newspaper of your destination area may also provide some leads. So might the nearest big daily paper where boonies businesses advertise to attract metro money.

When sleuthing around town it's best to leave your city-slicker ways back home. Drive the Jeep rather than the BMW. *Be* smart. Just don't *show* it. And bring every ounce of common sense you can muster. Just because someone has rented a storefront and hung out a shingle doesn't mean he or she has a viable business.

When it comes to actually locating possible businesses, often the best buys are also the best-kept secrets. Many stores and firms shun posting For Sale signs in their windows. "'Tain't good for business," observed one old-timer. That doesn't mean there aren't owners eager to sell. Your challenge is to find them. Become a detective! When something interests you, go in and ask to speak to the owner. Find a secluded corner and explain you're new in town and looking for a business to purchase. Interested proprietors will take it from there.

EVALUATING PROSPECTIVE VENTURES

What appears to be a sterling buy may turn out to be fool's gold when you dig deeper. And dig you must to be sure you're not investing in a marginal undertaking. First find out why they want to sell. Don't always take what you're told at face value. Perhaps the owner is indeed ready to retire or has a health problem. On the other hand, he or she may also have less benevolent reasons for wanting to sell: new competition, supplier problems, or a declining local economy.

Sift out the obvious by talking to people. Assume a relaxed, easygoing manner. Things don't happen at lightning speed in the country. Visiting with townsfolk is the most valuable research you can do. All sorts of useful tidbits will emerge. Especially hone in on members of local service clubs such as Kiwanis, Rotary, Lions, Optomists, and Elks. These are the business leaders.

Systematically analyze all aspects. This won't be easy. In cities you can look at "comps": comparable businesses and what they sold for. But in rural areas no such numbers exist. Don't let your emotions overload your intellect. Buy with your head, not your heart. That darlin' little antique shoppe could be the biggest albatross in town. And get professional help. Be wary, however, of hiring the same accountant or attorney as the business owner uses. That's like putting the fox in charge of the henhouse.

Stop by the library and look in the *Encyclopedia of Associations*. Find out what associations similar businesses belong to. Call them for norms, membership information, and industry surveys. See if they can recommend a member in a noncompetitive, similar area whom you could phone and chat with.

Check the competition. How long have they—and the business you're considering—been in business? Is there enough for all of you? Three video stores in a town of 3,000, for instance, is probably two too many. Has the business been profitable? If not, what's the reason? Can you *really* do something to turn it around? Do you honestly have the money, ideas, personality, stamina, and skills to transform it into a moneymaker? Are you smart enough to compete against your competition's *weaknesses* rather than their strengths?

There's another intriguing facet to doing business in Small Town America. In many situations, living quarters are part of the package. There's an apartment above the store or a house behind the shop. This can prove very economical. In such cases your living quarters' mortgage payments, utilities, taxes, and insurance are often shielded under the business umbrella. And if you purchase an inn or a similar establishment, food and auto expenses are also sheltered. When you start racking up these costs in an urban setting, pulling up stakes for the country often means prospering in paradise.

Many rural businesses are family-run. This can stir up a witch's cauldron of trouble—or be a practical blessing—depending on the family. What about your other half? Does he or she have the skills and the temperament to supplement or complement your abilities? For parents seeking to teach their youngsters a sound work ethic, there is much to be said for a country family business. It's not unusual to see three generations helping out in rural enterprises.

When it comes to the purchase agreement, be sure you understand what it encompasses. Does it include the actual land on which the business is located? What about the building itself? If not, what are the terms and restrictions of the lease? Is it transferable? Is the business name included? All the inventory? Equipment? Fixtures? Be sure the exact terms of the sale are clearly spelled out and you know about existing contracts that affect the business's operation.

For instance, who's responsible for any debts? Are there ongoing contracts, like a lease on a copier or telephone equipment, you must assume? Are there any outstanding claims or loans on the inventory, equipment, or fixtures? What about liens on the property? Don't just ask the seller. Also check with the county clerk and at the recorder's office in both the county where the business is located and the one where the owner lives. You may even want to conduct a Universal Commercial Code (UCC) search to be sure no liens are filed against the property or assets of the business. This is typically done through the Uniform Commercial Code Section of the secretary of state's office.

In addition to studying the seller's books, also ask to see actual tax returns—personal as well as business. If there's a discrepancy between the owner's salary as stated in the company books and his personal income tax, this bears close scrutiny. Sometimes owners "fudge" on their books. This can have disastrous ramifications for the new purchaser. One man recommends dividing the down payment into three chunks. One is paid immediately, one midyear, and the last portion at the end of the year. You'll know by the end of the first increment if the books were honest. If not, you've only lost one-third of your money. Sales revenues and owners' salaries are easily manipulated.

Your diagnostic work will include such research as whether the profit picture reflects steady growth. The previous owner's attitude or poor health could have sapped a growing business. It's amazing how *one* simple idea can change the direction of a venture. In a retail shop, does the inventory turnover (meaning how fast it sells and must be replaced) match national averages? New systems of managing inventory can make an enormous difference in retailing. And providing outstanding customer assistance may be the key for a service business.

A WARNING TO THE WISE IS SUFFICIENT. . .

Investigate before you celebrate. Be sure you don't inherit a bucket of worms. The Environmental Protection Agency (EPA), for instance, in their zeal to protect ground water supplies, is clamping down on gas stations across the U.S. Many service station operators are being forced to close because their underground gasoline tanks don't meet EPA regulations. Woe to the poor soul who buys such a station.

Another area to watch is "grandfathering." No, we don't refer to the jolly older man. In this case, grandfathering means a rule or law that is waived for the present owner. Let's say a new sign code is enacted, but Joe Smith is allowed to keep his big, flashy sign because it was already in place when the law went into effect. Often, however, this latitude is not extended to the new owner. What a blow that could be if one of the primary reasons you bought Joe's place was because of the dominant advertising sign!

In certain endeavors it's wise to budget way ahead and take seasonal lulls into consideration. Rural businesses often fluctuate between soaring highs and disheartening lows. If you blow all your cash from a good month, you may not have enough to carry you over in a bad one. Seasonal businesses that depend on tourism are especially vulnerable. We know one motel owner who had such a profitable summer that he went out and bought a new Cadillac to celebrate. Then winter came. Business plummeted. Because he hadn't put something aside to see him through the lean season, he lost his place when he couldn't pay the taxes and insurance in the off-season.

In retailing, figure that the money you invest in inventory is gone. "What?" you exclaim in horror. Think about it. You never actually recoup that money until you sell the business. Why? Because you must constantly replenish the inventory! A dwindling inventory means sagging sales. Sure you make a profit when you sell merchandise, and you may learn to buy more shrewdly, but the bulk of those original inventory dollars will remain tied up in your goods.

One detracting aspect of rural entrepreneurism is that your personal life isn't always your own. Most people in town know where you live—whether it's above the store or out on County Road 364. They're your friends, your neighbors, your acquaintances. And the unwritten country code is you help your neighbors.

This means getting a carburetor for Larry's pickup so he can get his little girl to her physical therapy appointment early tomorrow morning—even though you officially closed two hours ago. It means opening the restaurant to make hot chocolate and sandwiches for the search and rescue team when they're called out at 4:00 AM on a dreary Sunday morning. It means going down to the shop to find a spool of turquoise thread so Bessie can finish the bridesmaid dresses she needs for the wedding tomorrow. It means being part of other people's lives—and allowing them to be part of yours. Not such a bad trade really.

WHAT'S A BODY TO PAY?

Reckoning the true value of a business is about as scientific as catching catfish with a bamboo pole, string, and a safety pin. Some say a going concern is worth the value of its equipment, plus the wholesale cost of its inventory, plus one or more year's anticipated profit. Most small businesses are rarely sold for more than a year's gross sales. This, of course, may be two to three times higher than the annual pretax income.

Then there is the issue of measuring goodwill. Let's say you want to buy a service station. How can you figure a fair price for the business that takes into account goodwill and business contacts, in addition to the value of the equipment and inventory? Many methods can be used. The bottom line is you're trying to set a value on the assets and earnings record of the firm. The simplest way is to determine the payback period. This is usually two or three years. That is, the net profit for two years would equal the goodwill value. Goodwill, while an intangible quality, means a lot. Community support and individual patronage can make or break a business.

And speaking of paying, one of the delightful aspects of buying a rural business is that the owner is often willing to finance the sale. With a decent down payment, many sellers will carry the paper themselves.

We know of one situation where a business was purchased with no money down. The buyer pledged a percentage of the profits on a monthly basis until a specified figure was reached. This arrangement worked well for both parties. The seller avoided a lump sum tax liability. Because he also charged 11 percent interest, he realized more overall than if he had gotten the purchase price in full initially. And the deal was structured so the seller's investment was secured by a note on the assets of the business.

Another important way the previous owner can aid you is by agreeing to stay on for a period of time and teach you the ropes. He or she can introduce you to suppliers, take you on buying trips, and explain how to display items for faster turnover. More importantly, the seller can introduce you to customers and fill you in on their idiosyncracies.

If you can't involve the seller in your financing package, ask the local bank if they will consider the business itself as collateral. Then you can get a chattel mortgage. This puts a dollar amount on all the business assets (excluding real estate) and requires that you not dispose of any of them until it is paid off.

While we're on the subject of money, never *never* invest all your liquid assets in a business. Keep some cash in reserve, probably 20 to 30 percent. You never know when broken water pipes will hit you with a devastating plumbing bill, when the furnace will conk out, or when a dismal quarter will require you to dip into your reserves for living expenses.

But maybe you're leery of taking the do-it-all-yourself plunge. If so, the next chapter offers a wondrous collection of tips on franchising.

11

◆

Investigating the Franchise Alternative

With downsizing continuing, people realize the days of the protective parental company are over. No longer can we depend on our employers to safeguard our positions. The era of 25-year watches is gone. The alternative is to create success for yourself.

If building a business from the ground up sounds a bit too risky for your taste, franchising may be a viable solution. With less than a 5 percent failure rate, it provides the enterprising Countrypreneur with a welcome safety net. Franchising is a practice in which the company owner (the franchisor) licenses the right to use the name, product or service, and procedures of the company to an investor (the franchisee). It's a multibillion dollar industry that appeals especially to former corporate middle managers who appreciate having some structure. Ever-increasing participation fuels the franchising frenzy.

It provides an easy-entry opportunity for small investors to get into business. Franchise owners are not cookie-cutter people. Variety can be found in every area, from the type of franchise purchased to the style of doing business. If you're a risk taker, it can be your route to a business empire. It has been said the only difference between a franchisee and an independent businessperson is that the franchisee is smarter. Approached properly, this business concept is almost recession-proof.

Franchisees have training, marketing expertise, and business consulting at their fingertips. Investing in a franchise offers many advantages including having a *proven* product or service at your disposal.

Identification with a brand name offers instant credibility. And start-up costs will typically be lower than those in an independent business because of volume purchasing power for products or equipment.

Before deciding if franchising is for you, consider a couple of important points. With this method of conducting business, investors pay for the right to use the existing system and market existing products or services. If yours is a total entrepreneurial mind-set, think carefully about whether following someone else's guidelines works for you. Though there is plenty of room for creativity, you are buying into an already tried and established idea.

Another point worth considering is the expense involved in buying into a franchise. Those interested in this sort of opportunity can expect to pay an initial fee, royalty, or both. Initial investments run anywhere from $3,000 to $500,000. Royalty fees range from 3 to 10 percent of gross sales. Additionally there can sometimes be an advertising fee of 2 to 5 percent. Potential participants should plan to provide part of the capital themselves. The wise new businessperson also creates a personal cash cushion to cover the first year of start-up. This way, more money can be funneled through the infant franchise, creating more growth at a faster rate.

FERTILE FIELDS

The recent expansion in this area is phenomenal. From 1990 to the present date, franchising has continued to multiply profits for savvy folks who had the foresight to become involved.

The International Franchise Association's (IFA) *Naisbitt Report* predicts that "By the year 2000, franchise sales will account for half of all retail sales. Almost any service imaginable can be franchised . . . ." According to the IFA, a new franchise store opens every 16 minutes, bringing the number of outlets to more than half a million. Franchised outlets account for more than one-third of all retail sales in the United States, compared with one-tenth only ten years ago. Will this growth include rural America? You bet!

Although some organizations choose to limit themselves to upscale malls, many flourish in Small Town USA. One of the advantages of taking a franchise rural is the excellent word-of-mouth advertising. Citizens of these areas share new finds freely, so remember to make a dynamite first impression on them. With this in mind, you'll find that small populations yield rapid market penetration. Networking is easier because of strong community ties.

One of the franchises going to the country is Mr. Rooter. More people are on septic systems and few plumbing companies think of locating in remote areas. Locals appreciate franchises setting up shop in their areas. It gives them access to services they've not had in the past. Other familiar rural franchise names include Snap-On Tools, Dairy Queen, Sonic Drive-ins, and Pizza Hut.

SEPARATING THE WHEAT FROM THE CHAFF

With franchising, being in business for yourself doesn't mean being *by* yourself. Support networks are vast. Most franchisors offer advertising guidance, training and professional advice, marketing and accounting know-how—even advice on start-up procedures, finance avenues, and location choice for your new business. Products and services are tried and proven. Operations are in place; problems already faced and handled. You'll find a kaleidoscope of opportunities. With such limitless prospects, the new franchisee is bound to find a niche personally customized to his or her needs.

While some are skeptical of the market for franchises in rural America, most are singing its praises. Not all potential choices would work, of course, but many could thrive in the fertile soil of America's hinterland. Base your choice on your present skills: What do you already enjoy doing? This will be a long-term time investment, so whether you enjoy performing the services rendered should be a major component in making your choice.

After you've narrowed down the list of possibilities, figure out what your proposed community needs. Our dry cleaners burned a few years ago. A replacement was a welcome addition. In a village of 2,000, another accounting service may not be a very good idea if they already have two or three. Choose something that fills a void and your success will be much greater. A small town will view a new service as an exciting event. Folks will drop by to see what you're about. If no one else offers what you do, you have the local market sewn up.

If your chosen area draws tourists, explore recreational franchises or sweeten the deal by starting up a candy franchise. These go over like gangbusters with tourists.

Many small towns don't have janitorial services. Oh sure, there are those who profess to be housecleaners. But there's no quality control, no standards of operation, and many aren't reliable. In addition, those working independently in this area have to find their own clients. Bringing in an established franchise and offering training to these people, working around their schedules, putting them on salary, and giving them encouragement and support might just be the ticket to improving their situations. And higher standards of service would certainly be an asset in clients' eyes.

Looking at market inclinations in franchising is helpful in guiding you to your choice. This is a hotbed of change, so be sure you're looking at a trend versus a fad. Is your choice something that will have high demand ten years down the road? Or will it flash and burn like a shooting star?

Environmental franchises are an up-and-coming idea in remote areas. Many folks have never had the convenience of dropping off recyclables in town. Either locals don't recycle at all, or they save mounds—then make a monthly trip into the city to dispose of them.

And don't overlook the fastest growing segment of our population. Senior citizens will soon be the largest slice of the American pie. Many flock to rural areas for retirement. If exercise programs are a favorite, look into Take Time, Incorporated, an exercise chain for mature consumers. Other franchises that cater to this group include travel agencies, interior decorating, home services (i.e., lawn care and maid service), accounting and tax assistance, health aids, and recreation.

Other hot franchising opportunities include quick automotive services, children's goods, party supplies, temporary services, house inspection, carpet cleaning, pest control, and chimney sweeping. Explore all businesses that interest you, but make sure you look to the needs of your new neighbors. Giving them a service they've previously had to drive miles to get will make you a valued new asset in your community. Be unique, but practical.

IF HOME IS WHERE YOUR HEART IS

A cost-saving alternative is the home-based franchise. Extremely practical, start-up costs here can be limited in some cases to just a computer program and training. Franchise fees for a home-based business can be under $10,000.

If this lights the fire beneath your motivation, look for a customized product or service and deliver it to your clients' homes. A clever entrepreneur with a decorating bug could have samples organized in a van, while keeping base operations at home. Companies handling glass and marble lend themselves to delivery and home service. Again be imaginative. Very few rural citizens have access to home services. If you handle it with pizzazz, you'll find yourself in high demand.

MATCHMAKER, MATCHMAKER

Finding the franchise that's just right for you can be a challenge. But if you follow a selection system, you can make the job much easier. If there is something you don't have much experience with but you have a strong interest in, don't limit yourself. Travel Agents International, for example, prefers to recruit people who have no experience. As we've counseled before, prioritize your life. If you want to spend evenings and weekends with your family, then don't go into the hospitality industry. Weekends mean big money for this field. Folks wanting success here need to make their full energy available when it is most needed.

Make sure those you are considering have been around for awhile. One of the advantages of going with franchising is the product and the market have been proven. If you go with someone too new in the field, you could be setting yourself up for failure.

If you're more adventuresome and have a desire to cash in big, you may look at buying additional franchises down the road. Adding more salespeople or additional units is one avenue to increased profits. This freedom is great for the person who isn't happy with a plateau. When your first location reaches its peak, continue to grow. Go to surrounding areas opening the same type of business, or stay where you are and open complementary organizations.

For example if you go with Mr. Rooter, you might think of opening other home improvement franchises. Some ideas could be painting, interior decorating, or cabinetry. You can perform many services for the same client base. In this way you can boost your opportunities for increased earnings.

Use the resources available in looking for your location. Remember that most franchisors offer this service. And don't feel restricted because of your remote location. Franchisors look for accessibility. Can 20,000 people comfortably reach the location by car? Traffic counts are key factors in deciding this important point.

FINDING SPECIFIC HELP

Many excellent tools are available to smooth out the wrinkles in your quest for the ideal franchise. By far the most valuable resource we've found to date is the IFA. Anyone checking into buying a franchise should contact this organization. They offer several inexpensive publications. *Investigate before Investing* is a booklet with tips on evaluating a franchise. *Answers to the 21 Most Commonly Asked Questions about Franchising* is vital to newcomers in the field.

The IFA also publishes the comprehensive *Franchise Opportunities Guide*. It lists IFA members, all other franchises, and additional important information. Updated twice a year, it always has the most current data available. It's a marvelous place to prospect. After looking through it carefully, you may come up with a list of 20 possibilities initially. This directory includes tips on choosing a franchise and what to do before you invest. IFA is also a ready source for advice and encouragement on finding the right franchise. Ask for their *Publications and Products Catalog*. You'll find everything you need from books to audiocassettes.

If computer software is more your style, their *Franchise Edge* is a Windows-based program that lists more than 5,000 franchises. Multiple search functions allow the user to search with various parameters including industry category, company name, and investment range. Legal advice and financing sources are also included. Latch onto this and other IFA tools by writing IFA Publications, 1350 New York Avenue NW, Suite 900, Washington, DC 20005. Or call 800-543-1038 for further information.

The FTC provides a package of information about the FTC Franchise and Business Opportunity Rules free of charge. Write Public Reference Branch, Federal Trade Commission, Washington, DC 20580, or call 202-326-3128.

The Franchise Annual is a comprehensive guide covering over 4,200 franchises in its 1996 edition. It's chock-full of advice on the technical aspects of becoming a franchisee. Help is available in checking agreements and interpreting laws on earnings claims here too. You can find it at Info Press, Inc., Box 550, Lewiston, NY 14092, 716-754-4669.

The *Directory of Franchising Organizations* (published by Pilot Books, Pilot Industries, Inc., 103 Cooper Street, Babylon, NY 11702, 516-422-2225) offers a listing of franchise opportunities. They give addresses and approximations of initial investments, classified according to industry. This information makes easy work of narrowing the field of choices. Simply choose areas of interest within your individual investment range and write for information.

PUTTING FRANCHISORS UNDER THE MICROSCOPE

In the 1850s, Singer accidentally developed the first franchise network to distribute and sell sewing machines. But it wasn't until the 1950s and 1960s that the practice was actively pursued. Companies getting in on this initial surge were Holiday Inn, Dunkin' Donuts, Roto-Rooter, McDonald's, Midas, and 7-Eleven. Unfortunately at that time there was very little regulation and many fly-by-night organizations took advantage of small businesspeople looking for big opportunities. As a response to this problem the Federal Trade Commission developed the Uniform Franchise Offering Circular (UFOC) a disclosure document required by the federal government.

Ask for the franchisor's UFOC. If you have a difficult time getting this document from a prospective company, it's likely not a safe choice. The UFOC puts in writing the company's history, principles, business experience, and franchise program. It covers everything from accurate earnings claims to forecasted sales. You'll find out what restrictions to expect on goods and services offered by the franchisee. This document also spells out what obligations, assistance, and supervision can be expected from the franchisor. An outline of fees and royalties is included. It's a virtual who's who of the company. Biographical and professional information on company officers is complete and up-to-date.

You can also examine the franchisor's profit and loss statements. Peruse annual reports. Seek documents that offer a wealth of information such as initial fees, financing arrangements, territorial rights, past bankruptcies, and standard operating statements. Also look for listings of privately held franchises versus company-owned outlets, plus copies of contracts and agreements. Check with the state attorney general's office to see if there is any record of complaints against the franchisor.

Above all, be informed. Be sure to have a lawyer who understands this area review the information. Consulting with an accountant who specializes in franchise agreements is also a wise move. Trusting those who know always works best. Do your research and hire expert advice.

The UFOC will also have a listing of current franchises. Spend time talking with these people. Ask lots of questions! Listen carefully to their answers. What kind of training did they receive? How's business? Are they able to meet desired goals? How well does the franchisor work with them?

You can get invaluable "insider information" by chatting informally with a franchisee in a noncompetitive location. To get a feel for things, befriend someone in an area similar to yours and ask to take a look at their franchise agreement. You can find out how much it will cost you to open your franchise and sometimes even expected salary levels.

Once you've narrowed the field, consider going to work for one of the existing franchises. Whether done openly or incognito, this can be a source like no other for finding out how well franchisors work with franchisees, what training and support really is available, and how much freedom there is to grow.

Always visit the franchisor's headquarters. Meet the management. Find out if you agree with their business philosophy. See the quality of work at home base. If the atmosphere is disorganized and unproductive, beware! If there are problems with the heart of the corporation, the extremities will surely suffer.

While you're there, ask to audit their training program. Is it meaty? Realistic? Upbeat? Be sure headquarters is committed to ongoing support of their franchisees. Their concern with providing for success assures you continued, expert guidance. If your chosen franchise is a member of IFA, you can be comfortable with the professional standards to which the company adheres. Members have agreed to abide by the IFA Code of Ethics.

Use the following "Franchise Evaluation Checklist" to assess the strengths and weaknesses of the franchises you are evaluating.

For many, the "extended family" aspect of franchising is the key to success. Working with a team that cares about how your business is progressing is always encouraging. If this is the avenue for you, fully exploring all possibilities will yield satisfaction and opportunities for great prosperity. In a crowded market, franchising is the key to market share and profitability. You can catch the wave of this burgeoning field and ride the crest to success and financial security in your new country home.

We discuss creative financing in Chapter 15. Just remember that the best alternatives don't always come from a bank. Some franchisors offer aid to prospective franchisees. Investigate that option. And spend time digesting the information in Chapter 17, "Persuasive Marketing Strategies to Boost Your Bottom Line." They will help you excel.

Franchise Evaluation Checklist

❏ Do you have a complete description of the business?
❏ Does the franchisor have a proven success record of at least five years in actual franchising?
❏ How many franchises has the company sold?
❏ What are the total costs for entering the franchise (including initial investment, equipment purchase or rental, training costs, etc.)?
❏ Does this fit with your ability to invest? Don't forget to include the costs of a building site, storefront, needed vehicle, etc.
❏ Did the company supply you with an up-to-date UFOC?
❏ Is the company strong financially?
❏ Is it interested in a long-term relationship?
❏ Does the company have a good reputation and credit rating?
❏ How fierce is local competition?
❏ Does the product or service meet a local need?
❏ Is territorial protection defined and guaranteed?
❏ Have you checked with other franchisees concerning the business ethics and continuing support of the franchisor?
❏ From whom will you purchase inventory and supplies?
❏ Who handles advertising?
❏ If the franchisee is responsible for advertising, do you have the capital and know-how to back this up? Does the franchisor tack on an extra fee?
❏ What fees are required? Is this too big a cut from your anticipated profits?
❏ Are most franchises in the system succeeding?
❏ What are the continuing costs for maintaining the franchisor/franchisee relationship?
❏ Under what conditions can the relationship be renewed or ended?
❏ Have many franchisees left the system? When? Why?
❏ Will you have the power to sell your franchise?
❏ Did your attorney and accountant review the contract?
❏ Have you found out if the state attorney general's office has any record of complaints against the franchisor?

Two main associations seek franchise reform and fair practices. You may want to check with them: American Association of Franchisees & Dealers, P.O. Box 81887, San Diego, CA 92138, 800-733-9858 and American Franchise Association, 53 W. Jackson Boulevard, #205, Chicago, IL 60604, 800-334-4232.

Some people prefer working from their home. Both franchised and nonfranchised businesses blossom here. The next chapter gives you the inside scoop on accomplishing near miracles without setting foot outside your house.

12

◆

Home Suite Home
The Information Age Option

What do Domino's Pizza, Hallmark Cards, Ford Motor Company, Apple Computer, Nike, Playboy, Amway, and Baskin-Robbins have in common? They all started as home businesses. One in five businesses is started in the home today. According to Link Resources, 44.7 million people now work at home at least part of the time. Twenty-eight percent of them run a full-time home-based business (HBB), while 29 percent operate a part-time enterprise. Every day more people agree "there's no place like home." What used to be perceived as a humble industry now enjoys newly found prestige. The "virtual" office is a reality.

WHO'S WORKING FROM HOME AND WHY?

Who are those participating in this ten-second commute? While many twentysomethings are reluctant to ride the corporate treadmill, most home-basers are around 40, married with a child or two, well-educated, and have an average household income of slightly over $50,000 a year. Fully 99 percent of the readers polled by *Home Office Computing* say they are happier working on their own; 98 percent would recommend it to others.

Why did they escape corporate confines where office politics are filled with quibbling rivalry? "I wanted to be my own boss," report 64 percent of *Home Office Computing*'s readers; 50 percent say, "I wanted more control over my life." Only after these two reasons does money influence the decision. The desire to meld family obligations with work responsibilities is a recurring theme among home-office enthusiasts. Thirty-one percent made the change to spend more time with their loved ones. Some believe HBBs arc doing more to restore family unity than education, philosophy, and social services put together.

A Montana mother of small children who lived 25 miles from the nearest town couldn't justify commuting and baby-sitting costs, especially when most jobs offered only minimum wage. She created a home business (a telemarketing service bureau) that's mentally stimulating and income producing.

"There is work beyond 'day care and crafts' for mothers who want to remain home with their children," observes Jane Williams. In 1986, she launched Bluestocking Press from Placerville, California, a town of 8,000 located in the Sierra Nevada foothills. With the help of her family, she publishes educationally oriented books and a 50-page book catalog.

Her children, Katie, aged 11, and Ann, aged 8, have always been home schooled. "This means we interact within each other's working and living environments throughout the day," says Williams. "The kids understand what work is, what it takes to put food on the table. They participate in those jobs they're skilled enough to do. Katie is a dynamic phone receptionist and handles customer service work. Ann fills book orders."

This mother is an outspoken advocate of home schooling. "It brings the real world into children's lives more effectively than conventional education," she observes. Williams—who can be reached at Bluestocking Press, P.O. Box 1014, Placerville, CA 95667, 916-621-1123—sells books on the subject.

This is a familiar refrain as baby boomers hunger to sink deeper family roots. Couples with children can better balance family and dual careers if one or both parents work at home. This also gives career-oriented women who want to nurture their children the opportunity to plant a foot in both worlds.

Judith Wunderlich thought she had it all—until she realized that she had less of what mattered. Wunderlich rarely saw her baby. Supermom would rise at 4:30 AM for an hour-long commute to her fast-track management job in insurance, then return home about 7:30 in the evening. Frustrated and exhausted, she finally quit and started a home typesetting business in Bartlett, Illinois. Today Wunderlich runs a $300,000-a-year temporary employment service out of her home. Her two children play in an adjacent room.

Top Ten Home-Based Businesses

1. Consulting
2. Computer services/programming
3. Business support/services
4. Financial support/services
5. Independent sales
6. Graphic, visual, or fine arts
7. Writing
8. Marketing/advertising
9. Construction/repair
10. Real estate

Source: © 1991, *Home-Office Computing* magazine.

What other sorts of businesses are run from the home? Virtually everything. Notice on the "Top Ten Businesses" recap from *Home Office Computing,* an excellent magazine, that consulting leads the pack. In this age of corporate retrenchment, budget-conscious companies are keeping a lid on costs by outsourcing to independent contractors. Mail order and desktop publishing also flourish in home environments. Of course, so do day care, gift basket services, janitorial firms, and public relations agencies.

While traditionally work-at-home people have been writers, artists, and others whose occupations required they work alone, that's changing. The ranks are swelling like a cresting river. Teri Ross of Minnetonka, Minnesota, designs sportswear at home. Those offering financial counseling services have a rosy future. Clients who prefer to cocoon needn't even leave their homes. Everything can be taken care of by phone, fax, e-mail, or overnight delivery service.

Those who do word processing from their homes say their business is recession-proof. When the economy turns down, companies cut back on secretarial help and use outside services like theirs. Personal shopping services are thriving. Reports one woman who runs such a business, "With fewer employees, those who still have jobs are often asked to work overtime . . . they're reluctant to (refuse) for fear of losing their jobs. So they hire me to shop for them."

In North Dakota, home-based manufacturing is as busy as a plant running three shifts. People knit sweaters, create jewelry, and fire pots. And they're learning how to take their products to market all across the

USA. Home-based franchises—such as Pet Nannies, Decorating Den, and Computertots—perform services at the client's site.

Network marketing, once castigated as pyramid scams, has cleaned up her act and is making millionaires out of ordinary people. Today she dresses in fine suits, wears tantalizing perfume, and exudes an aura of respectability. She's even changed her name. Now most call her "network selling." The secret is individual contact, done out of homes and apartments across the land. The potential for profits is geometric growth. With the right product, the right organization, and the right timing, it can be an extremely viable HBB. After all, in the new millennium, we won't go to the store—the store will come to us.

ACHIEVING THE THREE "Fs"

People set up home businesses to get the "Three Fs": freedom, flexibility, and financial independence.

Having freedom is a wonderfully liberating feeling. Anyone who works in a city has two choices: live in the city and face high rents, congestion, and crime; or move to the suburbs and endure long daily commutes. Entrepreneurs who work at home can live almost anywhere. Sophisticated ad agencies are run from farmhouses. In-demand consultants, some of whom have an international client base, operate out of posh country homes.

Flexibility is another plus. You don't have to battle the elements, the traffic, or the clock. You can work any hours you want. Have young children who need attention during the day? Work evenings or while older kids attend school. Flexibility applies in other ways as well. You might start your HBB as a sideline or do it part-time while you hold down another job to earn a base income. This allows you to build clientele and cash flow. In some cases, it's practical to start a home-based endeavor while still located in the city, then take clients with you when you move.

There's also financial independence. When you work out of your home, the price for office space is always right. You can operate on a shoestring when combining your work and your residence. "If you have a problem," advises one home-business operator, "don't throw money at it; throw your mind, your energy, your spirit." Besides overhead and start-up costs being lower, multiple tax breaks may also be available.

The Tom Scheibal family of St. Helena, California, runs an antique shop and bed and breakfast out of their home. Tom Scheibal reports, "With the expense and tax write-offs I get on a place that's also my home, I do a lot better financially than I could on a regular job."

We also know of a source of inexpensive crime insurance for your business equipment when you're home-based. In the case of burglary, residents in many states are eligible for a federal crime insurance program that actually subsidizes the cost of insurance. This lowers the premium because Uncle Sam pays part of the bill if your place is burglarized. To see if your state qualifies, call 800-638-8780. Chances are you can get a rider added to your homeowners insurance to cover computer equipment and business furnishings. You may also want to investigate business interruption insurance, disability income protection, and business life insurance.

Two wonderful resources on the subject of HBB are *Working from Home* by Paul and Sarah Edwards and *Homemade Money* by Barbara Brabec.

MAKING IT WORK FOR YOU

When people go from the corporation to the cottage, many need an "attitude adjustment" (though not the kind Hank Williams, Jr., sings about). What we refer to is an upbeat outlook that expects and projects excellence.

It's especially important to alleviate any shreds of amateurism. To look and feel your professional best, dress the part. You can slouch around in a bathrobe only so long before an important business contact shows up unannounced and catches you looking like you're heading to the bedroom rather than the boardroom. Forget heels or a necktie, but do be presentable.

Consider spending a bit extra on your written materials. A snazzy business card, letterhead, and brochure shout *professionalism*. For a home-based business, these are your windows to the world. Be sure they sparkle! Carry business cards with you everywhere. Marilyn made a good contact at a hotel swimming pool one day and was able to fish out a card from between the sunscreen and the room key.

Other actions can help establish you as a serious Countrypreneur. If it's possible to set up a separate business entrance, do so. This is especially true if clients will be coming to your home. And be sure the yard, porch, and foyer aren't littered with toys, coats, shoes, or other inappropriate items. Make sure, too, the family dog doesn't terrorize would-be clients.

You may want to make arrangements for UPS or Federal Express to pick up letters and parcels from your home. (Put up a large sign with your name and house number on it.) Additionally, it's a good idea to think of your mail carrier as part of your team. He or she will be delivering more than usual to your address. Be kind, patient, and generous with this person. By the way, if you live in an apartment, consider referring to your apartment number as your *suite number*. The post office doesn't object and it comes across more businesslike.

Some HBBs affix a lockbox outside for the convenience of their clients or customers—not to mention themselves. Good accounts receive a key. These people regularly drop off work to be completed and retrieve it when done. This cuts down the interruption factor.

Even if you didn't punch a company time clock, you were expected to be at work at a designated time. You may find it helps to establish regular office hours now too. Then when the urge to do the laundry, tidy the house, or lie down for a nap seems overwhelming, check and see if you're "off work." Maintaining a schedule makes it easier to get into a productive rhythm.

And setting firm deadlines for having projects finished will keep you out of trouble. Making "to do" lists is another good strategy. Put the task you least like to do at the top, then reward yourself when you've accomplished it. Play with the dog, eat a frozen yogurt, or listen to a few minutes of your favorite music. Remember, you're the boss.

Give yourself permission to enjoy yourself! This is your chance to finally try your wings. Yes, at times you'll be on an emotional roller coaster. One day you're elated because you just put together a big deal; the next day you feel overwhelmed by all the work to be done. But you'll get through those times.

Of course you need to know your personal bottom line. If you nurture your business well, chances are it will flourish. This could present a real dilemma. Do you want to expand beyond your home? Will the prospects for extra profits be worth what you'll give up? There are definite trade-offs.

Marilyn: When I worked out of my home, I was a lot more freewheeling. If it was a beautiful day and I wanted to sunbathe or putter in the yard, I did it. That night I might work until 11:00. Because I met my clients elsewhere, I also had the latitude to work in sweats and be completely comfortable.

Now that we've grown to a staff of six and moved into office quarters, it's a different story. I feel obligated to be at work when everyone else is. While my country lifestyle still permits some informality, sweats and slippers would be stretching it.

USING EQUIPMENT AS YOUR STAFF

Does it seem impossible you'll be able to perform dozens of tasks all by yourself? Can you handle correspondence, market for new prospects, track bills, cut invoices, take inventory, do the bookkeeping, update the mailing list, service the business you generate, and perform other record-keeping tasks? Yes! With several electronic helpers. A telephone and a computer allow you to deliver the one-two punch that knocks out these chores like they were rank amateurs.

Today, many entrepreneurs take it a step further. Their "electronic cottages" are the ultimate in high-tech wizardry. The phone system has several lines and sophisticated features. The computer sports a modem, fax capability, and software with the latest bells and whistles. Complement this with a laser printer and copier, and they have a state-of-the-art office right in their homes. Those who are doing desktop publishing from home might add a scanner to the list of equipment helpers.

How expensive is setting up such an office? Dan Janal left his job with a mid-sized New York PR firm. He invested $5,000 in equipment. "My income has more than doubled," reports Janal. In fact, he now has to hire freelancers to handle the extra workload. Would you believe all this is happening out of a *hallway?* He turned the long hall from his kitchen to his bedroom into Janal Communications.

When you live in the boonies, the telephone is your lifeline to the world. When you work out of your home, it becomes doubly important. Handled properly, prospects need never know you're comfortably ensconced in the spare bedroom, looking out at the horses in the pasture while nibbling on a bagel. By all means, get a separate line for your business. Nothing is less professional than calling a business long-distance and getting a four-year-old who wants to chat. Answering "hello" brands you as a novice. Talk with phone representatives and learn what options are available to make your work easier, more efficient, and more professional. Automatic dialing, for instance, is a real time saver when you repeatedly call the same people. Call conferencing might be useful. You may want call waiting.

Also give considerable thought to how the phone is handled when you're not home. If you use an answering machine, be sure it allows unlimited-length messages. It's a good idea to get one equipped so you can pick up messages remotely. Voice mail is a preferable alternative; answering services are better yet. People prefer to talk to other people. A further option is to make a deal with another local business or a neighbor to answer your calls. You pay them to take messages and set appointments for you. To do this you'll need a call-forwarding device, which requires two phone lines.

Fax-on-demand allows you to respond to prospects' and clients' inquiries without any interruption. Prices have really plummeted so this could be a wise business purchase.

Of course, you may need employees—who would also no doubt like to work from their homes. Technologically linked work groups often function on a project basis. Together they deliver services or products they couldn't provide alone. They accomplish wondrous things via computer, telephone, and fax. Distributing the production in this fashion makes you a "virtual company." Many successful Lone Eagles who need to fly with birds of the same feather take this approach.

DESIGNING YOUR PERFECT HOME OFFICE AND GETTING ORGANIZED

A home-based office can be professional, functional, and great-looking. Your office is a tool, just like the telephone and computer. So consider ergonomics—the relationship between people and their environment—when setting up shop. Home offices are becoming so popular, Faith Popcorn coined a new word to describe them: hoffices. She forecasts they will be the newest real estate development. As if in answer to that prediction, a recent *Denver Post* article quoted Andy Ades of Ades Design as saying, "We're probably putting offices in more than half the homes we're building in the Evergreen [Colorado] area."

No longer relegated to the back of the house, today's office in new home construction is usually in a main part of the house, often close to the entry. This preserves privacy for the living area and allows easy access for business visitors. An adjacent private bathroom is important too if the business will have outside visitors. The traditional study/ library feel is popular. Features like a bay window, wood paneling, and bookshelves provide a special ambiance. French doors with beveled glass give the room a "grand" look.

When constructing an office space, beefed-up electrical wiring is an important consideration. The handful of typical wall outlets can't handle today's office needs. You may want to add floor plugs to accommodate a desk in the middle of the room. It's a good idea to include a closet for resale value. With built-in shelving, it can store office supplies out of sight and have hooks for prospects' coats. Think about lighting too. Recessed and track lighting, which can be clustered over computer work stations, function well.

The more windows the better. They help combat feelings of isolation. Blinds—rather than drapes, curtains, or shades—are the foremost window cover. You can tilt them slightly, or completely, and change the whole mood of the room. We had fun decorating one home office with shutters, which created a similar effect.

Size is all in the way you look at it. What one person calls a "compact office" another dubs a "walk-in desk." Be assured, however, you'll expand to fill the space. Any space. Make it as large as possible.

The physical layout should be arranged to accommodate your work style. Having two desks—or an adjacent work surface—is extremely helpful when approaching a big project. If you want to churn out the work, forget high-backed chairs with arms. While imposing looking, and outstanding for napping, these plush monsters aren't practical unless your job just involves thinking. A sturdy steno chair gives you greater movement and better back support. Comfort increases productivity.

The atmosphere you create in your office is very important to your psychic well-being. You can transform a plain room into an enchanting oasis with thought, planning, and imagination. Surround yourself with things you love. Maybe it's a couple of exquisite antique pieces, or perhaps a quality stereo player and classical CDs. Include photos of loved ones. It's refreshing to look up and see the face of someone dear. Don't treat your workplace one-dimensionally. Include memorabilia, a collection of treasures, houseplants, an aquarium, whatever delights you.

To break the monotony of staring at a computer screen all day, Barbara Brabec filled an entire wall with artwork and photographs of Bengal tigers. To her, this is the most exquisite wild animal in the world. "When my eyes are tired and I need a stretch, I lean back and gaze into all those beautiful amber eyes staring back at me and feel a sense of peace that is hard to describe," relates Brabec.

Clutter is to a home office what an accident is to a freeway. It impedes the flow, causing movement to grind almost to a halt. Clear your work area of all nonessential items; handle only work-related tasks in this area. It's easy to be distracted when you work at home. That's one of the reasons you want to organize yourself well. Police paper relentlessly. As you open mail, sort it into appropriate stacks: to do, to pay, to file, to read. If in doubt, trash it. Reading materials grow like bacteria in a friendly culture.

Don't agonize, organize! To be productive, establish "action needed" and "pending" files. Decide on a way to file things so you can retrieve them quickly. Set up a tickler system to remind you of items or tasks needing follow-up. Find out your personal *peak time*—when you are most creative—and handle the toughest jobs then. By taking these simple precautions, you'll boost your efficiency immensely.

COTTAGE INDUSTRY COEXISTENCE: MELDING BUSINESS AND PERSONAL LIFE

While using your residence as your office has many advantages, it also has drawbacks. Sometimes it's a minefield waiting to shatter your serenity.

Take chatty neighbors, for instance. (Yes, please take them!) They figure when you're home, you're not *really* working. In their eyes, you're fair game for coffee and gossip and favors. Now you get to use all your diplomatic skills. Try to keep on good terms while you explain firmly that you have important obligations and can't get your work done when there are unnecessary interruptions. Be careful not to encourage them in the beginning, however, because *you* miss the water cooler chats.

Friends also need to be educated to reconsider every time they want to contact you. Set aside an hour in the day when you're least productive and designate that as "caller time." Train your friends to phone during that period. And help them realize you can't take off to join them to fish, or go to an auction or fashion show. (And maybe you can—especially if you make an arrangement with the boss [you] to make up the time.)

Of an even greater challenge is your family. It's impossible to make a two-year-old understand that mommy isn't to be bothered. With children that young, your choices are to hire child care, work when they're asleep, or get your mate to baby-sit. That is, unless your job requires little concentration and can be done while Lindsey or Christopher is toddling around the house chattering like a magpie. As they get older, youngsters can participate in the business itself. Then instead of feeling alienated, they feel included.

Marilyn: When I began my freelance article-writing career some 25 years ago, I got my sons involved. They both took typing in school. I would write a standard query letter soliciting an article assignment, then have the boys retype the letter with different editors' names and addresses. This allowed me to send out multiple, customized queries. And it gave the kids spending money since they made 35 cents per letter. (Wow! What a difference computers have made in our lives.)

Family privacy and lifestyle patterns are disturbed by a HBB. Your teenage daughter will resent having to keep the stereo low because you're meeting with a client in the next room. Your husband won't look kindly on you when he can't get to the Ping Pong table in the rec room because you've confiscated it to lay out a wedding gown pattern. Or your wife may not understand why you can't fix the leaky faucet today. After all, you're just shuffling a lot of papers. Furthermore, your son may be testy when you won't stop to fry the fish he just caught.

ALL THAT GLITTERS ISN'T GOLD

Other traps wait to ensnare home-based business operators.

Sometimes it's difficult to separate your business from your personal life. The office is so handy, you're tempted to dash in and finish that project. Thus workaholics are born. Overwork is a habit prevalent among entrepreneurs. We love to lavish attention on our enterprises. It's even more seductive when the office is only a few feet away. Shut the door and hang a "closed" sign if necessary. That takes self-discipline.

On the flip side of the coin, so does *making yourself work!* There is no longer company structure to shape your day. When the business is in the home, it's easy to get sidetracked. You notice a houseplant drooping slightly and decide they all need watering. Or you look out the window and the grass seems unusually long. Better get to it. You remember the pot roast left over from last night and long for a snack. The commercial for Oprah said today's theme is right up your alley. Friends call your business number during office hours and you don't have the heart to cut them off. A neighbor arrives with a plate of brownies hot from the oven. It's distraction with a capital "D."

To combat this productivity gobbler, take yourself seriously. Other people will adhere to your rules about work only if you do. Stay focused. Handle routine household chores in your off hours. Stay away from the TV. Avoid nibbling. Many new HBB operators gain weight when they first start working from home.

Explain to your school-aged children early on about this being your new work and why it's important they not interrupt you unless it's an emergency. (Help them define what an emergency consists of.) Lay out snacks for them when you make your own lunch, then take around 30 minutes when they arrive home to hear about their day. They'll sense if you're "squeezing them in," so relax and be prepared to listen. Once they've been heard, they'll happily go their own way. If they feel rushed, however, you can bet they'll find an urgent need for you within the hour. That's how children are.

Perhaps the most difficult aspect of working from home is the isolation factor. Most of us who come from a busy office, store, or manufacturing environment go through withdrawal; we're struck by feelings of exile and loneliness. Being alone in a home office is unfamiliar. There is no one to bounce ideas off of. No one to praise our work or share a story. The quiet and inactivity engulfs us.

The best antidote for these feelings of separateness? Become part of something. Get out among your peers on a regular basis! Join a local service club that meets weekly for breakfast or lunch. Consider organizing a local brainstorming group of four or five other Countrypreneurs with whom you can kick around ideas and discuss problems. Or find a buddy and set up an informal mentor program. Get involved in your trade association and attend out-of-town workshops, conventions, and trade shows. Don't forget to include your spouse. He or she can be your greatest supporter, sounding board, and strength.

You'll also feel less isolated if you treat occasions to run business errands as mini social functions. Visit with the bank teller as you make a deposit, stop and chat a few minutes when you bump into acquaintances at the post office. And tease the UPS or Fed Ex courier when he or she comes with a delivery.

Company can also be as close as your computer's "on" switch. As we've mentioned before, various electronic bulletin boards and newsgroups allow you to tap into special interest groups. Here you can conference with distant colleagues, send messages, and trade tips with other small business owners. Respected small business leaders Paul and Sarah Edwards even run a special working-from-home forum at http://www.HomeWork.com. Log on and lose the blues.

Many other Web sites cater to small business owners. If you visit http://www.smartbiz.com you can even register to be reminded of important upcoming dates via e-mail. To research opportunities for starting a HBB, check out http://www.ro.com/. To interact with other small-business owners be sure to go to http://www.Entrepreneur-Mag.com. And AT&T Home Business Resources has lots of goodies at http://www.att.com/hbr/check/bestbus/index.html. They list *Entrepreneur* magazine's 100 best home businesses, which are ranked by minimum investment (from $1,500 for mini-blind distributorship to $315,000 for a bed and breakfast), stability factor, risk factor, average profit, industry growth, etc. Some of these sites also have links to other informative home pages so your fun can go on and on.

Another way to combat the blahs is to get a pet. (Clients typically love being greeted by our dog and stroking the luxurious coat of our cat. They don't get that amenity in big-city offices.) A dog, cat, or bird is good company and makes the house seem less empty. And have you ever thought about *appreciating* that quiet? Turn negative emotions into positive ones by acknowledging how nice it is not to be constantly interrupted by coworkers.

ZAPPING THE ZONING ORDEAL

Zoning restrictions can present another hurdle. Many communities have strict laws about the *secondary* (or business) use of a home. These rules vary. One town may allow professionals—whom they consider to be doctors, lawyers, dentists, etc.—to work from home. (There is much controversy today about which additional occupations qualify as "professional.") Other places permit virtually anyone to run a business from home as long as it doesn't become a neighborhood nuisance. Still others prohibit HBBs completely.

If you plan to use your residence as your office, it pays to check out local regulations carefully. In small villages, contact the town hall. Other sources for information are the planning department, zoning commission, or building inspector. Determine for yourself that the zoning is appropriate.

If it isn't, there's hope. Your recourse is to apply for a variance. This means you ask the ruling body to make an exception in your case. If your business enterprise won't markedly increase the neighborhood traffic flow; cause a parking problem; be noisy, odoriferous, or dusty; or require unsightly signs or storage facilities, you'll probably get your way. Most neighborhoods have a live-and-let-live attitude if you keep your premises neat, are quiet, and don't create undue activity. Naturally a computer operator is much more likely to get a zoning variance than someone who plans to do mechanic work. Most of us wouldn't want to live next door to a person who tunes up hot rods all day.

Do be aware that many towns limit the number of employees you can have working at your home. In some cases, it can only be the owners; in others, one employee is allowed. More lenient laws permit as many as three people. A few HBB operators stretch that by having more workers, but using them part-time, rationalizing that two half-time people equals one full-time position.

Some proponents of home occupations complain that archaic zoning laws, irate neighbors, even unions, have combined to thwart their intentions. In extreme cases, assertive entrepreneurs have been known to contact their congressperson to intervene in their behalf.

If you contemplate purchasing property in an exclusive subdivision, watch out for CC&Rs: conditions, covenants, and restrictions. The deed to your house may prohibit running a business out of your home. Sometimes you can even get around this, but don't count on it. Contact the homeowners association and request a special dispensation or ask them to amend the restrictions.

For those interested in starting a manufacturing enterprise at their residence, it's of interest that the federal Industrial Home Work Act of 1943 was repealed in November of 1988. That opened the door for doing certain kinds of garment manufacturing in your home. Some experts feel it has far-reaching implications and will nullify many local zoning regulations.

We'd advise you not to proceed illegally. If you operate a business in violation of zoning ordinances, chances are excellent that a disgruntled neighbor will report you. This can result in an injunction to cease business, forcing you to close up shop that very day!

On the other hand, some communities are actually launching subdivisions targeted to *attracting* HBBs. Market Place in Oak Creek, Wisconsin, for instance, consists of 20 homes built especially to accommodate home occupations ranging from dentists' offices to craft studios. And each home in the Eaglecrest subdivision in Foresthill, California, was designed to include a teleport containing a personal computer and modem so occupants can link to computers—and employment.

A village in Lynwood, Illinois, has taken this concept a step further. There a development has one-acre lots in which the front is zoned for a single-family residence and the rear is dual-zoned to encourage commercial use. Residents have drafted restrictive covenants governing the neighborhood businesses and find the roomy lots give their neighborhood a country atmosphere. That's progressive zoning!

Restrictions are being relaxed everywhere in response to our new ways of working. In Cochise County, Arizona, they passed a law permitting "minor home occupations" (whatever *that* means) that have no outdoor signs or outside employees, and take up only a limited space. Owners of such businesses will no longer have to go through zoning hearings. And Davis, California—which prides itself on fostering energy efficiency—is considered very permissive toward home businesses. Air pollution is greatly reduced when cars never leave home.

To fully prepare yourself for launching a successful HBB, we recommend you get into the other chapters in this part of *Country Bound!*. They contain valuable tips on starting your business, becoming an entrepreneur, marketing your new venture, plus staying prosperous and personally content.

You may work from home, however, and still be employed by someone else. We promised earlier to tell you about a fascinating concept called telecommuting. Your time has come. Turn the page and learn about this modern-day way to stay connected, yet separate.

13

◆

Telecommuting
Bringing Your Job Home

"**W**ho will ever use it?" people asked in 1878 when Alexander Graham Bell published the first phone book. "Who wants a letter in one day?" others scoffed when Fred Smith started Federal Express. "Nobody needs a computer on their desk!" ridiculed some when Steve Jobs and Steve Wozniak launched Apple Computers.

How times change. Telecommuting has significant potential to protect the environment, improve economic competitiveness, and bring families closer together. It will enhance our quality of life by allowing workers to reside in more far-flung locales. During the great blizzard of '96—which left thousands of workers on the East Coast housebound—many found that rather than being disruptive, telecommuting was a pleasure.

UNDERSTANDING WHAT IT IS

Exactly what is "telecommuting"? The term was coined in 1973 by Jack Niles. It is the process of transmitting, or communicating, information electronically. While there are varying definitions, most agree telecommuters are people who are employed by companies but who do much of their work at home. They are connected to their corporate offices by computer-network phone lines. This term is synonymous with the moving of work to people, rather than people to work. Of course, position responsibilities and individual personalities must mesh if this technology is to be truly exploited.

Many believe working for a salary without leaving the house is the shape of our future work. It's much more than the separation of worker from office. Ultimately, it will be a total transformation of the structure of the workforce. Teams of employees meet for brainstorming, conferences, or training sessions via computer. Corporate headquarters brings them all together several times a year for rallies or retreats.

Until a decade or so ago, the only practical method for communicating quickly over long distances was by telephone. Today fax machines enable us to send printed sheets, handwritten notes, graphs, drawings, and photographs across the country almost instantly. Modems allow computers in one location to send, receive, and access information from computers in another. And video conferencing permits participants in various locations to view a document on the screen, then work on it simultaneously.

This technology allows *anyone* to do almost *anything* virtually *anywhere*. Location is no limitation. Occupants of households thousands of miles from headquarters can process insurance claims, reorganize financial data, or answer 800-number calls. A major catalog sales firm has more than 100 employees working out of their homes accepting long-distance orders. From a farmhouse outside a small Colorado town, a computer program designer serves clients on six continents. A speechwriter telecommutes instead of braving Manhattan traffic each day. Decentralization is here. The "virtual" office has arrived. Options are infinite.

HOW TELECOMMUTING ANSWERS PERSONAL NEEDS

This opens stimulating alternatives to dreary daily commutes under gridlock conditions. You may only go into the office occasionally. Such travel becomes much more tolerable when it occurs only once weekly or monthly. Many can move further from their workplaces—finally becoming country bound.

The more affluent will find this new structure allows them complete latitude to make decisions that are not location-specific. They can relocate anywhere; they'll simply catch a plane into the office the few times each month they must make a personal appearance. A new breed of worker will emerge: people who are cosmopolitan, yet proudly provincial.

Telecommuting supports family values. Variable work schedules contribute to this. In some positions it doesn't matter when the work gets done, as long as it's accomplished in a timely fashion. Enter flextime. Maybe you'll work evenings or weekends sometimes. The choice is yours. So is the time with your family and the childcare costs.

Some large companies—AT&T; Johnson & Johnson; Sears, Roebuck & Company; Wendy's International, Inc.; American Express; Levi Strauss & Co.; and J.C. Penney—have instituted telecommuting programs for certain positions. And a few progressive government bodies—the city of Los Angeles and the state of California Franchise Tax Board, for instance—have climbed on the bandwagon. The highest concentration of telecommuting is in the southern California area. Companies there were encouraged to start programs in the early 1980s to cut down traffic congestion. But this movement is still largely a national oddity.

We foresee growing legions of individuals chanting "home sweet office." People who love their jobs don't want to get away from it all. They want to bring it with them. If you yearn to be part of this, chances are *you* will need to take the initiative. You'll have to cut your own deal with your boss. Think through the concept and put together a proposal outlining why it will benefit him or her if you telecommute in your present job. Tell your boss how telecommuting will reduce absenteeism, because you can be "on the job" at home, in spite of minor illnesses or family emergencies.

Many in the corporate world are reluctant to endorse telecommuting. Their greatest fear centers on how they manage and measure the performance of employees who perform tasks off-site. Supervisors are understandably more secure when they can see people work. They're intimidated by absentee workers. Another concern is that everybody will want to try it.

And many feel it will create administrative hassles. This is partially true. Yet there is a price to pay for everything. Have these same managers looked at the escalating cost of office space or the eroding effect of absenteeism? Both are minimized by telecommuting. Even more promising, studies repeatedly show that productivity goes up when employees work from their homes.

Working solo needn't feel isolating. Mark Kurtz, who lives in Montrose, Colorado, has a foreign exchange phone line between his residence and his employer, CareerTrack of Boulder, Colorado. This line, also known as a "metro line," permits Kurtz to maintain a Boulder local phone number at a flat monthly rate. Since there are no long-distance phone charges, he can have extensive phone discussions with his colleagues. Problems can be solved spontaneously, and occasional social chats remove the feeling of working alone. The company also provides him with videotapes of staff meetings, so he can keep in touch with "some of the subtle cultural stuff."

FROM THE CORPORATE PERSPECTIVE

From a company's viewpoint, this increased productivity is the major advantage of telecommuting. Travelers Insurance Company, which has a telecommuting staff of 80, cites productivity increases of 20 percent. This is no fictional figure plucked from a dreamer's head. The human resources department determined this number by examining the amount of actual lines of code generated by programmers.

The two "Rs" offer more reasons telecommuting is gaining in popularity. They are *recruitment* and *retention*. In our increasingly competitive job market, the ability to attract prime people is a serious consideration. Many professionals would prefer spending a majority of their work time at home, rather than having their off-hours gobbled up by long commutes. "Recruitment is a prime reason for offering work-at-home [arrangements] to employees," reports Travelers' Diane Bengston. The geographic boundaries of a company's hiring pool widen, because candidates need not live near the worksite. This is an innovative way to entice talented people.

Travelers' retention statistics are impressive. After two years in the program, 28 of 35 participants remained. Says a spokesperson for Blue Cross, "We have a waiting list a mile long, the error rate has plummeted, and no one has ever quit as a cottage coder or keyer." Telecommuting appeals to employees as a benefit. It's perceived as a "perk."

Especially in metropolitan areas, companies must comply with public aims to improve air quality, employ the disabled, and reduce traffic congestion. This movement helps with ordinances, legislation, and regulation covering all three mandates. California's Regulation 15 requires companies with 100 or more employees to develop commuting options for their workers. Obeying these trip-reduction and air-quality statutes must go far beyond ride sharing.

How practical is telecommuting? A survey conducted by JALA Associates indicates 20 to 30 percent of workers have location-specific jobs requiring they be in a particular place. This firm, which consults with corporations interested in telecommuting, predicts 20 to 30 percent could work part-time at home. About half of the overall workforce could work at home or in a regional office, they say.

What are the criteria for this method of accomplishing tasks? First, the job has to be physically portable and require a minimum of unscheduled face-to-face contact. Second, it must be measurable, with a definite beginning and end. Otherwise managers have no reasonable way to gauge how their people are doing.

Supervisors will be additionally challenged. They must hold a tight reign on scheduling. And it's vital their out-of-office people be kept informed. Managers should also focus on results rather than processes.

Most larger firms have found specific training helpful in preparing workers and managers for a successful journey into this new job-handling adventure. Managers improve communication and planning skills. They learn to overcome their reluctance to allow employees to work without close supervision. One supervisor comments, "I do a lot of management by wandering around. I just do it [now] through remote telecommunications. I think I am still a pat-on-the-back coach." Another observes he can count on his people to give him at least 40 hours a week. "Maybe not 9:00 to 5:00," he says, "but I don't enforce that."

Experienced workers make the best candidates. "Usually telecommuters are people who have been on the job long enough to solve their own problems," says Gil Gordon of Gil Gordon Associates, a New Jersey-based management consulting firm. "They must be confident and intelligent enough to function independently."

Link Resources National Work at Home Survey data shows that telecommuting is growing rapidly among two key groups: They include large organizations with more than 1,000 employees and small firms with fewer than ten employees.

Business guru Tom Peters admits to being a broken record: "Don't just bash hierarchy, destroy it—if you want to survive," he challenges managers. In his *On Achieving Excellence* newsletter, he calls telecommuting "perhaps the ultimate bureaucracy-bashing tool." Peters practices what he preaches. He confesses to spending two-thirds of his year in Vermont—as the telecommuting manager/owner of his businesses, which are headquartered in Palo Alto, California.

COMMUNITIES ALSO BENEFIT

This workplace strategy addresses several hot national issues: air pollution, traffic congestion, and improved child care options.

Environmental impact can be significant. It decreases the need for mass transit, reduces fuel consumption, limits the demand for transportation infrastructures, and improves air quality.

In a speech presented at the University of California at Irvine, John Niles, president of Global Telematics, stated, "The telecommuting phenomenon gives economic development activists a new option for long-run regional improvement." He pointed out that not only growth, but *quality*, should be considered by sophisticated economic development proponents.

Telecommunications has been hailed as having as dramatic a potential for rural America in the 1990s and beyond—as did railroads in the 1870s and interstate highways in the 1950s. As the traditional staples of rural economies—agriculture, mining, and manufacturing—falter, telecommunicators will infuse these idyllic isolated places with new life. People who are free to perform their work from any location often pick more bucolic surroundings. Like Alexander Graham Bell, Fred Smith, and Steve Jobs, the pioneers in this exciting field are pointing the way to the future and reviving thousands of dying communities. In the process, they are creating a more fulfilling future for themselves and their families.

But what if you plan on going into business for yourself? Let's discuss all the particulars that go into setting up a successful enterprise.

14

◆

Pivotal Start-Up Considerations

Now that you've pinpointed precisely *what* you want to do, let's explore *how* best to do it. We'll decipher all the damnable details—chop the elephant-sized job of start-up considerations into easily digested, bite-sized pieces.

Going from paycheck to president can be one of the most exciting— and potentially intimidating—adventures you'll ever embark upon. Our goal in this chapter is to equip you with the gear to make your pilgrimage easy and successful. Hindsight is a tragic teacher. Here we outfit you with the foresight essential for gaining prosperity.

We'll look at the structure your enterprise might take—sole proprietorship, partnership, or corporation—plus registration and licensing procedures. Business incubators will be examined. So will creating a mission statement and business plan, and deciding on a location. Additionally, the subjects of finding reliable suppliers, not to mention qualified employees, will be addressed.

BUSINESS STRUCTURE OPTIONS

An early decision involves what business classification to use. One report showed that 13.2 million businesses were organized as proprietorships, 4 million as corporations, and 1.6 million as partnerships.

Let's briefly examine the pros and cons of these three options. (You'll also want to check with your accountant or a tax attorney.)

Sole proprietorship.   In this business structure, you operate as a self-employed individual. The majority of fledgling businesses begin this way because there are no legal setup fees and you alone call the shots. Profits or losses are considered part of your personal income. Even if you begin this way, you can always incorporate later.

Incorporation.   If your plans are large-scale and aggressive, it probably makes sense to *incorporate*. The drawbacks include setup costs and annual fees, greater regulations from state and federal authorities, more complicated accounting procedures, unemployment taxes covering yourself as an employee, higher Social Security taxes, plus loss of the ability to operate in a freewheeling way.

There are also distinct advantages. The normal (chapter C) corporation can pay many of the legitimate business expenses from pretax dollars. These include medical and disability coverage, liability insurance, perhaps even a portion of life insurance—all of which can be written off as a cost of doing business. And you can participate in employee benefits not available to unincorporated owner-operators: tax-sheltered pension plans, profit sharing, and bonuses.

Incorporating also typically gives you personal protection. As a legal entity, it shields you against individual liability, thus protecting personal property that could be considered fair game in a lawsuit. Once incorporated, you can also attract investors by selling shares in the business. (Be sure to get expert advice when doing this.) One further consideration: If a sole proprietor or partner dies, the business is legally dissolved and must be reorganized to continue. Not so with a corporation. It has permanency.

Subchapter S.   Some small businesses use a simplified *subchapter S* corporation. While this offers some tax advantages, it doesn't let you write off insurance costs. This structure does, however, allow profits to flow directly through to shareholders. It is especially useful as a tax shelter when losses are involved, providing there is other income to shelter. In this variation on the corporate theme, the IRS allows business owners to declare all income and losses on their individual returns.

General partnerships.   While these work for some people, they can also be fraught with problems. In a general partnership, each person is completely responsible for the debts and obligations of the whole partnership. What that means is your partner can incur bills and make promises you don't even know about, and *you* will be held financially responsible. If the relationship turns sour, your partner can really do you in!

Limited partnerships.   In this business arrangement, there is at least one general partner and one limited partner. The general partner is fully liable for all obligations and controls the business. The limited partners have just that—limited liability and rights of control.

It's wise to hire an accountant or attorney to advise you about the most advantageous business structure for your individual needs. Each person's requirements are different. Saving money here can end up costing you a great deal in the long run.

NAME REGISTRATION REQUIREMENTS

Naming your business is an exciting, creative activity we cover fully in Chapter 16, "Image Building: Creating Powerful Attention-Getters." But be aware that once you've decided on a name, in most states you have to register it. Get particulars from the state corporation office, the county clerk, or the chamber of commerce. If you are using anything but your full legal name, you are operating under a "fictitious" name. Sometimes this is also called a "dba," which means "doing business as."

Many states also require you to publish this proposed trade name to allow anyone already using such a name to object to it. Several weeks elapse as the notice must appear repeatedly. Find a small weekly newspaper where many other fictitious name ads appear. It will be cheaper to advertise there.

LICENSING AND REGULATORY PROCEDURES

Talk with the local chamber of commerce to determine what steps must be taken—and places contacted—to get yourself properly taxed, licensed, and regulated. (That one should have to request help with such dastardly duties!) Procedures vary from state to state, county to county, town to town. Some states have a business start-up kit that condenses the process and allows you to fill out all your papers at once.

In some places, occupations like barbers, taxi drivers, psychologists, kennel owners, child care providers, plumbers, and architects all require a special license, examination, and/or approval from an appropriate state agency. If your new enterprise involves food or liquor, you can definitely count on needing a state license. The same probably holds true if what you plan involves hazardous substances or could pollute the air or water. Additionally, check with your city clerk's office to verify whether your new occupation falls under any special city licensing regulations.

Every business must have a federal tax employer identification number. This number is needed for filing tax returns and will be requested by other firms with whom you do business. It is obtained free from the nearest IRS office.

Most municipalities also require you to have a local business license. Costs are usually between $20 and $100 and must be renewed annually. Check at the town hall or chamber of commerce for details.

And if you're opening a retail establishment, or purchasing goods to be resold, you'll need a resale tax number. This lets you buy merchandise for resale without paying tax. You will, of course, need to collect taxes when you sell the item, then later remit that tax to the state. For more information, contact the state tax office.

When you apply for a seller's permit, you'll be asked to estimate your anticipated revenue. This is a time to be humble. If you indicate you expect terrific sales, you'll likely be instructed to leave a hefty deposit against future taxes, plus file quarterly tax reports. On the other hand, those who expect meager sales often dodge the deposit completely and need only report annually. For more information about tax laws and how they'll affect your new business—plus good general financial advice—you'll want to get your hands on *Small Time Operator: How to Start Your Own Small Business, Keep Your Books, Pay Your Taxes, & Stay Out of Trouble!* by Bernard Kamoroff, CPA.

There may be some advantage to registering your business as a trademark. For information on this subject, contact the U.S Department of Commerce, Patents and Trademarks Office, Washington, DC 20231, 703-308-4357. Or look for professional help in the Yellow Pages.

THE TELEPHONE: LIFELINE TO OPPORTUNITY

Telephones can ring up huge profits for most businesses. You'll probably want a business line rather than a residential line. While business lines cost more, they also give you a listing in the Yellow Pages—usually an important asset. In most areas there is also a feature dubbed "call waiting." This technological option is both a blessing and a curse. Although it allows you to know when another caller is on the line, it's also a rude interruption of the original conversation. It may make more sense to have two lines installed, one primarily for outgoing calls.

Some folks on shoestring budgets opt to have a residential phone installed and answer it simply with the phone number or "good morning/good afternoon." While this is definitely a cost savings, because you can also take advantage of low long-distance rates, technically it may be illegal in some places and cuts you out of Yellow Page listing opportunities.

Phones also give the little business a way to appear big. You can get remote call forwarding (also called a foreign exchange) where it appears to customers you have a local number. In actuality, you pay a flat monthly service fee to have those calls forwarded to you, but the customer never knows the difference. You may be 100 miles away and have a local phone number. Think about how you're going to advertise and whether this would be advantageous.

Professionals and some other businesses will want a dedicated phone line for their fax machines. As fax communications grow ever more popular, it will become less and less attractive to have this machine sharing your regular telephone line.

In Arkansas, Texas, Oklahoma, and other states, a new service is ringing up impressive demand. "Personalized ring" gives an existing phone number additional flexibility by allowing two additional distinctive rings. What this means is you could conceivably operate three different businesses from the same phone number. You'd know which company was being called because each would have a different-sounding ring. This new business feature costs around $10 per month and includes a white pages directory listing at no additional fee. It's now available in most Southwestern Bell Telephone markets, from US West Communications, and some other "baby bells." With this custom ringing feature, it's like being on a party line with yourself.

If you're seeking regional or national orders, a toll-free number garners extra inquiries and sales. Because many toll-free numbers now begin with 888, be sure to state in your promotional materials that the call is free. The general public does not yet understand this. Many companies also use toll-free numbers for customer service. Costs have plunged the past few years. Today, installation charges typically range from zero to $50, monthly fees go from $6 to $20, and rates per minute vary from 16 to 31 cents. In this highly competitive market, sometimes unadvertised specials make it even more attractive. Ask around about deals. The ultimate cost depends on usage. Naturally if those calls are racking up sales, the more the merrier.

However, toll-free numbers aren't always necessary. While they're a plus when trying to entice the average consumer who has to pay his or her own phone bill, if your prospects are in the corporate sector, don't bother. They'll call anyway because the cost isn't coming out of their pocket.

And what's available for those who must spend a lot of time on the road and want to get really sophisticated? Today there are cellular phones, fax machines, computers, modems, even message centers in automobiles to turn the business traveler into an entrepreneurial whirlwind.

LOCATION, LOCATION, LOCATION

For most retail stores, restaurants, and lodging accommodations, the key to success hangs on a hook labeled "location, location, location." If you're in any of these fields, deciding precisely where in your new community to situate your business will have a profound impact on your survival.

Retail stores in small towns depend largely on foot traffic. Who your potential neighbors are may be more important than your store site itself. You're looking for retail compatibility. Planning on opening a women's shop? If you find a suitable spot next to a busy beauty salon, grab it! You'll automatically have a certain number of women passing each day. A fabric shop, drugstore, children's shop, five and dime, or craft store are other desirable neighbors. It works in reverse if you want to open a hardware store. Find a location that's adjacent to a sporting goods store, men's wear store, barber shop, auto supply store, etc.

Downtown versus a strip mall is a decision many new businesses face. Take a careful look at each and think about the purpose of your business. If you're selling carpet, appliances, or furniture, for instance, the mall or even a remote location is probably fine. People will make a special trip to visit your facility when they need one of these high-ticket items.

On the other hand, if you're dependent on getting many of your sales from impulsive drop-in trade, you'd better take a hard look at downtown. The sad fact is, however, in many small towns the downtown section is a depressing collection of boarded-up buildings and discouraged merchants hanging on by their fingernails. Think long before you join such a group, even though the price may seem ridiculously low. You're better off paying more and being where the action is.

Speaking of action, especially if you're wavering between downtown and a mall, investigate if either has an active merchants' association. This is usually separate from the chamber of commerce. An association strengthens your business though group advertising programs, group insurance plans, and collective security measures. They can be especially effective coordinating common themes, advertising events, and promoting special activities during holiday seasons. Affiliating with an association gives you more clout. Very active ones have been known to get grants for civic improvements and to successfully lobby for highway exit changes.

Grocery stores, service stations, and other outlets at intersections will out-pull those in the middle of the block because they can depend on two distinct traffic streams and more window area. For certain stores, window display space is a big consideration.

If you don't have enough of your own, consider doing what we recommended to one of our clients. Contact nearby stores that don't need their window space and put together an informal lease where you pay them a little each month to show your merchandise in their window. Simply add a sign directing passerbys to your establishment. This is also smart advertising reinforcement.

When you're evaluating traffic flow, pay attention not only to the number of cars (or people) who pass by, notice also *when* they pass, and if they appear to be your kind of customer. Heavy early-morning and late-afternoon traffic is great for gas stations and convenience stores, but it does little for specialty retailers. Those in the entertainment industry would look for a surge during evenings and weekends.

Use the following "Traffic Flow Worksheet" to keep accurate records. Analysis of the characteristics of passing traffic often reveals patterns and variations not apparent from casual observation. If a traffic study is important to you, try contacting the planning commission, state highway department, city engineer, or an outdoor advertising company to see what data they can provide. And if you're making a pedestrian survey, be sure not to count people twice.

One final bit of advice for those opening stores: conduct a site history. Ask surrounding merchants what businesses operated in the location you're considering and how long they were there. If you discover a series of failures at a particular site, either back off or investigate very thoroughly to be sure you won't be the most recent in a long list of losers.

If you're a professional or have a company seeking office space, much of what we've said still applies. A new attorney or CPA would do well to locate in a spot where he or she is very visible to the locals. But nothing too radical. People expect these professions to have traditional offices. Ad agencies and writers, on the other hand, might set up shop in a loft, a renovated Victorian home, a remodeled barn, or the second-story quarters over a retail store. For larger firms wanting to make the right move, we recommend the *Company Relocation Handbook* by William Gary Ward and Sharon Kaye Ward.

Don't decide on a location based on your personal preference. Because it's within walking distance to home, is such a darling place, or belongs to a friend are not valid criteria. Your first consideration should be for your customer or client.

The one remaining issue is whether to lease or buy. That's a personal decision that will be partly dictated by your financial capability, tax situation, and future plans. If you chose to lease, here are some pointers and questions to ask:

1. The higher the vacancy rate, the cheaper the price.
2. If the landlord isn't willing and cooperative in the beginning, it will only get worse.
3. Cost per square foot depends on your location within a larger building (upper floor, corner office vs. the basement, etc.).
4. Is there a clause that allows you to sublease?
5. How long is the term of the lease? (The longer the lease, the lower the rate.)
6. Can you negotiate a lease with an option to buy?
7. Is the lease flexible with a realistic option to renew after a specified number of years?
8. Is the landlord willing to put in writing any special promises regarding repairs, remodeling, and maintenance?

Traffic Flow Worksheet
(Use chicken scratches (⊬⊬) to keep track)

	Mon.	Tues.	Wed.	Thurs.	Fri.	Sat.	Sun.	Total
7 AM								
8 AM								
9 AM								
10 AM								
11 AM								
NOON								
1 PM								
2 PM								
3 PM								
4 PM								
5 PM								
6 PM								
7 PM								
8 PM								
9 PM								
TOTAL								

MISCELLANEOUS DETAILS

Develop a mission statement for your business. In 30 to 40 words, capture the essence of your objective. Who will you serve? What will you provide them? How will you do it? This should be carefully crafted, well thought out, realistic. It describes the products or services you plan to provide and the intended market. It will help you get—and stay—focused.

People often ask us what the most important thing is in starting a business. We answer in two words: cash flow. You can have the greatest idea since the pet rock—but if you can't stay afloat until it catches on, all is lost. In the early life of a business, you should be lean and mean. This is not the time for extravagance. On the other hand, don't fail to calculate all you need for start-up costs. A common problem is not borrowing quite enough and having no cushion. It isn't necessary to *spend* it all, but be sure to request adequate financing.

Of course cash flow is impacted by what you charge. If you're going into a retail business, the markup is usually double the wholesale price. For those manufacturing a product, determining how much to charge is a prickly decision. It's influenced by four factors: (1) your direct and indirect costs, (2) the profit you want to make, (3) your competitors' prices, and (4) urgency in the marketplace.

Here's a formula for computing a fair price. First, look at your direct material costs for a month. What do you have to pay for the raw material used to make an item? (You may need to divide batches to get the price of a single item.) Second, what are your direct labor costs? What do you pay employees—or yourself—to produce the item? Don't forget to factor in fringe benefits; they usually equal about one-third of the salary. Now figure your monthly overhead expenses, such as rent, utilities, insurance, packing and shipping supplies, delivery, etc. List all overhead items and total them. Then divide that total figure by the number of items produced by month. So you have:

$$\frac{\text{Materials} + \text{Labor} + \text{Overhead}}{\text{Number of items per month}} = \text{Total cost per item}$$

Now it's time to add something for profit. Find out what the competition is charging. If you have a new, rare, or handmade product—or a needed personalized service—people may be willing to pay a little more.

We discussed zoning restrictions in Chapter 12. Be sure you don't overlook this consideration. Only certain parts of a town are zoned for commercial use. While sometimes you can get a variance, this involves red tape and lapsed time.

Naturally your new entity deserves its own checking account. We advise getting all the other necessary registrations and paperwork out of the way first, though. Most banks will want to see your articles of incorporation (if your company is a corporation), your fictitious name registration, and your federal ID number.

Select a banker, accountant, lawyer, and insurance agent whom you trust. Their expert advice at this stage can save you thousands of dollars later. Purchase and learn bookkeeping software in advance so you have everything in place *before* you open for business. And don't forget to include insurance premiums when figuring start-up costs.

You may also want to hire a business or marketing consultant. A major advantage of hiring a consultant is that he or she brings fresh and objective expertise to the table. Perhaps you need help setting up a computer system, developing a business plan to present to the banker, or creating a results-oriented marketing campaign. When working with a consultant, explain what you need and ask for a proposal outlining costs and time lines to accomplish your goals. A competent expert can help you think though your venture and avoid problems before they arise.

Another option for guidance is the Small Business Administration (SBA). The national toll-free number for their answer desk is 800-827-5722. This information hotline can tell you how to get in touch with a local SBA office, start up your own business, get financing, and access their counseling and training programs. Here you can also learn about SBA publications and videos, plus get information about programs for minority and women business owners; international trade; and veteran affairs.

The SBA district and regional offices can tell you about any conferences, seminars, or counseling services offered in your area. Additionally, the Service Corps of Retired Executives (SCORE), a group of retired business persons and professionals, provides free training to small business. The district and regional offices sponsor Small Business Development Centers throughout the nation. To find help online, visit the SBA's home page at http://www.sba.gov/.

Also check with local colleges and universities to see what business courses they offer. And if you're a computer buff, don't overlook going online to ask questions. You'll get immediate feedback.

To pull everything together, review the following "Start-Up Stimulator Checklist." It will serve as a memory jog to help you take into consideration various possible items or functions. Not all points will apply, but it should keep you from overlooking essentials.

BUSINESS INCUBATORS AS EARLY GUARDIANS

A business incubator shelters and protects a new enterprise just as the outer shell does a soon-to-be-born chick. Incubators customarily house somewhere between five and 30 new businesses under one roof, each with its own office or suite. Typically, guidance on obtaining financing, management and marketing acumen—even such fringe benefits as secretarial services, conference rooms, faxes and copiers—are part of the package. This setup sees to it start-ups don't operate in a vacuum. Usually there is great camaraderie and networking between

Start-Up Stimulator Checklist

- ❏ Accounting/Bookkeeping/Tax preparation
- ❏ Advertising/PR plan
- ❏ Alarms/Security systems
- ❏ Answering machine/Service
- ❏ Auto renting/Leasing
- ❏ Banking services
- ❏ Business consulting plan
- ❏ Chamber of commerce/Other memberships
- ❏ Computer consulting
- ❏ Computer equipment/Supplies
- ❏ Computer repair/Service
- ❏ Copy machine
- ❏ Data processing
- ❏ Delivery/Messenger service
- ❏ Equipment
- ❏ Fax machine
- ❏ Federal ID tax number
- ❏ Graphic design/Desktop publishing/Typesetting
- ❏ Insurance
- ❏ Internet access/E-mail
- ❏ Janitorial service
- ❏ Leasing space: Office/Retail/Warehouse
- ❏ Legal services/Lawyers
- ❏ Licensing requirements
- ❏ Loans/Start-up capital
- ❏ Meeting facilities/Conference room
- ❏ Mission statement
- ❏ Name (dba) registration
- ❏ Office furniture
- ❏ Office machines/Typewriters, etc.
- ❏ Office supplies/Business forms
- ❏ Printing
- ❏ Secretarial service/Word processing
- ❏ Shipping and mailing supplies/Service
- ❏ Signage
- ❏ Space planning and design
- ❏ Telephone equipment/Pager/Cellular phone
- ❏ Trademark/Service mark registration
- ❏ Transportation and moving
- ❏ Trash removal/Recycling plan

incubator participants. They share the common bond of being new businesses. This approach is used to help launch fledgling enterprises; rarely does a firm stay in an incubator longer than two years.

Of course, the tiniest of towns don't offer this option. It takes about a 25,000 population base to support an incubator. For a free state listing, check with the National Business Incubator Association, 20 E. Circle Drive, Suite 190, Athens, OH 45701, 614-593-4331.

Another option is to establish a buddy business relationship with another new entrepreneur. Contact the chamber of commerce or economic development office to see who else is just opening up. You might be able to share costs of office supplies, bags, shipping materials, direct mailers, etc. Such a strategy is really helpful when suppliers have minimum-order requirements. And you can also use each other as brainstorming partners and for mutual emotional support.

LOCATING RELIABLE SUPPLIERS

One disadvantage of living in remote areas is that you are sometimes a distance from needed suppliers. Additionally, distributors who service rural areas often maintain low stock levels. We've learned several ways of coping with these frustrating dilemmas. One is to plan ahead. Think through any project or your inventory level needs and make a materials list of what you will need. Then when you travel to a bigger town on a buying safari, you won't forget vital items.

If you're taking over a retail shop, consider approaching your vendors about replacing old stock with brand new merchandise. Our friend Rebecca, who purchased a bookstore, used this approach successfully to stock her store with all the latest best-sellers. It required no out-of-pocket expense for her, as she simply rotated old inventory for new.

Another wise tactic if you're stocking a retail establishment the first time is to visit wholesalers *in person*. Get acquainted. Sell them on how successful you're going to be, and play one against the other for the best prices. This will also allow you to personally pick the most desirable merchandise, be aware of any closeout specials, and negotiate a better discount for your large initial order. Of course, attending a trade show or exhibit in your field is another excellent way to find out what's hot and establish supplier relationships.

And consider taking items on consignment. When we added a little gift shop to our hotel in First Try, we carried a lovely assortment of fine Indian jewelry—all on consignment. The arrangement worked well for both parties. We had no money tied up in inventory and the lady who owned the jewelry had a new outlet to sell her wares.

It makes sense to talk to locals about your needs. In small towns, people often don't advertise for business. People just know they're there—everybody except newcomers like you, that is. Ask around. You'll be surprised at the vast number of folks right in your own community who offer the very services you may need, or who carry items you require.

Until you've established a business track record, you'll need good personal credit and must be willing to personally guarantee business accounts. Prepare a sheet detailing credit references and your bank account numbers so you appear businesslike. Another approach is to put up a deposit against which you make purchases. After six months or so of prompt payment, most companies will give you credit. Also consider asking your sales representatives for letters of recommendation once you've been in business for a few months. Get creative in proving you're a sound business risk.

If you plan on doing extensive building, repairs, or maintenance, it might make sense to set up a separate "dba" company. Ours is called Valley Service. We've established accounts with vendors all over Colorado and enjoy discounts of from 20 to 50 percent off retail prices. How so? We resell the items to one of our corporations. You'll also need a federal ID number if you're reselling items and want to avoid paying sales tax.

A wise lady once told us, "It's not how you *sell* things, it's how you *buy* them that spells the difference between success and failure." Sam Walton pinpointed buying strategies as one of the primary contributors to Wal-Mart's achievement.

PROSPECTING FOR QUALIFIED EMPLOYEES

Most businesses grow out of the inspiration and perspiration of one person or couple. Successful ones, however, ultimately expand to the point where the founder(s) can't handle everything.

Taking the leap from doing it all yourself to hiring help is a big step. Frankly, finding good employees is one of the greatest challenges facing industry today. Ferreting out competent people with strong work ethics isn't easy. But there are some gems out there waiting for those willing to look carefully.

Get the word out that you're looking. Now is the time to make the Gossip Monger work *for* you. Tell not only the president of the bank, but also the tellers. They're the ones who have day-to-day contact with area residents. Mention it when you get a haircut, at the grocery store, when filling your car up with gas. Tell your accountant, insurance agent, and attorney. Alert the chamber of commerce director. Talk about your opening at service club meetings, church, and other community gatherings. While the people you speak with may not be qualified or interested themselves, chances are one of them will have a daughter, cousin, or neighbor who might be ideal. This is how things often work in Small Town America.

When you run across someone who impresses you, plant a seed. We frequent a particular restaurant in town and got well acquainted with one of the waitresses. In the course of chatting with her, we learned she had taken a two-year secretarial course a couple of years before. She was working as a waitress because she made enormous tips in the summer. But when winter came, her hours were cut and tips plummeted. We'd observed Susan was pleasant, efficient, and well organized in the way she approached her job—traits that would follow her in any working situation. So one day Tom invited her to come and talk with us if she ever decided to make a change. A couple of months later, we hired Susan.

Help-wanted ads are another natural employee prospecting tool. And they're so cheap in little local papers. It may make sense to set your ad apart by putting a box around it and using larger type. This is called a classified display ad.

Let's suppose you've run an ad and received several intriguing résumés. What if you're just moving to the new town? You have no office in which to interview applicants. And using a restaurant or hotel is awkward. We solved this problem by asking for help from our real estate broker. She put us in touch with a local insurance agent who was kind enough to not only let us use her suite of offices one Saturday, she even had her secretary there to greet our prospective employees! How's that for small town hospitality? We found three new hires, and Kathy acquired another insurance client.

Because our business is rather specialized, we used to think we had to recruit from the larger cities of Denver and Colorado Springs for key positions. We spent hundreds of dollars on ads in their major newspapers to lure prospective employees to our small town. We got lost among the hundreds of other advertisements. Save your money.

What do urban opt-outs do who want to move to a particular small town or area? They get the local paper! Your ad here will do double duty—not only alerting locals about the job opening, but also serving notice to those seeking to relocate. Over the years, we've hired people from Clearwater, Florida; Cincinnati, Ohio; plus Breckenridge, Colorado Springs, and Lamar, Colorado. They all saw our ads in the local paper, or friends and loved ones alerted them to the openings.

If you must find a person with very specific expertise, try running an ad in a national trade journal or newspaper targeted to your industry. These specialized publications are a conduit between job hunters with experience in a given field and companies with openings. Be sure to highlight the fact that you offer an opportunity to pursue their chosen career while experiencing greater quality of life and a lower cost of living.

Don't overlook checking into federally funded placement programs such as the Job Training Partnership Act (JTPA). We found a delightful employee this way. While Hugh was a capable administrative assistant, he knew nothing about our particular business or word processing program. JTPA paid almost half his salary for six months, plus footed the bill for him to go to school and learn WordPerfect. Our part of the bargain was to train him and provide an ongoing job. What a win-win situation! This help with payroll is also a real financial boon. Just be sure you aren't totally gobbled up in the training process.

If you employ certain types of people, such as dislocated workers or people who have lost their jobs because of competition, your business may qualify for a federal tax credit under the Targeted Jobs Tax Credit Program. It can even be used in conjunction with JTPA. For more information contact the Office of Employment and Training Programs, Room N4469, U.S. Department of Labor, 200 Constitution Avenue NW, Washington, DC 20210. You can also call the U.S. Department of Labor's Employment and Training Administration at 202-219-6871 and request a Program Highlights sheet on the Targeted Jobs Tax Credit Program and the Job Partnership Training Act.

Another way to supplement your own efforts is to hire interns and work-study students from a local high school. Some internships provide free help in exchange for training; in others you pay the trainee a reduced salary. Check with the local school. Carol came to our facility two hours a day for a full semester. She learned about the real world of business and we had free clerical aid. This is also a practical way to prospect locally for bright young people to add to your permanent staff.

And because grant money runs out before the need does, colleges also help students finance their educations by helping them find employment. Work-study programs can be found at virtually every school. Sometimes financial aid is available to the employer. At any rate, you'll likely find exceptional help at reasonable rates.

Gallopade Publishing Group got discouraged trying to hire qualified people. Their innovative approach was to do just the opposite: Get workers for free! They started an official apprenticeship program, ran ads in area newspapers, and were flooded with super candidates fighting each other for a chance to learn the publishing business firsthand.

Perhaps hiring freelance subcontractors to assume responsibility for different aspects of the business is a workable solution for you. In this alternative you find other firms or individuals to whom you can spin off some tasks. Maybe an advertising/PR firm takes over your marketing, or a secretarial service does your letters, updates your database, and handles mailings. The primary advantage of subcontracting is that it's easier in many ways. You don't have personnel problems, payroll deductions to figure, or such facility-related matters as rent or lease payments, insurance, or building upkeep.

Of course, you still have to find appropriate firms to work with. In a small town, you may already know someone suitable. If not, ask around. Here again, word-of-mouth recommendations—or cautions—are the best source of information.

When you begin a new business relationship, be sure your expectations match theirs. To avoid later misunderstandings, be clear initially about such things as precisely what services they will render, deadlines to be met, plus how and when they will be compensated. Don't lock yourself into a long-range subcontracting commitment until the relationship has proven itself.

By now you should feel confident about the details involved in beginning a business. But where will you get the funds to start this new venture? Dozens of ideas await you in the next chapter.

15

◆

Generating Capital to Launch Your Venture

Going into business without adequate preparation is like trying to determine the nature of the ocean by studying a cup of water. You need the right tools, whether they be money, expertise, or imagination. This chapter is about all three.

Now that you know you want to go into business for yourself, creating "adventure" capital to make your dream come true is the first step. There are more ways to generate cash than there are instruments in an orchestra. Some are more viable than others for the person desiring to set up a rural enterprise. You're sure to find innovative ideas for raising money as we explore and exploit these methods.

Some of the most visible possibilities—banks, government programs, and venture capitalists—may be the *least* important sources of business capital. Most new firms gain financial support one of two ways: through their owners or via private investors. The role of the private investor is underestimated and undervalued because it is neither institutionalized nor documented.

How much do you really need to get started? According to a study done by the National Federation of Independent Business, one out of three new businesses starts with $10,000 or less. And you can use that to leverage a venture in the $50,000 to $100,000 range. The next most common capital investment amount is from $20,000 to $49,000.

TAPPING INTO PERSONAL RESOURCES

You may want to refer to the section on "Cashing Out with Your Urban Equity" in Chapter 4. For many of us, our metropolitan real estate is just the nest egg needed to launch a country business.

Have a passbook savings account, CDs, or annuities? Most people are tempted to use these to start new businesses. Don't. Once it's gone, it's gone. On the other hand, there's an old axiom that says, "Thems that got, gets." Never was this more true than when approaching your banker for a loan. If you have $7,000 in savings, there is little hassle in borrowing another $7,000. The lending institution probably won't even require your account as collateral. Now you have $7,000 of other people's money (OPM), plus your original $7,000 (less the amount of interest on the debt, of course). If you reverse the process, though— spending the $7,000, then trying to borrow that amount—you have about as much chance for success as the guy who went bear hunting with a switch.

You may be able to use other assets to capitalize your business. Do you receive rents from real estate or dividends from stock? What about royalties from a book, song, computer software, or invention? One acquaintance used her hefty divorce settlement to start a new rural life.

According to the *Boston Globe*, many baby boomers may *inherit* the nest eggs they need to start businesses. Due to historic gains in the stock market, high real estate prices, and the growth of millions of family-owned businesses, baby boomers can expect to inherit an estimated $8 trillion in cash and other assets over the next 20 years!

In the meantime, consider your credit cards. Many a creative financier has breathed life into a small business thanks to multiple Master-Cards or VISAs. In fact, some folks plan years ahead to use this strategy. They amass as many cards as possible, use them regularly, and pay punctually. As a reward, the card companies keep raising their credit limits. We know of one person who borrowed almost $30,000 on his credit cards. The downside is interest rates for this money are exorbitant. The debt service cost could be devastating.

Building a good personal credit history will go a long way toward helping you in business. Borrowing increasingly larger amounts from your bank, S&L, or credit union—and repaying promptly—is a good start. If you anticipate doing your own thing, get any personal loans *before* you quit your present job. Bankers are understandably skeptical of the newly self-employed. Business start-ups usually can't get unsecured loans. In most cases, the business owner must put up collateral—his or her home, plus a combination of other personal or business assets. And most banks require your personal guarantee, sometimes even that of your spouse if the collateral assets are jointly owned. Often your individual financial statement becomes the basis for the loan.

Be aware that there are different levels of bank officers. While a regular loan officer at a branch may have a limit of $10,000, a senior loan officer at the main location can go much higher without requiring committee approval. Usually the higher you begin, the better your chances. If you dead-end at the local level, ask how to contact a regional investment bank specializing in financing small companies. There you'll gain access to a wide range of lenders and investors, including pension funds and insurance companies.

Perhaps you have a vested interest in a retirement fund or pension plan. They often make loans at reasonable rates. Consider this as a revenue source.

If you're a mature person, lump-sum retirement benefits may well pave the way to an exciting new enterprise. There are all sorts of annuities: IRAs, Keogh plans, plus myriad private and government pension plans. Some 6,000 government plans cover federal civil service, military, state, and municipal employees. Of course, each has different rules about the years of service required, age of eligibility, payouts, etc.

Former executives laid off as a result of mergers and downsizing sometimes receive a cash settlement called a *golden parachute*. It is meant to ease the bumpy ride back to employment. Instead, a golden parachute often aids the leap to freedom. Outplacement specialists estimate that more than 20 percent of the people they see as a result of downsizing go into business on their own. Many executives open consulting practices, thus capitalizing on expertise developed in the corporate world. These newly minted outsourcing service providers target their past employers and take over a corporate function previously handled in-house.

Life insurance is another funding option. Possibly a sizeable chunk is lying there in cash value. Presto, magic! Such loans require no qualification and carry attractive interest rates. If you took out a policy before 1965, for instance, you can typically borrow an amount equal to the policy's cash value for about 6 percent interest.

But what if you've got lousy credit and need an infusion of quick cash? One nontraditional answer for a loan might be a pawn shop. Yes, you read right. You won't get big bucks here and the neighborhood may make you feel about as welcome as a furrier at an animal rights convention. Yet if you need a few hundred or a thousand to shoestring an idea, it's a possibility. Such assets as stereo systems, expensive watches, diamond rings, sterling silver sets, musical instruments, guns, and family heirlooms are most likely to turn the most cash.

Another unorthodox seed money source is unemployment insurance. In Washington they've started a pilot program with 500 unemployed applicants. Called the Self-Employment Demonstration Project, it lets jobless workers use their unemployment checks to start their own businesses—up to a maximum of $7,000. The aim is to reduce unemployment and boost small business development.

REACHING BEYOND YOURSELF

In these days of troubled S&Ls, many potential small businesspeople turn to F&Fs: family and friends. In 65 percent of the cases, the start-up capital needed for a new business is obtained from personal savings, relatives, and friends. Yet many people shun approaching their relatives and friends. If you believe in the business enough to put yourself on the line, is it fair to *protect* your loved ones from participating? Try to find family, neighbors, colleagues, and buddies who are on your wavelength. Sure, some will give you a reception as cool as the backside of a pillow. But you'll never know unless you ask.

There are various ways of structuring such arrangements. Prepare a written document specifying terms and conditions. It must be clear whether the lender will get equity in the new business, sit on the board of directors, or have any say in day-to-day operations. Family-owned businesses are enjoying a resurgence. Just be sure yours doesn't have so many strings attached it braids into a noose around your neck.

MONEY FROM HEAVEN

Another popular source of start-up money is to find an "angel." This term refers to a private venture capitalist not affiliated with any institution. Often these people are successful entrepreneurs who yearn to relive the thrill of the chase. Usually an angel won't require you to put up any collateral; rather he or she will want a piece of the action. In his book *Finding Private Venture Capital for Your Firm,* author Robert Gaston estimates there are some 720,000 angels committing somewhere in the range of $56 billion annually. The angel's average equity investment is $64,000. That's in sharp contrast to professional venture capitalists, who more typically finance companies seeking upwards of $2 million. An additional way an angel can serve as your guardian is by offering advice. Those who enjoy the challenges of start-ups can help a fledgling entrepreneur ask all the right questions.

So where do you find these investment cherubs? Check your database. Go through your Rolodex. Ask around your professional community. Talk with lawyers, bankers, and CPAs. Search out people in your industry who have made money. Or visit one of the 100 or so venture capital clubs around the nation. You can get the *Directory of Venture Capital Clubs* by sending $19.95 to the International Venture Capital Institute, Inc., P.O. Box 1333, Stamford, CT 06904, 203-323-3143.

Angels usually want returns of three to five times their investment in about five years. They are not just *financing* your operation in return for a simple payback on the loan. Angels are *investors*. They expect substantial ownership in a company and strong growth potential. That can present a problem. Some start-ups give away too large a slice of the pie and ultimately harm themselves. Know and be able to articulate the difference if you want to appear credible.

SECURING CONVENTIONAL BANK FINANCING

Money is expensive any way you look at it. There would be no problem if you were a Fortune 500 company and could borrow at the prime rate. But you're not. So the banker will expect to get several percent above prime as a precautionary way to hedge his or her bet and protect the bank's investors. When someone quotes 5 percent above prime, that means if prime is 12.0 you will pay 17.0. Today, variable interest rates are popular because they allow lending institutions to further protect their profits.

There are techniques for talking your way into money. One is to practice giving a 20-minute presentation. Ideally, rehearse with a video camera. Short of that, stand in front of a mirror and use an audiocassette recorder. Monitor your eye contact, comfort level, and voice projection. Dress conservatively for your interview. Bankers are known to be a restrained group. Don't inflate your numbers—it smacks of amateurism. If you're selling a product, be sure to take samples with you or prepare an impressive "dummy" mock-up.

Not every bank feels the same, so if you're appalled by what one says, try another. Geography also impacts your ability to borrow. In high-growth parts of the country, money is easier to get. Some states have laws that prevent banks from taking actions that other states encourage.

In some places, small-town banks don't handle commercial loans. They aren't like car loans that turn over fast. Yet counter to expectations, research shows that some local rural banks take a strong role in providing start-up capital for new businesses in their area.

It's wise to apply a dual strategy: Work through local lenders, but also take additional steps to access federal and state financing programs. Secure as many diverse sources of capital as possible. Cultivate them deliberately and vigorously. Use the following "Financing Structure Worksheet" to help you keep track of your use of funds and potential sources. It's important to match the figure in the Monthly Debt Service column against your monthly cash flow. You must have adequate income to cover this debt. Look at each month individually and make any necessary adjustments promptly. Also take into consideration seasonal changes, especially if you're in a tourist-oriented business that has wide income swings.

Finally, don't rely on a handshake. Always get commitments on paper. Then your dream isn't vulnerable to the whims of banks or investors. Everything is subject to change. Rates vary. Policies are revamped. Bank officers retire. And hopefully your negotiation acumen improves.

If they're unwilling to give you a real estate mortgage, inquire about a chattel mortgage on your equipment or inventory (if applicable). Equipment is typically financed over three to five years. Working capital is usually financed over three years, buildings and land over seven.

You may be able to convince a banker to go with deferred payments. This option takes into consideration business swings and is especially helpful for tourist-oriented enterprises. You pay more during the good months and less during the slow ones. This helps you get over a hump until the cash flow comes in line to cover the debt service. Payments may be structured 75/25, for instance, with the highest amount due during the seasonal tourist time.

How much can you get? At the most, 70 percent of the total price. And then only if you've put together a dynamite business plan (which we'll discuss shortly) and have a strong personal financial history. If you're purchasing real property, the terms of the mortgage can vary significantly. Naturally the longer the loan, the less your monthly payments—but the more overall interest you'll pay.

Financing Structure Worksheet

Use of Funds		Source of Funds					
Use	Total Projected Amount	Lender's Home	Term of Loan	Estimated Interest Rate	Collateral*	Amount of Loan	Monthly Debt Service†
Land	$						
Building construction/Renovation	$						
Machinery and equipment	$						
Furniture and fixtures	$						
Leasehold improvements‡	$						
Contingencies/Emergencies	$						
Working capital/Inventory	$						
Total Cost	$		Total Sources = $				$

*Property or securities pledged by the borrower.
†Cost of principal, interest, and possibly taxes and insurance.
‡Improvements to the physical property.

Here's one strategy that works beautifully for some people. Take as long a term loan as you possibly can, even if you think you could handle a shorter one with a higher payback arrangement. Then *double* your payments every month. That extra money goes toward the principal and retires the loan faster, saving you a fortune in interest. It also gives you a safety net. If business gets sluggish, you aren't stuck with arbitrary high monthly mortgage payments.

Be wary of *balloons*. Unlike the colorful toys of your youth, this means a massive payment that comes due at a distant point. It can quickly drain all the color out of your future. When the time comes, you must either fork up all the cash or pay to refinance.

FRANCHISE FINANCING: USING THE TEAM APPROACH

Franchisors are bullish about financing. Banks and other lending institutions recognize these businesses as solid investments. They realize the franchisor has a vested interest in the franchisee. This interest translates into support. And it's that support that gives new franchisees their excellent chance for success.

Some companies provide expert guidance for their potential investors. A Dallas-based franchise, I Can't Believe It's Yogurt, employs a full-time staff member to help qualified franchisees find financing. The company even works with a special lender who knows all about its track record. Other franchisors also address the complicated chore of completing applications, aiding prospective franchisees in wading through loan paperwork. And some headquarters have aligned themselves with large leasing companies that help their affiliates finance equipment and vehicles.

When Gina and Mark Edwards decided to buy a franchise in Apopka, Florida, they struggled to come up with the required amount. Their choice, Pak Mail, stepped in to assist in several ways. The company helped negotiate the shopping mall lease, putting in penalty clauses if the project didn't finish on time. And the Pak Mail area distributor waited for his fee of $7,000 until the couple's store was operating. "We were fortunate to have a good franchise like Pak Mail behind us because they did some things that helped us get through that first year," says Gina Edwards.

Even more exciting, many franchisors are digging into their own pockets to bolster prospective recruits. Robert Tunmire, president of the Waco, Texas, Dwyer Group, says, "We will finance three-quarters of the initial franchise fee, allowing our franchisees to pay us back $50 a week at 12 percent interest." Another franchisor that will fund a large portion of the franchisee's investment is Steamatic, Inc., of Fort Worth, Texas. "We finance 100 percent of the equipment-and-supply package for qualified applicants," states Scott BeVier, senior vice president of Franchise Development.

Debra Janos learned her business from the ground up. She joined Merry Maids as a part-time cleaning person eight years ago. Soon she was working full-time, then managing the office. Janos quickly realized the potential and set about to buy a franchise. Although she worked three jobs, she couldn't come up with the needed $28,000. So Merry Maid's parent corporation, Service Master, stepped in with $10,000 in direct financing, enabling Debra to set up shop in Las Vegas.

Franchise financing can be achieved in other ways too. Dan Smith wanted to open a Juicy Lucy's outlet in Naples, Florida. But he couldn't handle the hefty $325,000 to $375,000 fee. So he got creative with the developer of a strip shopping center he determined would be a good location. He formed a partnership, working out a build-to-suit arrangement in which the mall developer incurred the cost to construct the fast food outlet, then charged Smith a monthly rental.

In this arrangement, the developer assumes the risk. In exchange the developer gets "a solid tenant who generates an instant income flow in their center even before the rest of the project is completed," says Smith. His investment amounted to the $25,000 franchise fee, $25,000 for working capital, plus a $95,000 loan package for equipment leasing. Comments Smith, "My liability is half of what it would be if I had bought the franchise outright." Which all goes to prove franchise financing is alive and well—and using the team approach to partner for profit.

GETTING THE GOVERNMENT ON YOUR SIDE

Seed capital from Uncle Sam—or his state, county, or local counterparts—has financed many a fledgling business. Government funding programs are especially accessible to women, minorities, the disabled, and companies that create new jobs to escalate the area's economy.

SBA loans.   Negotiated through a conventional lender (also known as a sponsor), SBA loans are guaranteed up to 90 percent by the Small Business Administration. They must be paid back in eight years and carry interest rates slightly lower than a commercial loan, usually two or three points above prime. But just because these loans are government backed doesn't mean they are easy to get. You'll still need a powerful business plan to get you in the door with bankers or to attract investors. Cash flow projections are also necessary. The paperwork you do almost guarantees you'll have the answers for bankers too. The SBA has a very informative Web site. Access it at http://www.sba.gov.

If you're a budding entrepreneur who can do with $25,000 or less, the SBA has launched the Micro-Enterprise Development Program. Money is allotted for intermediary lenders who want to serve America's smallest businesses by arranging these short-term, fixed interest rate loans. This may be an answer for you.

Small business investment companies (SBICs).   The SBA also licenses these private investor firms, which can borrow up to twice as much from the SBA for each dollar of private capital they have. They move quickly and are relatively uncomplicated to deal with. For a list of SBICs and their specialties, contact the National Association of SBICs, 1199 N. Fairfax Street, Suite 200, Alexandria, VA 22314, 703-683-1601. The directory is $20.

Rural Business and Cooperative Development Service (RBCDS).   Money has also been available over the past couple of years from the RCBDS. The SBA's 1995 budget allocated $500 milllion of guaranteed loans to help the private sector create jobs and improve rural economies.

State funds.   All 50 states have some sort of program designed to help small businesses raise capital. They're competing with each other to make their business climates more attractive to smaller firms, in order to add jobs and boost tax revenues.

Pennsylvania's Ben Franklin Partnership Program hands out seed grants up to $35,000 to qualified companies doing product research in technology. "One of the principal activities of the Ben Franklin program," explains Andrew T. Greenberg, Pennsylvania's executive deputy secretary of commerce, "is to provide grants for cooperative research and new product development between businesses and universities in our state." Their grants typically range between $5,000 and

$50,000 and are available to individuals or companies for early-stage research. Recipients must match the funds.

Ohio has a similar plan dubbed the Thomas Edison Seed Development Fund. Once an entrepreneur's research project receives approval, the seed program directs the funds to an Ohio academic institution, which conducts the research for and with the entrepreneur.

The United States Department of Agriculture (USDA).   The USDA is responsible for about 29 money programs that Countrypreneurs can use to begin or enlarge a business. For example, the Business and Industrial Loan Program can be used to start almost any kind of business as long as it is in a town of fewer than 50,000 people. And the USDA's Farmers Home Administration (FmHA) wants to promote economic stability and job creation in rural areas. It guarantees loans up to 90 percent of the principal advanced, to bolster weak rural economies and create jobs. For more information, call 202-720-4323.

ENTERPRISE ZONES: WAITING BONANZAS

Another intriguing option available to some budding entrepreneurs is enterprise zones. Currently there are about 500 state zones in 37 states. And the federal government is expected to set up about 100 federal enterprise zones soon, one-third of which will be in rural areas. The concept is to create a pro-business atmosphere and bolster lagging area economies. These zones encompass tax incentives and credits offered to businesses that expand or locate within certain areas around the country.

Cuba, Missouri—a village of 2,100 people located 75 miles southwest of St. Louis—is one example of how this program turned a town from gloom to boom. When two factories closed in 1984, unemployment soared to 18 percent. Enterprise zone incentives coaxed more than a dozen new industries into Cuba. They, in turn, spawned 750 additional jobs.

Although not all businesses qualify for all incentives, here's a sampling of some tax breaks: triple investment tax credit and new business facility job credits. These are for firms that create new jobs, add value to agricultural products, or provide health insurance to their employees. Other inducements include state sales tax and use-tax exemptions for manufacturing equipment, tax credits for research and development or the rehabilitation of vacant buildings, even local government tax incentives. For more information contact the American Association of Enterprise Zones at 1620 Eye Street NW, Suite 300, Washington, DC 20006, 202-466-2687 or the economic development group for the area.

While financing a fledgling business is never easy, there is another source that may be willing to back your start-up. Community development funds are available in some areas. These are for businesses likely to have a direct and positive impact on the community, such as job creation. If you find this source, investigate the ratio of dollars lent to jobs created. Organizations that manage such funds provide loans at or above prime, or sometimes money in exchange for stock.

In Wiscasset, Maine, Coastal Enterprises, Inc., raises funds from private foundations and corporations as well as from the state itself. In turn, it dispenses loans and puts together equity investments in small businesses. Since 1977, it has raised about $9 million and financed some 150 enterprises with credit of up to $50,000. To determine where such funding is available, contact the National Congress for Community Economic Development, 11 Dupont Circle, Suite 325, Washington, DC 20036, 202-234-5009.

DEVELOPING A BUSINESS PLAN

No matter where you go for funding, chances are you'll need a well-thought-out business plan to unlock the vaults of the financial community. This is a formal walk-through on paper of everything you and a potential investor or lender need to know about your venture.

Including appropriate and detailed financial documents is essential and will automatically raise your octane rating in their eyes. These documents should encompass profit-and-loss and cash-flow statements, and a balance sheet showing assets and liabilities for the next three to five years. Experiment with different growth rates: high and low scenarios. If you're still in the red, you'll also need a break-even analysis.

Of course for new businesses, conservatively calculated estimates must suffice for much of this information. Remember when creating your business plan that sound, stable management strategies go further than pie-in-the-sky projections. Prepare what you hope to accomplish, based on reasonable, conservative projections; also do a worst-case scenario.

Not only will this vital written plan help you see where you're going, it's mandatory if you hope to interest investors in your enterprise. It should provide a detailed description of your company, its products or services, management, market, competition, history, marketing strategies, and forecasts. Fuel their interest. Tell why your company is special, why your product or service is unique, and why you expect success. Any financial institution or individual investor wants to know there is meaning, purpose, and commitment behind a company seeking funding. A good resource for developing this document is *Anatomy of a Business Plan* by Linda Pinson and Jerry Jinnett (800-621-9621, extension 3650).

And if you're purchasing an existing building or business that has been appraised, study that appraisal. They often contain errors. Look for flaws; check the overall level of accuracy. A solid appraisal attracts financing just as the Indy 500 attracts racing wanna-bes.

Pay attention to the physical presentation package. Your plan is a direct reflection of you. Give it clout by providing an attractive, well-organized, easy-to-read proposal. For help in preparing a business plan, call your local SBA office for the nearest location of the Service Corps of Retired Executives (SCORE) and the Small Business Development Center. Most SCORE and SBDC services are free. Local universities and community colleges also offer useful courses.

The area economic development group may also be of help. Their whole purpose is to entice businesses to their area, so it only makes sense that they assist worthy ventures in obtaining necessary start-up loans. Coordinate your visitation time to avoid holidays, peak vacation times, or weekends. Ask very specific questions. Rather than saying, "Do you have any ideas on how I can finance this business?" go with something like, "What three local avenues do you feel are most viable for potential financing?" and "Who should I see there?"

MORE FUNDING IDEAS

When searching for capital, creativity, persistence, and action are the keys. Here are a few random thoughts on other possibilities.

What about using sympathetic suppliers as a form of short-term financing? A major vendor that will wait 90 days to be paid may be just what you need to get a new establishment off the ground. If you're looking into a franchise, talk with the franchisor about providing financing.

If you're a super salesperson, you may be able to convince a banker to finance *purchase orders* for your product. (They sometimes do this on receivables for established customers.) Here's how it worked for one firm: When they got a purchase order, it went to their outside accountants who verified that the order was accurate and the purchaser was creditworthy. Then the bank advanced them 40 percent of the value of the order. This equaled their production cost. When they billed the customer, they faxed a copy to the bank, which sent them another 40 percent. Finally, when the customer paid, the bank took its 80 percent of the bill, plus interest, and sent them the rest—which was their profit. In effect, they pledged their purchase orders as collateral to gain short-term financing.

Are you a start-up technology company? Corporate giants and global conglomerates are a rich source of capital. While it's difficult to find the key players, once you've identified the corporations most likely interested in your technology, contact the corporate development director. But be wary. More than one inventor has inherited heartache along with hard cash by climbing in bed with a giant corporation.

Another option for aspiring entrepreneurs is *bootstrapping*. While you won't get any money here, you may save a bundle and help cover your start-up expenses. This is an arrangement to supply something other than funding to a new business. Such strategic alliances frequently come as a result of good networking. Companies that would benefit from your success, or individuals who simply support you in what you're trying to do, may be willing to loan you an office, or let you use their production facilities or computer system after hours. Perhaps a colleague will give you access to her conference room if you need to impress clients. Maybe a business associate will have his secretary accept phone calls for you. The opportunities here are bound only by your imagination, contacts, and chutzpah.

Of course, if you're buying an established business, one of the best sources for financing is the present owner. This is especially true when times are tough and money is tight. After all, who's better acquainted with its potential? (Short of that, talk with area real estate personnel about other local businesspeople who might be receptive to a shared risk proposition.)

Sellers are often anxious to make installment sales to postpone or reduce their capital gains tax on the sale. Have you noticed ads that say "only 29 percent down?" That's a tip-off that the owner wants to spread the actual proceeds of the sale over a period of years to avoid IRS penalties. The IRS regulation allows the seller to report income in the year of actual payment if he or she receives less than 30 percent of the total amount in the year the sale occurred.

Marilyn: Being a good detective can pay big dividends. That was so in our case. When our telephone communication was abruptly interrupted on the remote ranch we operated from in southern Colorado, we had no choice but to make a hasty retreat or lose all our clients. We pinpointed five other Colorado communities to consider, then hastily began looking for real estate. The odds weren't good. We had no time to sell our ranch, and thus had no down payment for new property.

By calling the Federal Deposit Insurance Corporation (FDIC) and inquiring about the towns we were considering, I learned that Buena Vista had suffered a bank failure a couple of years previously. After making friends with the area coordinator, I discovered a few pieces of property still on the FDIC's rolls. I ended up knowing more about them than any of the local real estate brokers.

As it turned out, one was a 4,000-square-foot church with an accompanying rectory. Because it was a unique property and they'd been unable to sell it, the price was amazingly low. It was perfect for our needs. We could convert the church into offices and live in the rectory. Because we had an excellent company credit rating and Tom was a relentless negotiator, we purchased the church and accompanying house in our corporate name—without even a personal guarantee. We offered $5,000 less than the asking price and a 15 percent down payment, which we scraped from corporate funds. Miracles do still happen. You just have to give them a nudge!

To explore properties available through the FDIC, prepare yourself to wind through miles of red tape. One option is to go to their online Web site (which loads very s-l-o-w-l-y). At http://www/fdic.gov/you want to click on "assets." This will send you through myriad choices including properties in order by price, by property type, by state, or by zip code. We chose the price option, then narrowed it down to $50,000 to $100,000. Here, among dozens of others, we found a retail store for $55,000 in Fort Arthur, Texas; a single family house for $53,000 in Victorville, California; a triplex for $54,900 in Sanford, Maine; and a farm for $92,400 in Cape Vincent, New York. For your convenience, we also list the FDIC regional offices in Part Three. When you call, ask for the owned real estate department.

With the FDIC, you purchase property "as is." For instance, we had to install a new furnace in the building we bought. You also receive only a quitclaim deed, which might concern some people. They prefer buyers who come with financing in hand, but they do underwrite loans in some situations.

Also, don't overlook the possibility of finding a great piece of property at a bargain price by scanning the local paper for tax sales. Auctions are another common event in country areas and sometimes are a way to acquire real estate cheaply.

A company can always make it through thick and thin—providing the thick isn't the owner's head and the thin isn't the capital! We hope you've found ideas here to fatten your funding. To help you leapfrog the competition, we next discuss how to create a powerful image.

16

$\bullet$——$\blacklozenge$——$\bullet$

Image Building
Creating Powerful Attention Getters

Part of the exhilaration of having your own business is the initial creation process. There are many exciting decisions to be made in the beginning. One is the image you will project. What will you name your new baby? How you christen your venture can dramatically enhance its chances for success. Would a slogan help solidify your identification? What about logos, letterhead, and business cards? Does your enterprise need an eye-catching sign? We'll cover all these important topics.

ESTABLISHING YOUR IMAGE

If you are the only restaurant, gift shop, attorney, doctor, or repairperson in town, skip this part. (And realize you'll be living in a very tiny village!) But if there will be similar outlets or professionals operating in the area, the identity you project becomes of paramount importance. This is also true on a national scale if your client or customer base is located all over the country.

Have you ever noticed that in some hardware stores the employees are especially knowledgeable? Maybe you've observed that the atmosphere of a certain clothing shop is unusually inviting. Perhaps you have auto repairs done by a favorite mechanic because he washes the exterior and vacuums the inside of your car—along with performing the required technical service. Maybe you patronize a certain chiropractor because he never keeps you waiting more than five minutes.

Each of these establishments has developed a certain image. The hardware store is known for its helpful workers. The clothing shop has created an appealing ambiance by decorating in a winsome way, playing classical guitar music, featuring a fragrant potpourri, and offering free herb teas and gourmet coffees to customers. Shopping there is *an experience*. The auto mechanic makes your life easier. The chiropractor values your time. What's the atmosphere in your store: friendly, avant-garde, homey, funky, sophisticated?

Image revolves around how people perceive you. It's your firm's ability to satisfy expectations. And it sends a potent message about your capabilities and caring. Image-building should be PROactive, not reactive. This isn't the place for tippy-toe, soft-shoe stuff. Image involves visibility, charisma, respect, personal responsiveness.

And if you take image-building seriously, you'll consistently romance your prospects in every way possible. You'll woo them with carefully crafted collateral materials: business cards, stationery, brochures, flyers. Your signs will reflect the same image, as will your interior design and the very *feel* of your place.

Even the way you answer the phone projects your image. Is it friendly, unhurried, and professional? A favorable reaction gives you an important competitive edge. It contributes directly to why folks get their wrenches, jeans, auto repairs, or back adjustments from you. Apply this knowledge to your own operation.

Developing an image applies to virtually every business. Let's say you find a mobile home park for sale below market value. While purchasing such a business is iffy because most park owners are struggling to maintain decent occupancy rates, such a venture can be turned into a gold mine by clever packaging. A major challenge is to replace the stigma of "trailer court" with something prestigious and fun. Let's do some brainstorming and see if we can create a different image.

What if we were to make this into a theme park? After all, nearly everyone loves visiting Disneyland and other theme parks. How about a ranch motif? Here's what we would do to position this mobile home park as distinct and desirable. There are cottonwood trees on the property and a pond nearby, so let's call it Cottonwood Ranch.

To establish the mood, an old stagecoach greets visitors at the main entrance. Streets are renamed Rawhide Road, Buckboard Boulevard, Sagebrush Street, Lasso Lane, Chuck Wagon Court, and Desperado Drive. Rustic signposts mark each corner. Corral fencing—complete with wagon wheels and hitching posts—divides the lots. The club-house, dubbed "Wranglers' Roost," is redecorated with ranch-style fur-niture; branding irons, horse collars, and Indian rugs adorn the walls. The playground is called the "Kids' Korral" and includes blocks for building forts, a couple of sturdy old wagons, and wooden ranch crit-ters—in addition to the normal swings and slide.

To further carry out the theme atmosphere, *homesteads* are rented rather than spaces. The staff wears western garb, and the manager—sporting a sheriff's badge—answers the phone "Howdy. Cottonwood Ranch." What about creating a spokesperson—maybe Bucky Bronco? He can appear in ads and on brochures, be featured on "Wanted" post-ers that detail the rules, even appear on T-shirts available for sale at the office and clubhouse.

If budget allows, and you want to carry the ambiance further, you might arrange to lease and stock the nearby pond for fishing. And of-fering free monthly hay rides or cookouts for park residents is almost guaranteed to build a waiting list. Of course, this idea would also work perfectly for positioning a campground or RV park. Be our guest. (And if you use it, write and share the results with us!)

For small-town residents, quality of life is everything. Give it to them. Remember the law of karma: the more you give the more you get back. Go out of your way to satisfy people. Approach business with the attitude of being a good neighbor, always ready to please. Negative comments travel faster than lightning. Make sure what's said about you is good.

DECIDING ON A SEEMLY—OR SENSATIONAL—NAME

Names, like fashions, go in cycles. Initials and acronyms are said to be passé. Trends in naming are moving away from letters and numbers because experts have found these symbols have minimal name recog-nition. If people don't think of your store or firm when they need your products or services, all is lost.

Today comfortable, environmental sounding names are in. So are approachable or friendly monikers that show you care about people.

Your company name must both distinguish you from the competition and be appropriate to what you do. Be sure to check the competition. Choosing something too similar makes about as much sense as squatting on a land mine. It should be memorable, easy to pronounce, and fitting. It's also a good idea to invent a name that has your product or service *within it* to avoid confusion.

Consider your customer or client base. Suitable names will vary widely depending on the age level of your prospects. Twentysomethings have different buttons than boomers or retired folks. Don't settle for just one idea; list lots of possibilities. Then rank them. When you go to register your name, you may find it already taken. One large corporation ended up being christened with a meaningless group of letters because their first four choices were already in use.

To help you identify possibilities and stimulate your thinking, check the following "Naming Notions" list to energize your thought process. Once you've come up with some ideas, get feedback from other people—especially those who are prospects. Something may be clear to you, yet as cloudy as a neglected aquarium to others. A name with a misleading connotation can be a real detriment.

Independent Business magazine runs an annual naming contest. One year, readers voted the winners to be Juan in a Million, a restaurant in Lubbock, Texas; Twice Sold Tales, a used bookstore exchange in Pine Grove, California; Loch Ness Lure Company, a lure manufacturer in Crossville, Tennessee; and Bottoms Up Diaper Service of Clackamas, Oregon.

Sometimes the facility where your business is housed dictates the name. George Risolo located his florist shop in an empty bank building and renamed the company the Flower Bank. Furthermore the shop has a bank motif. Customers can order flowers from the drive-in windows and deliveries are made from an armored truck by workers dressed like guards. The Norwalk, Connecticut, florist took in $27,500 one Valentine's Day. Perhaps what you do lends itself to a clever naming twist.

Businesses heavily dependent on Yellow Pages advertising—such as plumbers, mechanics, travel agents, florists, heating and air-conditioning, repair shops, pet groomers, locksmiths, etc.—are wise to choose a name that falls early in the alphabet. This is also true of companies that do business nationwide. One of our firms, About Books, Inc., receives several inquiries each month from our listings in national directories. Certainly appearing at the head of the alphabet doesn't hurt.

Before we leave this topic, let's also examine the pros and cons of using your own name for your business. One woman, who planned to work out of her home, elected to call her business Sara Steinman Productions. Upon learning zoning restrictions didn't allow her to post a company sign outside her house, she was pleased about this choice.

Naming Notions

Agency	Management
Annex	Market
Arbor	Mart
Associates	Maxi
Association	Mini
Bazaar	Mobile
Beat	Outlet
Browser	Park
Bureau	Partnership
Cache	Peddler
Call	Place
Camp	Plaza
Carrier	Plus
Cellar	Portable
Center	Practitioner
Channel	Productions
Clinic	Products
Communications	Provider
Company	Rental
Connection	Repair
Consultant	Salon
Corner	Shelf
Corporation	Shop
Cottage	Shoppe
Deals	Society
Design	Source
Emporium	Specialist
Enterprise	Stall
Equipment	Store
Exchange	Supply
Expeditions	Systems
Forum	Trader
Foundation	Trading post
Inn	Training
Institute	Tours
Junction	Vendor
Gallery	Villa
Group	Village
Incorporated	Wagon
Lodge	Wares
Loft	Warehouse
Lounge	Works
Mall	

You see nothing stopped her from hanging a sign inscribed with her name! Thus business visitors could easily find her.

One advantage of using your full legal name and nothing else is you don't have to register it as a trade name. If, however, you tack on terms like *Company* or *and Son,* in most states this puts you back in the trade name category. Of course, using your personal moniker has the disadvantage of not giving prospects any hint of what you do and making you appear small.

CREATING A WINNING SLOGAN

Is there a slogan in your future? Many businesses benefit from originating a saying connected to their product or service. Perhaps the most famous is "Where's the beef?" Wendy's soared to huge profits when this catchy phrase debuted several years ago. Other national giants use similar marketing strategies. "You're in good hands with Allstate" assures potential buyers that they'll get kid-glove treatment from the insurer. And the self-deprecating "With a name like Smucker's, it has to be good" pokes delicious fun at the company.

Such maxims aren't just for corporate giants though. A ski resort has as its motto "*Snow* ahead, make my day!" An ingenious florist plays on the beer commercial by saying "This bud's for you." And the Lock Ness Lure Company has as their tag line "We catch monsters!" If you decide to coin a slogan, have the following handy: a thesaurus, rhyming dictionary, a sense of humor, and lots of imagination.

GENERATING LOGOS, LETTERHEAD, AND BUSINESS CARDS

Once you know who you're going to be, have developed a slogan, and know your physical location, it's time to prepare stationery and cards. Many businesses hire a graphic artist to also design a logo. This is a symbol that helps identify you. We chose to name our public relations consulting firm Accelerated Business Images (ABI) partly because it has excellent visual potential. Then we worked with our artist to develop a logo that connotes movement, thus symbolizing the progress we achieve for our clients.

Keep in mind the image you want to portray. What's your "look"? Are you going for sophisticated elegance or popular glitz? A traditional or contemporary feel? Coordinate your letterhead, envelope, and business card. Choose a color other than white so your correspondence stands out from the crowd. And be sure you include all pertinent information—such as your phone area code, zip code, fax number, e-mail, and URL if appropriate. When using a post office box, it's also wise to include a street address for in-person deliveries. Adding the street address also eliminates the fly-by-night image. Avoid tiny type. As the population ages, prospects' eyes appreciate larger print.

We contend business cards are severely underrated. They're like having a sales tool right in your hand. What's a well-thought-out and creatively executed business card of today? A mini billboard! Just as freeway billboards tout certain items, so can your business card.

Our About Books, Inc., firm handles everything to do with books that isn't illegal or immoral. To aid people in getting a better handle on specifically how we can help them, we itemize these services on our card (manuscript critiquing, editing, typesetting, design, printing, marketing, publicity, consulting, seminars). If you want to get even more mileage out of your card, consider using a double-sided, tent-style card. These have a fold along the top and print on both sides. We originated such a card for a boutique and used the inside for a listing of ladies' sizes and favorite colors. Then each customer was encouraged to fill out a card for the man in her life. That simplified gift-giving for hundreds of husbands, boyfriends, and dads. Of course it also brought extra business into the boutique.

To be more unusual, design your card vertically instead of horizontally. For some enterprises, using a florescent paper stock is a smart idea to attract attention. We know a plumber who had his card done on a rubberized magnetic material. It sticks to the refrigerator door and serves as a constant reminder of who to call in case of plumbing problems. Some people like to include a photograph, or even do the whole card as a color picture.

And consider whether you can do a cross-promotion with another business. We know of a fellow who got his business cards paid for by tying the location of his crafts gallery to that of a nearby hotel. On the back of his card, he drew a map that showed the location of his shop in relation to the hotel. The hotel then made his cards available to guests, who often visited the gallery.

EVALUATING SIGNAGE NEEDS

Virtually every business that isn't home-based requires a sign. This is not only excellent advertising, it helps prospects find you easily. Again, your sign should reflect the image you want to communicate. Integrate it with the other design aspects of your business. Clarity and simplicity are the bywords in sign design. Don't get cluttered. You want your company name and maybe the logo. Period. No slogan, no phone number, no distractions. And before you go too far, check on any regulations. There will no doubt be ordinances you must obey.

Eye appeal leads to "aye appeal." Colors should complement the surrounding buildings. Shy away from subtle shades; strong contrasts make for easier reading. Speaking of readability, be aware that to be seen about 100 feet away, letters should be four inches tall. If you have a sign on the highway, however, letters must be more like three *feet* high to be read at a distance when traveling fast.

Perhaps what you do lends itself to an unusually shaped sign. This gives additional visual clues. A music store might design its sign as the outline of a musical note, a bowling alley in the image of a bowling ball or pin. For automobile-related businesses, how about the profile of a car? An optometrist's office sign might take the shape of eyeglasses, while an aquarium supplier could do well with a fish image.

Don't overlook other signage opportunities. Perhaps your business lends itself to advertising on vehicles. Commercials here can take the form of metallic signs, decals, or lettering on the actual auto body. A Taylors, South Carolina, man who owns an electrical wiring company transformed his truck into a roving billboard. He puts metallic signs across his side doors and along the back, then parks his truck in high-visibility spots like country club parking lots and commercial construction sites. "I've gotten at least 100 jobs in a year from having the sign on the truck," reports owner Bobby Cox.

Now that we know our distinct image and have christened our enterprise, not to mention designed stationery and a sign, let's move on to that most fascinating of topics: marketing strategies! After all, it's the selling of your products or services—and the resulting livelihood—that holds special appeal for everyone.

17

———◆———

Persuasive Marketing Strategies to Boost Your Bottom Line

Doing business without marketing is like winking at someone—in the dark. *You* may know what you're doing—but nobody else does. Marketing is the vital cog in the wheel, regardless of whether you offer a service, own a retail store, head a professional firm, make your living as a wholesaler, or manufacture a product. Here we'll show you how to get attention without weighing 300 pounds, throwing public tantrums, or disgracing the national anthem.

POSITIONING YOURSELF FOR GREATER PROFITS

Positioning is simply looking for a hole, then plugging it. It's doing something to set yourself apart from the crowd. Granted, in Small Town USA the crowd is more sparse. But don't delude yourself into thinking that means you needn't differentiate yourself. If you want your market share (and some extra), seek ways to carve out a special niche. Try to identify and serve a segment all your own.

To better understand this concept, let's look at cookies. Some are chewy, others crunchy. There are ones like Grandma used to make, nutritious ones, gourmet ones, low-fat varieties, gigantic cookies that are almost a meal in themselves, and, on the other side of the spectrum, bite-sized morsels. All of these cookies' manufacturers are going after their own sweet section of the market. They're avoiding cookie-cutter approaches by positioning their product to appeal to certain consumers.

Will you become known as the place where a person can find almost anything in a given line of merchandise, or will your inventory be customized and selective? If you're in mental health care, will you cater to children, teens, adults, or downsized executives? As a physician, will you let people walk in without an appointment or might you make house calls? If real estate or appraising is your thing, do you plan to specialize in residential property, commercial holdings, or raw land?

Thinking of opening a restaurant? It might offer American, Italian, Chinese, Mexican, or other ethnic cuisine. And it could take the form of a deli, gourmet fare, home-style cooking, fast food, family style, even a cafeteria. The ways you can segment the market go on and on. Do you deliver? What about catering parties and special events? Is the town large enough to support a nonsmoking eatery? Can you play on a unique location? Maybe you will situate your restaurant in a charming church, railroad station, or historic landmark.

Suppose you want to start a maid service, but there are already a couple of them in town. Don't go head-to-head in the traditional way. Come from a different perspective. You could market a "luxury package" of special services to affluent households. Or maybe a monthly "quik 'n heavy clean" program for mature people who can't afford weekly service but need periodic help with difficult tasks.

Of course before you can sharpen your focus to set yourself apart, you must know the competition. Find out who your potential rivals are. Evaluate what they do well and what they do poorly. Now scrutinize your own situation. What could you do better, faster, and more innovatively? Go with your strengths.

Consider creating a mobile moneymaker. By offering free pickup and delivery, you save customers time and endear yourself to them. What about Chinese fast food to go—or delivered? Setting up a mobile operation where you outfit a van or truck and take your enterprise on the road might make sense for certain occupations. Want to do alterations, repair small appliances, or groom dogs? All three could fall under the "Have van, will travel" category.

Look for ways to give your business an exotic or adventurous twist. A motel, shop, or restaurant might offer escapist entertainment by implementing a Polynesian, western, or futuristic theme, for instance. Appeal to our five senses in any way you can by adding sensory value: taste, smell, sound, light, color, texture. Make the experience "sensational."

For specific ideas, study the following "21 Ways to Separate Yourself from the Herd." Find your special niche; then really take care of your customers or clients. Proper positioning, teamed with genuine caring, makes the difference between doing business as usual—or doing business unusually well.

---

21 Ways to Separate Yourself from the Herd

1. **Price point.** Are you expensive, moderately priced, or cheap? Establish your image and let customers know it.
2. **Size.** Small can be beautiful; play on your personalized attention.
3. **Atmosphere.** Are you laid-back? Sophisticated? Hip? Continental?
4. **Hours.** Do you stay open late (or early) to accommodate working people?
5. **Days of operation.** Should you consider opening weekends? Holidays?
6. **Location.** Are you convenient? Easy to find? Handy for walk-by traffic?
7. **Portability.** Could you put your business "on the road"?
8. **Ease of purchasing.** Do you offer credit cards? Lay away? Financing? Phone orders? Purchasing via the Internet?
9. **Convenience.** Can people get in easily, find what they want, and pay quickly?
10. **Gimmicks.** Do you have an environmental angle? A theme decor?
11. **Delivery.** Do you offer pickup or delivery?
12. **Guarantee.** Do you have a unique money-back guarantee or service warranty policy?
13. **Packaging.** Could you use innovative, reusable, or fun packaging?
14. **Giveaways.** Do you offer free gifts to potential customers? To purchasers? For referrals?
15. **Piggybacking.** Can you combine two businesses to better serve people and improve your revenue stream?
16. **Samples.** Could you offer samples to entice prospects?
17. **Seminars or demonstrations.** Should your product or service be showcased to attract prospects?
18. **Contests.** Would some form of competition focus attention on you? People love contests—and winning them.
19. **Age/sex segmentation.** Should you slant toward women, men, teens, adults, retirees?
20. **Service.** Do you offer extraordinary assistance to your customers/clients?
21. **Technological edge.** Will a fax, modem, cellular phone, bigger computer, toll-free line, e-mail, or a home page on the Internet open new doors?

DEVELOPING AN EFFECTIVE MARKETING PLAN

Once you've determined your distinctive difference, it's time to develop a marketing plan. This written blueprint will serve as the springboard for launching all the possible ways you plan to generate profits. Naturally it will vary, depending on the kind of business you're in and whether your area of influence is local, regional, national, or global. To stay focused, refer to your mission statement.

Let's take a moment here to brainstorm potential markets. Not all of them will be limited to your local economy. Will you incorporate systems to bridge you to a regional or national market? What about exporting internationally? Don't flinch! These days, state and local governments are more than willing to help connect you with outlets in other countries. They can furnish market studies or help you locate embassy officials willing to link you to foreign businesses interested in selling your wares. With the walls coming down in the global arena, international markets are on the rise. If these prospects interest you, contact your state office of economic development in the state capitol.

Marketing takes a different tack in rural America. If your business is dependent on the locals, make certain your neighbors know you. Go out of your way to make new friends. If you're asked to dinner, go and enjoy. Your new neighbors are also your new prospects. Find the long-time residents and make them your friends. Join the chamber of commerce. If you're a churchgoer, find a good church and become an active member. Making sure people know who you are and what you do is half the battle.

Some marketing plans are heavy on publicity and promotional events; others stress telemarketing or direct mail. Still others emphasize radio, magazine, newspaper, or Yellow Pages advertising. Another firm might rely on public relations (PR) and community involvement. One-on-one selling works wonders in some situations, window displays and prominent signage in others.

In most cases, however, there needs to be a good marketing *mix*. That means a balance of various sales and promotional approaches. Seldom will a venture be successful by using only one of the above strategies. If marketing strategies don't come easy to you, get professional help. The entire life of your business is dependent on getting off on the right foot. For that reason, we're often called on by start-ups to assist them in developing a strong overall marketing philosophy and strategies to carry it out.

When we give speeches around the country, we ask how many people hate "selling." Most hands shoot up. Then we suggest that people think of it rather as "building relationships," helping people meet their needs. This really takes the pressure off.

BUDGETING: HOW TO BE AN ASTUTE SPENDER

First, a few words of clarification. In discussing a marketing budget, we don't just mean costs of advertising. Public relations and promotional tactics need to be factored in too. They usually have a much greater payback than outright advertising.

The most typical methods for computing what to spend are (1) earmarking "all we can afford," (2) matching or outspending the competition, or (3) allotting a percentage of sales. Let's examine these. Number one is hopeless. You can *afford* nothing. It's all been gobbled up with the move, purchase of the property and inventory, etc. Right? Number two is also fraught with problems. When you enter a spending race, everyone loses because an unrealistic amount of profits is funneled off for advertising.

Number three, on the other hand, holds promise. This formula is used more often than any other method. For an existing business, it's simple and provides a sense of security. Of course if the previous year was weak, you run the risk of perpetuating a downslide by allocating a lessening amount for marketing. This is a dangerous trend, so take such situations into consideration before deciding what you will spend.

We recommend that you first contact all the trade associations that represent your kind of business. Locate them in the *Encyclopedia of Associations* at the library. Talk to the executive director or some other key person to determine what the industry standard is for a marketing budget in your field. This is information gleaned from much trial and error. Benefit from your peers' experience. Now contact owners of similar successful business ventures in other, noncompetitive areas. Explain that you're just starting and need some advertising budget advice. Most people are happy to help.

Treat advertising as an investment. Naturally in the beginning, expenditures will exceed income. You may allot as much as 15 or 20 percent of your first year's expenses to marketing. Wise new entrepreneurs plow all possible profits back into advertising, promotion, and sales activities in the beginning. But—hallelujah—not everything costs money. Be sure to tune in carefully to the tactics contained in this chapter. Many of them are shoestring ideas to greater profits.

SECRETS FOR CAPTURING FREE PR

Tapping into no-cost public relations is one of the most FUNdamental aspects of marketing any business or professional practice. Yet many folks think you must be able to charm the lard off a hog to be effective in PR. 'Tain't so. What is important is being alert for every opportunity to focus attention on your venture and yourself.

The most common vehicle for doing this is the press release, which we prefer to call a *news* release in this electronic age. Do you realize that approximately 75 percent of all news is "planted"? By that we mean it is supplied by publicists and people just like you—rather than being dug up by reporters, producers, or editors. News releases cover a multitude of issues. Well-written ones are often used as is. Others are reworked to fit the style of the publication. Some are deemed worthy of greater attention; they result in full-blown stories done by a reporter, freelance writer, or editor.

We won't try to teach you how to write a powerful news release here. Kate Kelly's *The Publicity Manual* does a commendable job. *The Publicity Handbook,* by David Yale, shows how to develop a sophisticated publicity campaign that sends your message loud and clear. Don't think that just because you have a *local* service you shouldn't publicize it in the national press. Most people never get their names in print so they're in awe by those who do. Piano teacher Mollie Wakeman was interviewed in *Entrepreneur* magazine. "I know I won't get any new students from this mention," she observes, "but if I put a copy of this article where my students' parents can see it, they'll be so impressed I can raise my rates!"

This brings us to a significant point about publicity: secondhand PR is often *more valuable* than firsthand PR. What does that mean? Let us tell you about clients we helped in The Woodlands, Texas. They were a consulting and training firm with annual receipts of more than $1 million a year. No slouches, these folks. But while they were brilliant in their field, they were naïve in the ways of publicity. No less than the *Wall Street Journal* had run a piece about this firm and its founder. When the story broke, they celebrated their good fortune, then filed the article away in company archives. What a waste! We counseled them to print copies of any PR and use it *everywhere!* This is the ultimate in recycling.

Topics for News Releases

- [ ] The opening of your store, firm, plant, or office
- [ ] Announcement of new management
- [ ] An anniversary
- [ ] The hiring, or promotion, of a key staff member
- [ ] Being awarded a new contract
- [ ] Business expansion or remodeling
- [ ] Adding a new line of goods or service(s)
- [ ] The owner receiving an award, accreditation, or other honor
- [ ] Timely tie-ins with national holidays
- [ ] Demonstrations, plant tours, open houses
- [ ] Appointment or election to a board of directors
- [ ] Financial news
- [ ] Having an article or book published
- [ ] Special event or contest announcement
- [ ] Trend evaluations or reports
- [ ] Controversial rebuttals

Such pieces solidify your credibility. They provide an ideal, low-key reason to get in front of prospects and should be used as a mailing for anyone you're trying to woo. Also send copies to current clients or customers. Use them as enclosures in virtually everything you mail. And when soliciting additional publicity, include what has already been done. This helps establish your newsworthiness. The press likes to climb on an already-moving bandwagon. Some firms even have prestigious articles matted and framed to hang in their offices.

What subjects should your press releases cover? See "Topics for News Releases" for some ideas. This list is by no means comprehensive. Be creative! You're sure to come up with newsworthy topics and "angles" of your own.

Using the written word in other ways can assure you of more windfall visibility. How about letters to the editor? These are well-read platforms for getting your message, and your name, into the public's consciousness. Op-ed pieces, which are run in larger newspapers opposite the editorial page, do the same. These are essays about area concerns or timely topics. Or you may want to develop a flyer, quiz, or booklet of self-help information to be used as a giveaway. Professionals often find free quarterly newsletters to be viable tools to help them stay visible to prospects.

Besides print, don't forget radio and area TV stations. Media producers gladly book people who provide value to their listeners. Perhaps you can offer guidance for better health (by a doctor), hints on housekeeping (from a maid service), or effective parenting techniques (by a therapist). Then there could be tax guidance (from a CPA), Christmas gift ideas (from a gift shop owner or a craftsperson), and ways to keep your car in tip-top shape (compliments of a mechanic). The possibilities are endless. When you're interviewed by the media, you are perceived as the *expert* in the field.

Directory listings lead to good results for many companies. This is especially true for those who are not dependent on the immediate area for their well-being—such as consultants, speakers, writers, technological support people, and manufacturers. You'll find more than 14,000 annotated listings in *The Directories of Directories*. It lists business and industrial directories, professional and scientific rosters, entertainment, recreation, and cultural directories, directory databases, plus other lists and guides.

Scour it for appropriate directories, study the listings of your competitors, then craft an entry of your own that presents you in the best light. Fill out every possible line. The longer the listing, the more substantial you appear. If they allow up to 100 words for a description of your services, use all 100. Stress what you can do for prospective clients or customers: how you'll make their jobs easier, save them money, or expand their profits. Your aim here is to get them to contact you. Also notice if more than one section applies to what you do.

A study by the Association of Industrial Advertisers found that when buyers look for sellers, 35 percent find them in business directories. This tops sales calls, direct mail, brochures, Yellow Pages, even word-of-mouth. Get listed in all appropriate resources.

In whatever you do, offer outstanding service. Ask not what your customer can do for you, but what you can do for your customer! According to the American Management Association, 65 percent of the average company's business comes from existing, satisfied customers. Happy repeat customers are your best sources of free publicity.

DEVISING DYNAMIC PROMOTIONAL EVENTS

Promotional events will enhance your image, plus put more fun and profits into your business. It's important you allow time for planning and consider appropriate timing to increase results.

Events use kooky angles to create synergy. A baby shop might do something around baby pictures; a pet store might sponsor an ugly pet contest. A camera or film shop could back a photography show. Merchants can have "roll back prices" days to boost sales during slow periods. Sports and recreation—which can include everything from golf to bowling, hunting to fishing—lend themselves beautifully to special events. You can have people predict scores, guess attendance at activities, or estimate the biggest catch of the day.

Holidays are event bonanzas. How about a fashion show just before Mother's day or Valentine's day? Halloween brims with a cauldron of possibilities: A grocery store could have a pumpkin carving contest, a craft store might have a pumpkin decorating competition, and a bookstore might initiate a scary story contest.

You might even team up with others in the community to develop something purely for the enjoyment of area residents. Remember, doing good is good for business. Volunteering your time or expertise often pays big dividends. You'll make strategic contacts, probably receive exposure in local newspapers and the organization's newsletter, and best of all, feel good about what you're doing.

PROSPECTING ON THE INTERNET

While no one knows the magnitude of Internet usage for sure, current estimates range from 20 million to 60 million people worldwide. Millions more leap into cyberspace each year. Fully 20 percent of the U.S. population is expected to be online by the year 2000. Many assertive business people have decided to "tech it to the max." The Internet is a perfect vehicle for many boonies business people; it allows them to create a virtual enterprise with a worldwide clientele. Having a home page is like opening a retail store.

You can also use the Internet to capture business in your own backyard. By creating a Web site, a caterer could put up pictures of a lovely party, a couple of recipes that went over well, plus enthusiastic comments about the dishes from happy guests. Then she advertises her Web site in the local newspaper. A contractor might provide a list of frequently asked questions (FAQs), a couple of shots of his completed homes, and a bid request sheet. The options are endless.

A survey conducted by NetSmart found that over a fourth of Internet users have already purchased items online, while 46 percent ended up buying products at retail after first finding out about them on the

Web. A whopping 81 percent used the Internet to research new products and services.

We won't attempt to instruct you on how to develop and promote a site here; there are many fine books doing just that. Do be aware that putting up a home page (which actually ends up being more like 5 to 20 pages) is only the beginning. You must publicize your site so people visit, then devise clever ways to get folks to return. The most successful Web sites combine information with entertainment. After the prospect is informed and has fun, he or she is in a receptive mood to buy.

What sells on the Internet? Books are big; music does well; even buffalo meat sells. (Yes, partner, you read right. The Web helped double sales for Great Lakes Buffalo Company of Sheboygan, Michigan.) A car collector/trader has photos and information on classic cars on his site. As technology becomes more sophisticated and interactive, potential customers will be able to feel the fabric of a suit they're considering just by touching their TV screen.

A wide range of services is also being touted electronically. Stocks are sold aggressively over the Internet; so are travel services. A plastic surgeon has put his clinic online (these people can afford to come to you!) and also sells body and face creams. Advertising and PR experts glean new clients this way. Some attorneys provide remote counsel; a veterinarian provides long-distance pet advice; and an insurance agent wraps up policies online.

Proof that the Internet can make money for nearly any business is evidenced by an apartment owner in California. To make his 112-unit apartment building competitive in a saturated market, he converted one apartment into a classroom, then offered tenants ten free hours of Internet access each month. Within 30 days he had rented ten apartments as a result of the Internet program, increasing his cash flow by about $8,000 a month. Can you apply this concept to your business?

There is money to be made, no question about it. Sales generated through the Web grew from only $8 million in 1994 to $436 million in 1995. That's an enormous 5,350 percent gain in one year! The May/June 1995 issue of *The Futurist* magazine predicted that fully half of today's retail stores will disappear by the year 2000 as more customers flock to the commercial lanes of the information superhighway. "Rural areas could see a population boom as people decide they don't need the 'convenience' of living near shopping areas," the article reports. Shouldn't you be investigating how the Internet can boost your net (worth)?

ADVERTISING'S EXCITING OPTIONS

Developing an effective advertising campaign makes perfect sense for some businesses—and very little for others. In the professions, for instance, word-of-mouth and publicity are typically much more productive. But if you have a retail outlet or service company, advertising may play a large role in your overall marketing scheme. You'll use it to bring in new customers and maintain old ones.

We're talking here primarily about advertising designed to generate an immediate response and bottom line results, not *institutional* ads—those created to establish a position and reinforce an image. Probably the most promising are ads in the local newspaper or a "shopper" (which is distributed free), Yellow Pages advertising, direct mail, and radio commercials.

Ads come in two basic types: classified and display. Display ads cost more and consequently focus more attention on you. Some people go on a spree and blow their whole budget on one big ad. Don't. That's the wrong approach. Repetition is more valuable than size. Get in front of people and stay there: week after week, month after month. Every ad should include the store name and logo, address, phone, slogan, hours, Web site URL (if applicable), and what's known as a "call to action" to motivate people to respond.

Here are various options to make your ad more outstanding: Use a reverse (meaning white ink on a black background). If you choose a reverse, make sure you use bold enough type so that it can be read easily. Or include a screen where only 20 percent of the ink is used, thus creating a gray background. Use lots of white space so your ad looks open and inviting. You also might want to surround it with a heavy or distinctive border.

Classifieds can also be surprisingly effective. Especially in small towns, people really read the classifieds. We know businesses that keep a series of ads running constantly in the classified section.

Of course, the "where" is only one part of a three-legged stool. Without the other two vital components, it won't stand upright. Advertising is only successful if it is the *right message* to the *right audience* at the *right time*. Your timing might be lousy. More likely, you could be targeting exactly the perfect place, but lack an ad that motivates. Writing compelling advertising copy takes experience and skill.

In our busy society, more and more people "let their fingers do the walking." Yet 55 percent of all Yellow Pages users don't have a specific name in mind when they open the book. What an opportunity! These are prequalified prospects. They have a specific need to fill, whether it's finding a plumber, taxi, lawyer, appliance repairperson, beauty salon, air-conditioning and heating contractor, computer store, or whatever.

But because there's no place where you will be in more direct competition with rival companies, it's paramount you create an eye-catching, benefit-oriented ad. Layout, illustrations, type, headlines, body copy, border, and color, must work together to establish a dramatic whole. A key to remember is that you're not selling you or your business so much as you are selling *solutions to people's problems.* Tell readers about the benefits of doing business with you rather than the competition. Your aim is to be believable, to convey trust, to meet their needs.

Ads are placed in a given section according to their size. Half-pagers precede the quarter-page sized, and so on. If you determine this vehicle will contribute greatly to your success, purchase the largest ad you can afford. Yellow Pages advertising requires long-term planning and a sizeable financial commitment. You will be billed each month for a year. What you create today must be just as appropriate 12 months from now. Be sure you select the right listing or heading, maybe even get a cross-reference listing. It often pays to work with a professional consultant who understands the quirks of this advertising medium.

The same is true if you go into direct mail in a big way. For some, this is an immensely profitable endeavor; for others, an expensive and painful lesson. When entering into this area, be as careful as a nudist crossing a barbed wire fence. A successful national direct mail campaign must be orchestrated by someone who knows what he or she is doing. An excellent book on the subject is Bob Stone's *Successful Direct Marketing Methods.*

But if you're just concocting a flyer or postcard to circulate in the neighborhood, you can probably do it yourself. This medium works well to announce grand openings to those who live nearby, champion special sales, tell about a new line or service, or plug special events. Many direct mail promotions include discount coupons to increase traffic.

In fact, several merchants can go together on a discount coupon book. This goodwill builder is a real winner in tourist spots, charming area visitors and prospering local businesses. It could include two-for-one dinners, a percentage off lodging accommodations, or free items with the purchase of another. Other ideas are complimentary wine or dessert with dinner, free souvenirs with purchase of a recreational activity, plus assorted 10 to 25 percent discount coupons for a variety of merchandise. Such books can be given away at the chamber of commerce or made available at participating merchants.

Broadcast media can be very effective in stimulating traffic. In larger towns where there are several radio stations, you can target those who like classical, country, rock, or easy-listening music. If you want to sell to teens, the rock station holds potential, while upscale merchandise will move better when advertised on the classical station.

Because the radio tends to be background listening for most people, incorporate attention getters into your commercials. Special effect sounds, silence, unusual speech patterns, and good voice inflection help grab listeners by the scruff of the neck and shout, "pay attention to me!" Commercials usually run as 15-, 30-, or 60-second spots. Be sure to repeat your name and phone number two or three times. One other clue: refer people to the telephone *white* pages rather than the Yellow Pages—where they'll also be exposed to all your competition.

Commercials can be purchased as *ROS* (run of station), which means they will be aired any time the station is on the air, or *prime time,* the busy driving hours when people are usually traveling to and from work. In rural areas it doesn't pay to spend the extra money to get prime time.

Often the production of your commercial is free, as long as you're willing to settle for the station's staff. They have facilities for producing a taped commercial and often disc jockeys who will lend their voices to your cause. While you have less control over the results, live ads sometimes do double duty, especially if they feature a popular DJ. Listeners assume he or she is endorsing your product or service.

For a cost-effective ad buy, consider your church or temple directory, a local theater program, or the high school yearbook or sports calendar. This kind of affinity marketing gets people to notice your name and feel good about buying within their community.

MORE INNOVATIVE SALES TECHNIQUES

Seek out ways to expand your horizons. You can do this by exploring methods to get businesses or individuals to use more of what you supply. Suppose you're a window cleaner. Why not encourage local merchants to paint their windows for Halloween, Easter, and Christmas? The merchants will attract fresh attention to their establishments, community beautification increases, and you will have a fresh supply of windows to clean.

Along this same line, diversify to multiply. Seek ways to create more to sell. Let's say you own a beauty school. How about starting refresher courses for those who haven't worked in a while? Or business courses for operators who plan to open their own shops? Why not sell cosmetics, jewelry, or beauty books to generate more revenue?

Look for opportunities to gain strength in numbers. Five bed-and-breakfast inns in the Eugene, Oregon, area have banded together to create a phone loop to be sure they don't miss phone calls. Each B&B has two phone numbers—its own and the group's. Using call-waiting and call-forwarding, the group number rings at the first inn, then at the others in turn if no one answers. By working together, these entrepreneurs boost their occupancy rate and better serve their clientele. When one inn is full, it also refers guests to others in the group.

Testimonials and referrals are like money in the bank, especially for professional practices and service businesses. Cultivate them. It's harder to sell *intangibles* like consulting, repairs, maintenance, or health services, for instance. There is no garment, appliance, or gift for consumers to see. So when you get verbal accolades, ask the person to put it in writing. Respond to a written compliment with a prompt, sincere thank-you. Then request permission to use it. Weave these kudos into future ads, brochures, and sales letters. Frame and hang them in your office or store. They help establish your credibility.

Word-of-mouth praise can't be bought at any price. Yet it's an invaluable sales tool. A recent Whirlpool Corporation study proved Americans are six times more likely to base a buying decision on the judgment of others than on advertising. Such praise can be yours for the asking! A discreet sign in an attorney's office saying, "We Appreciate Your Referrals" might do the trick. A financial planner, insurance agent, or real estate salesperson might make a friendly follow-up phone call to check on a client's satisfaction and tactfully inquire about other individuals this person knows who could use some help.

It really behooves physicians to keep their patients happy. A recent *USA Today* article that looked at statistics shaping our nation found 50 percent of people choose their doctors based on recommendations from friends and relatives!

Especially if you depend on tourism, give your employees hospitality training. Be sure each person who interfaces with the public *exceeds* their expectations. Repeat visitors become next year's cherished customers. A courteous, informed, motivated staff creates ripples of customer satisfaction. Whatever your business, aim for this kind of value-based attitude.

Are you practicing suggestive selling? It's done all the time in better clothing stores and by conscientious waitstaff. Remember the last time you succumbed to a recommendation about the delicious, freshly baked pie for dessert? A carpet cleaning firm, for instance, might suggest customers also hire it to clean the drapes or wax wood floors. A phone order department could significantly impact sales on incoming calls simply by using telemarketing techniques to suggest related add-on items. And assertive consultants often convince their clients to hire them for additional services.

There are many ingenious ways to draw prospective customers into your establishment. Some restaurants post taste-tempting menus outside to lure hungry patrons inside. Others post signs offering free ice to attract travelers. A clever screen-printing shop owner uses his hobby to entice people. He has a showroom where he displays his Montana breweriana collection. Many who come to browse buy screen printed T-shirts. (He also parlayed his unusual hobby and business combination into an article published in *Screenprinting* magazine as well as area newspapers.)

Of course store display windows offer retailers opportunities limited only by their imagination. A map store owner decided to make what could be boring, one-dimensional displays into something exciting. In the coldest winter month she used a mannequin exhibiting a map of the Caribbean. At Thanksgiving she created turkeys made from maps of Turkey. And she always capitalizes on current events to display maps of places in the news.

A bookstore owner ties into holidays, or any other excuse she can find, to enliven her windows. At Easter, a giant rabbit is the centerpiece for an array of children's books. Her February windows are alive with hearts, cupids, and gift books. Around graduation there are symbolic decorations, plus books about job hunting and careers. Summertime is greeted with beach towels, sunglasses, and stacks of novels for lazy-day reading.

During slow times, offer financial incentives to boost business. While restaurants pioneered two-for-one dinners years ago, this can also be used by recreational facilities and others. A dentist or massage therapist might give a family discount. Another spin on this idea is used by one of our California clients. We helped this heating and air-conditioning company develop a special service insurance policy. It protects homeowners from expensive repairs—and generates up-front cash for our client.

The local paper might be your road to fame and fortune. Probe it for leads. We know of a diaper service that watches birth announcements, and a woman who owns an event-planning/bridal-service firm and garners leads by reading about engagements. One man who operates a small advertising/PR firm immediately contacts area people when they announce their candidacy for political office. He has picked up several clients this way.

Apply the 80/20 rule. This is a universal principle that works in every business. Simply stated, 80 percent of your business will come from 20 percent of your customers. Do you know who those 20 percent are? Find out! Get better acquainted. Focus attention on them instead of frittering away valuable time and resources on marginal accounts—or searching for new prospects.

How many times have you called or written for information about something you were considering buying . . . and never received anything in return? It amazes us how lazy some companies are about responding to a lead. Cherish every one. You never know which may be the pivotal point in your business—that one person who opens up a whole new window of opportunity. Furthermore, you never get a second chance to make a first impression. Handling leads promptly, effectively, and courteously is not only good manners—it's good business. Why bother to arouse interest, then ignore the prospect? Sourcing your inquiries is also crucial. This means finding out how or where prospects heard about you. Knowing what's working—and what isn't—is invaluable feedback.

Allowing consumers to put purchases on credit cards like VISA and MasterCard dramatically increases the profits of most businesses. But for certain kinds of enterprises, achieving this merchant status happens about as fast as getting your teeth straightened. Bankers are especially leery of mail order, telemarketing, and home-based merchants. The reason is risk. The bank assumes the financial obligation of returning customers' money if problems arise and the merchant has gone out of business.

While our big-city colleagues often bemoan the fact they can't get merchant status for processing credit card orders, we had absolutely no problem when we approached our small-town banker. Even if they're unwilling at first, chances are this will change. After you get known in the community, establish a solid reputation, and become acquainted with the bank officers, it's amazing how much easier it is to leap over stumbling blocks.

If you make and sell a product, your quest for sales outlets is continuous. Because you can only reach so many people by yourself, it makes sense to consider getting sales representation. Rather than hiring your own sales force, why not consider using independent reps? These people function as independent contractors who sell products for several different manufacturers and make a commission on what they sell. Some even have a permanent showroom in a merchandise mart. For your convenience, we've listed contact information for the major rep organizations in Part Three.

Ever consider bartering? Trading goods or services can be a realistic solution for mutual gain. It doesn't require out-of-pocket expense, yet it meets the needs of both parties. And it's as natural to country ways as congestion is to freeways. Maybe you're a printer with scant ability to do your own taxes. How about exchanging printing services with the CPA down the street who has oodles of tax expertise—and also needs new letterhead? Or you may find someone with a milk cow who hankers for your handmade pottery. Bingo! Everybody benefits.

Speaking of benefiting, if you want more ideas on how to publicize, advertise, and maximize your small business or professional practice, we've devoted a whole book to this vital subject. Get a copy of our *Big Ideas for Small Service Businesses* by calling 800-331-8355. As an additional brainstorming partner, see the following "Ross Marketing Idea Generator."

Have you ever noticed you have to give to get? Tune into the universal law that says "what goes around comes around." Be generous. Be helpful. Be thoughtful. Let your light really shine. The person who reaches out to fill the needs of others automatically finds his or her own cup running over. Go out of your way to share your business contacts. Write thank-you letters to worthy suppliers. Praise deserving employees. Show loyal customers you appreciate their patronage.

If your promotional efforts get stale, or your revenue drops, come back to this chapter and reread the ideas here. They will serve as a partner to jump-start your thinking and get you back into a marketing mind-set.

Suppose, however, that job hunting is where you really want to focus. Or your mate, who moved to accommodate you, needs employment. Where do you turn? Just keep flipping the page.

Ross Marketing Idea Generator

❑ Try to find an angle that makes your product or service controversial.
❑ Pursue newspaper features about your subject.
❑ Write op-ed (opposite editorial) pieces addressing your topic.
❑ Submit letters to the editor targeting related articles or stories.
❑ Join the chamber of commerce and local service clubs.
❑ Volunteer your time and expertise for worthy causes.
❑ Provide free articles to area newspapers or magazines.
❑ Conduct a survey or poll and announce the results.
❑ Offer exceptional service—always.
❑ Request testimonials from leaders in the industry.
❑ Ask your satisfied clients/customers for referrals.
❑ Prepare a "Here's What People Are Saying" flyer of comments.
❑ Do mailings to those on your Christmas card list, or in your address book, Rolodex, or database.
❑ Develop a PR mailing list of key contacts and major players.
❑ Practice overcoming typical objections to buying your products or services.
❑ Send local celebrities notes of congratulations on their accomplishments.
❑ Establish rapport with area legislators.
❑ Carry business cards—everywhere—always.
❑ Create an "event" centered on your outlet, product, or service.
❑ Establish a local, regional, or national award.
❑ Publish a newsletter.
❑ Launch a contest.
❑ Hold an open house.
❑ Tie in with a special national day/week/month.
❑ Create an internal bulletin board with photos of patients/clients.
❑ Found a regional or national association.
❑ Pursue radio and TV interviews.
❑ Clip and mail "FYI" articles and information to contacts.
❑ Give public speeches or mini-seminars at every opportunity.
❑ Look for ways to provide in-store demonstrations.
❑ Do co-op mailings with other compatible firms.
❑ Sponsor a team, group, or individual.
❑ Cultivate personal listings in who's who publications.
❑ Get your company listed in appropriate directories.
❑ Use creative signage to promote special sales or activities.
❑ Consider posters, balloons, even a blimp to promote your endeavor.
❑ Be alert to piggybacking with current news events and local hot issues.
❑ Seek out catalogs that sell related merchandise.
❑ Write a book to establish yourself as the expert in your field.

Ross Marketing Idea Generator (continued)

- ❑ Enter all contests for which you qualify.
- ❑ Have free drawings to generate an in-house mailing list.
- ❑ Team up with other merchants for special promotions.
- ❑ Send news releases to highlight your awards, accomplishments, etc.
- ❑ Become professionally certified or registered if applicable.
- ❑ Donate your products or time to community fund-raising auctions.
- ❑ Honor some deserving individual in your community or industry.
- ❑ Handle complaints quickly, quietly, and graciously.
- ❑ Follow up, *follow up*, FOLLOW UP.

18

———— ◆ ————

Finding a Rural Job
Gutsy Strategies Mother Never Told You

Americans have been pulling up stakes and pursuing prosperity elsewhere since the days of the Conestoga wagon. Many people are tired of working at the wrong job and not doing what they love. Downsizings, plant closures, and mergers are snuffing out the livelihoods of others.

Many of these individuals don't have the temperament or desire to run their own businesses. Or they're spouses from two-career families involved in a move to better their mate. They want to find a good job quickly in their new surroundings. If you fit this description, listen up. We give you tips to spin your fantasy of straw into a reality of gold. This chapter contains dozens of gutsy strategies for finding a satisfying rural job.

GETTING OFF ON THE RIGHT FOOT

Let's look at some overall recommendations: Find out if you can stay connected to your old job through telecommuting. Being electronically employed is a growing phenomenon. In this situation, you're linked to the home office via computer, modem, and telephone. You make a physical visit to your old job site weekly, monthly, or quarterly. (See Chapter 13, "Telecommuting: Bringing Your Job Home.")

When searching for a new employer, remember that government jobs are more secure and often pay better than private industry. Consider not only federal and state positions, but also those with county or town governments. (With this in mind, you may want to locate in the county seat if you seek a stable clerical job.) Sure, you'll probably have to pass a civil service exam. But if you develop a rapport with the hiring manager, he or she will help guide you through the examination maze.

"The next best employer to work for is the aggressive manufacturing or service firm with a national market," says relocation expert Bill Seavey. "These types of businesses are much less affected by the ebbs and flows of the local economy."

Perhaps you're a retiree seeking to supplement your income. Maybe you recently got out of the military, or you received early retirement from your company. Possibly your Social Security benefits just kicked in. Statistics show that nearly one in four people continue to work part-time for a few years immediately after they start receiving Social Security. And an additional 25 percent say they would do so too, if they found a good opportunity.

Many mature people prefer temporary, seasonal, or part-time jobs. Unfortunately, most of these pay little more than minimum wage. When applying for any position, stress your reliability, experience in the work world, and good judgment. Employers get tired of hiring and training young people over and over again. Once you're in, we'd wager you'll soon be getting raises, promotions, and pleas to work permanent, full-time hours.

If you're not willing to settle for this, fantasize! Imagine your fairy godmother will give you any job you want. What would it be? Write down your wish. Then ask yourself what you're doing to move yourself in that direction. If getting your ideal job seems unrealistic, break it down into components, suggests psychologist and career-change speaker, Dr. Lawrence Le Shan. If being a doctor is your dream, but you're too old for medical school, think about another health care position. For some, employment after retirement is a chance to finally get paid for doing what they've always dreamed of.

MOLDING YOUR CAREER FOCUS

Some skills transfer beautifully. Standard occupations—like teaching, nursing, and secretarial work—fall into this category. Electricians, plumbers, mechanics, and hairdressers can usually earn a living almost anywhere. And doctors are in demand in rural America.

Your career will often be molded into a different shape in the country. A rural nurse, for instance, isn't as likely to deal with severely ill people. Instead she or he may work in health promotion and prevention of illness. Also family planning, school physicals, and infant care occupy a lot of time. Sometimes there are other differences. Noel Ekin, a nurse who traded Houston, Texas, for the Arkansas Valley in Colorado, doesn't mind a daily 140-mile round-trip drive to work. There is no traffic. She brings a camera and leaves plenty of time to stop and take pictures of sunrises, sunsets, elk, antelope, and deer along the way.

A friend who taught at Lamar Community College in Lamar, Colorado, felt like she was part of Little House on the Prairie, compared to the megauniversity where she was before. But once she got her foot in the door of this community of 10,000, she ended up teaching classes in English composition, business English, business communication, and speech.

Many people are entering the teaching profession from other nontraditional fields. "Alternative certification programs, designed for career-switchers and other college graduates who lack education degrees, are gathering steam," reports *John Naisbitt's Trend Letter*. Over the past several years, thousands of former lawyers, computer analysts, engineers, and other professionals have entered teaching. And it's an occupation expected to draw heavily from the military sector as the Department of Defense downsizes. Two factors contribute to this surge of interest in teaching: people want to make a lasting contribution and salaries have increased.

Some people feel it's a poor act of stewardship not to use the gifts God gave them to care for their brothers or sisters. Nowadays jobs dealing with social change are attracting greater numbers. People in these public service positions often work with the underprivileged or the disabled. They also serve as city planners, recreation directors, or gerontology specialists.

RESOURCES TO EASE YOUR QUEST

Urban opt-outs who drool over jobs that keep them outdoors or in the heat of adventure will enjoy James Joseph's *Complete Out-of-Doors Job, Business and Professional Guide*. (The book is out of print, but try to get it through interlibrary loan.) It runs the gamut from game warden to archeologist, RV campground manager to forest ranger, timber grower to professional rockhound. If your quest is outdoor excitement, consider being a rafting guide, ski instructor, or wilderness outfitter.

More possibilities for outdoorsy types are listed in *The Caretaker Gazette* (2380 NE Ellis, Suite C-16RN, Pullman, WA 99163, 509-332-0806.) In one issue we noticed an ad for free rent if you pay for repairs and upkeep, a farming venture that promised possible partnership, and use of a fully equipped cabin and sauna for two months in exchange for caretaking. (Caretaking can be a great way to determine if you can hack remoteness. That particular cabin had no phone or power and required a one-third mile walk to reach it!) Another opportunity involved not only free housing and utilities, but also a stipend of $150 a month for feeding the horses and chickens. Under the heading for Environmental Positions, the *Gazette* lists scientific and supervisory positions, plus intriguing internships.

While we're making recommendations, another ideal national source for high caliber professionals is the *National Business Employment Weekly*. Published by the *Wall Street Journal*, it combines a week's worth of help-wanted advertisements from all the regional editions. While many of these jobs are in major metropolitan areas, some are located in more secluded places. Especially strong as a recruitment tool in the financial field, the paper also covers health care, high-tech, managerial, and executive opportunities. Additionally, it breaks the country into four regions and lists seminars and events for job seekers in the Weekly Calendar of Events. Helpful articles are also part of the package. For subscribing information, call 800-JOB-HUNT (800-562-4868).

Career women might find it useful to join the National Association of Female Executives. For $29 a year, you get a directory of 200 local chapters that can serve as instant networking links. Naturally, many are headquartered in major cities, but we also recognize several smaller towns among the chapters. Additionally, they publish a magazine and offer other benefits. For information, contact NAFE at 30 Irving Place, Fifth Floor, New York, NY 10003, 212-477-2200. Reach them on the Web at http://www.NAFE.com.

Think about other professional organizations to which you belong. Many, such as Toastmasters and swap clubs, will have chapters in or near your new destination. Look up members in the national directory and call them for advance help.

Consider associations where you hold membership when you're job hunting. For instance, the American Institute of Architects, the American Institute of Chemical Engineers, and Women in Communication all have nationwide databases to match job-hunting members with employers.

And lest we forget, this chapter would be incomplete without a hearty endorsement for Richard Nelson Bolles' *What Color Is Your Parachute?* This is the premier book for any job hunter or career changer. It's updated each year and has sold over 5 million copies. We defy even the most seasoned pro not to find some useful information here.

For many folks, rural relocation means they shift the approach to their careers. A Houston developer sold his business to become a carpenter. A geologist caught in Colorado's oil bust in the 1980s now applies her critical thinking skills to her job as a career counselor. A southern California stockbroker left his hectic lifestyle to join a most unusual brokerage house: Edward D. Jones. This firm, which believes that well-heeled investors can be found almost anywhere among the hills and dales of America, has more than 1,200 brokers living and working in towns of less than 25,000 people.

As we suggest throughout this book, you need to probe your avocations as well as your vocations, determine your likes and dislikes, and take a skills inventory. Everybody is good at several things. That's as true if you've been a homemaker all your life as it is if you've run a company that employed 800 people.

If you've supervised a home, you have been involved in purchasing (all those trips to the market), budgeting (making money stretch from paycheck to paycheck), and coordination (organizing car pools, preparing meals, doing laundry, cleaning, correlating kids' activities, running errands). Cooking is no doubt one of your competencies. Flower arranging, sewing, furniture placement, and other such activities may have given you a leg up on interior design. And when you organized and wrote all those PTA reports, or oversaw the whole Junior League cookbook project, you developed talents that have value in the job marketplace.

PLANNING YOUR JOB SEARCH

More likely, however, you come from a large company where the corporate culture is very different from that of small, rural firms. In Fortune 1,000 companies, there are personnel departments and many layers of buffers between where a person is hired and where he or she ultimately works. In our opinion, this breeds negligent hiring practices.

Interviewers in Goliath firms are influenced by degrees, prestigious schools, and impressive titles.

Not so the small-town businessperson. These Davids are concerned with *results*. They want to know if you can do the job and how you'll make or save them money. It's a whole different mind-set. They often base decisions on gut feelings. Credentials are secondary. Be sure to tune into this significant difference when planning your job search.

If you're a professional, also be prepared for the reaction that you're "overqualified." It's probably a reasonable concern. Your challenge is to convince a prospective employer that he or she is foolish not to hire you. Don't come on too strong. Underplay your achievements. Make it clear you don't expect to earn the same salary in Small Town USA that you collected in the city. If you're moving because you want more time with your spouse and kids, it's completely legitimate to say something like: "Although I made a substantial income last year, I also had to travel 60 percent of the time. I personally consider lower compensation with no travel to be a fair trade-off. Time with my family is a high personal priority." Then, without sounding like a cocky hotshot, describe how you can contribute.

Blend into the community and identify with its rhythms, needs, and wants. Reposition yourself both mentally and physically for this new environment. If you're an experienced executive used to responsibility and power, do some role playing to take the edge off your super sophisticated airs. Foremost in the minds of those making hiring decisions is "will this person *fit* into our team?"

To better connect with the individual who's interviewing you, evaluate his or her style—then mirror it. If he's about as upbeat as an undertaker, try to match this behavior. If she's warm and cordial, return her friendly demeanor. We're not saying change like a chameleon from one job interview to the next. But it is smart to take into consideration the mannerisms and attitudes of those in a position to offer you a job.

You can learn how to write a résumé in many books on that subject if you need help. A functional, rather than a chronological one works best for the country, however. A functional résumé catalogs your most important skills, then illustrates how you acquired and honed them. It's especially useful if you have a unique talent you want to showcase.

Think through what supporting materials you can provide. You've gotten letters of recommendation on company letterhead from former bosses. Right? What about personal letters or notes of appreciation? Have you received any awards or certificates of merit? Are there favorable performance reviews you can make copies of? If you're a writer, photographer, or artist, certainly you have a portfolio of samples to show.

The meek may inherit the earth—but only after it's been picked clean. Be ready to address the salary issue. " You must have a figure in mind," advises Richard N. Diggs in *Finding Your Ideal Job*. That means doing your homework. Find out what the usual wage is for your kind of work *in this area*. The last three words are the operative ones. It doesn't matter a crumb what people make for doing what you do in Los Angeles or Chicago or New York. In small towns, the salaries are considerably less. So are the living expenses. One way of checking out the going rate is to ask key people, "If you were applying for a position as a _____ , what would you consider a good starting wage?" Also be sure you know how the cost of living differs from what you're used to.

Diggs advises when you're asked, "What salary are you looking for?" to counter with, "Is there a set wage for this position?" If the answer is "No," you need to parry. You might say, "I feel I'm worth $_____ as a starting salary. But because *you* can't be sure of that yet, I'll place my request in the range of from $_____ to $_____ ." Put the first figure at something that's realistic for the area and that you can afford to live on. The second figure is what you'd *like* to have. (By the way, management thinks in terms of monthly or annual salaries for key personnel, not hourly pay. If you seek a high-powered position, you label yourself as a rookie when you give an hourly figure.)

Feel good about the company and the job? Then don't leave without asking for it! That's called closing the sale. Every successful salesperson does it. You might say something like, "I'm impressed with what you do here and know I can contribute to your growth. I can start this week or next. Which will be most convenient for you?" Remember most entrepreneurs or small business managers are put off by indecision. They'll assume if you're indecisive at the interview, that characteristic will also prevail on the job.

Don't forget there are other considerations besides salary. Will you get a company car? Are stock options available? What about a bonus plan? What are the employee benefits? It may come as a blow that many small-town firms don't provide health insurance. (By the way, if you've recently stopped working for a company with 20 or more workers, federal law requires that your medical coverage be extended at least 18 months. Although *you* must pay the premium, this is a convenient way to keep cost-effective coverage until you have time to shop for a new policy.)

Don't expect highfalutin titles in the boonies, unless you're working with a firm that has a national clientele. Bestowing titles is perceived as a waste of time in many small towns. People there are "just folks."

Job seekers who take a passive stance after the interview are usually left waiting on the curb. Be proactive rather than reactive. Send a prompt, (error-free!) thank-you letter to the person who interviewed you. Typed is best, but handwritten is better than nothing. (Do this even if you *don't* want the job. Why? Because this courtesy is so seldom extended it will set you apart. Small-town business owners talk to each other. Ralph Mercer may well mention you to Diane Bell, who just happens to need a new employee.) Not only is sending a thank-you gracious, it also serves as a reminder of your past meeting. It's a good idea to include one additional strength or accomplishment you didn't bring up in the interview. If you haven't heard anything in a week, follow up with a phone call.

Be politely persistent. Ask if you can provide any additional information. Calvin Coolidge had the right idea when he wrote, "Nothing in this world can take the place of persistence. Talent will not; nothing is more common than unsuccessful men with talent. Genius will not; unrewarded genius is almost a proverb. Education will not. The world is full of educated derelicts. Persistence and determination alone are omnipotent. The slogan 'press on' has solved and always will solve the problems of the human race."

When John F. Kennedy ran for the Senate in 1952, he collected 262,324 nomination signatures from all over Massachusetts. Only 2,500 were required. Persistence often prevails over talent in a job search.

Right beside persistence is networking. These two go together like salsa and tortilla chips. It's estimated about 75 percent of available jobs are never advertised. Personal contacts are the best sources of job leads.

Networking isn't just letting people you know, know—it's creating a ripple effect: contacting *their* contacts. Ask friends and acquaintances for referrals, for people they think might have some ideas. Talk with town leaders. Get permission to use their names when you contact the new lead. The best approach is *not* to ask strangers for a job, but rather for *advice* on how to go about your job search. This takes the pressure off them, yet it accomplishes the same thing.

And if they can't help, keep the ripple going by asking them for referrals to others. Executive search consultants coach their clients to try for three new names from every contact they canvass. This jump-starts the search from linear to geometric proportions. The secret to job-finding success often lies in pursuing people you don't know. (For further hints on how to network effectively, see Chapter 19, "Tactics for Staying Prosperous and Happy.")

Inform yourself about federally funded placement programs like JTPA (Job Training Partnership Act). Why do you need to know about this? Because potential employers may not, and it could be the leverage that gets you a job. You see, when someone qualifies for JTPA, the employer gets help paying them for the first six months. This represents a savings for the company of several thousands of dollars. The point of JTPA is to get jobless workers quickly into permanent, self-sustaining employment. While their requirements are that a person be economically disadvantaged, dislocated, or face significant employment barriers, in reality many people qualify.

We've spoken about volunteering elsewhere in *Country Bound!* Don't forget it as a job-hunting technique. Working as a volunteer or unpaid intern has opened many career doors in the past. You get on-site and visible, your cheery smile and efficient ways a constant reminder of how valuable you are.

Don't let yourself get discouraged. If you're having trouble finding an ideal position, look for a temporary job. Or put a classified ad in the paper and see if you can pick up some freelance work. People hire data processors, housecleaners, home care helpers for the aged, and handymen—to name a few possibilities—all the time.

For a list of additional tactics, see "24 Tips to Enhance Your Chances." While some are general, most work especially well in small towns. Included are suggestions for trailing spouses anxious to find employment in a new locale.

CHOOSING A COMPANY THAT'S RIGHT FOR YOU

Whether you go to work for an employer or not is as much your decision as it is theirs. Big career leaps should be made carefully. And in some cases, you'll have more than one job offer. So how do you decide between firm A and firm B—or if you want to go to work for either? You profile both prospective employers. Thanks to a cache of reports, news items, and inventive inquiries, you can compile stacks of information. Together, these items provide a portrait that's as descriptive as a paint-by-numbers picture.

24 Tips to Enhance Your Chances

1. **Read the trade journal for your industry.** Most have classified ad sections that list job openings around the country.
2. **Get on the phone to anyone you know at your new destination.** (Or anyone who has a friend who might know a friend there.) Find out how your skills fit the needs of your potential new home.
3. **Subscribe to the local newspaper** *and* **the Sunday paper from the nearest large city.** Sometimes important jobs are advertised in the city rather than the local paper. Or a headquarters office may hire district representatives to cover the area where you want to live.
4. **Check into career and job-search Web sites on the Internet.** Let technology help you in searching for your ideal work.
5. **Look into state certification or licensing requirements.** If your profession requires this, and you expect to move out of state, determine the new requirements immediately.
6. **If you're planning a career change and your education is irrelevant or (gasp) lacking, take a course ahead of time.** You don't need a B.A. or an M.B.A. But be able to say you're "studying" business or marketing or finance or whatever. Employers are impressed with adults who go back to school. It shows a conscientious, get-ahead attitude.
7. **Get some experience . . . somehow.** So you've never worked in this new field. Have you read books about it? Pored over the industry trade journals? Gone to a relevant conference? Talked to people in the profession? Learned the jargon? Can you *talk* the business? If not, get a good book on the subject that contains a *glossary*.
8. **Make an appointment with the personnel director of your spouse's firm.** Ask about possible employment at the new branch (if they don't frown on nepotism). Also request names of reliable employment agencies, search firms, or temporary help services they can recommend.
9. **If you're a relocating spouse, be sure potential employers realize your moving expenses will be borne by your mate's company.** This allows you to compete more fairly with local applicants.
10. **Check first in the hot industries.** These include services, finance, insurance, and real estate (known as FIRE). This is where much of the action is.
11. **Connect with the college placement office.** In addition to having lists of available jobs, they'll also know of any upcoming job fairs. And they can tell you things it would take you weeks to chase down yourself.
12. **Identify the local power brokers.** While many will hold elective office, some are simply respected old-timers who wield unusual clout.
13. **Attend chamber of commerce mixers and meetings of any economic development group.** This is where small-town business leaders network. If you socialize well, chances are you'll meet someone with an opening—or someone who knows about a position coming up.

24 Tips to Enhance Your Chances (continued)

14. **Look for a church affiliation early.** Religious organizations are a wonderful place to harvest job referrals. People will be anxious to help you. They want you to stay and be part of their church family.
15. **Watch for *hidden* opportunities.** Announcements appearing in the newspaper or chamber newsletter about new business developments or personnel changes often flag openings. Read these publications as soon as they're available and act immediately.
16. **Find out where the regulars hang out.** Go there yourself and eavesdrop on what's happening around town.
17. **Consider renting a local post office box and hiring an answering service.** If you're going to be writing or calling companies before arriving in town, make it *easy* for them to respond.
18. **Plan a vacation to check possibilities out personally.** Pound the pavement; it's the only true way to find out what's going on.
19. **Study the Yellow Pages for leads.** If it isn't clear what a business does, call and ask.
20. **Tap into any personal information network you've developed.** Ask for help from your real estate salesperson, insurance agent, lawyer, banker, etc.
21. **Respond to all possible ads.** That gets you in the door. If you don't qualify for this position, perhaps you can convince them to create a spot where your skills *will* be useful.
22. **If the town is large enough to have them, register with employment agencies and temporary help firms.** Working as a temp is an excellent way to check out potential employers, pick up gossip about jobs coming up, and showcase your talents.
23. **Notice if the local newspaper does a column on "new faces" or something similar.** If so, send in a black-and-white photo and a brief profile stressing your professional abilities.
24. **Take *something*, even if it isn't your ideal.** This eases the pressure and will give you a chance to get acquainted and look around while having a salary coming in.

Start by calling the area better business bureau. If there are a lot of unresolved consumer complaints, you'd better believe they won't be pleasant to work for! The BBB frequently has company histories on file that show the date of incorporation, who the owners are, and basically what the company does.

If your interview didn't give you this opportunity, finagle a first-hand look at the company in operation. Deliver something. Seek directions. Make every second count while you're on the premises. What image is projected? Is the atmosphere conservative or progressive? Cluttered or organized? Informal or rigid? Are there plaques or awards on the walls that give clues about their reputation or sense of pride? What reading materials are in the lobby? Of particular note is how employees relate to each other—and you! Ask yourself if this is an environment in which you could flourish.

Also check the largest area library. There may be annual reports on file, newspaper articles about their accomplishments or indiscretions, even copies of their promotional literature. Look up the owner or manager in various who's who directories, especially regional ones like *Who's Who in the West*. This often yields intriguing personal information like religious affiliation, alma mater, hobbies, etc. (Of course, doing this research *before* a prime interview will equip you with information for asking the right questions and developing rapport.)

If the firm has a net worth of from $500,000 to $1,000,000, it'll probably be listed in Dun and Bradstreet's *Middle Markets*. Here you'll find out about their main office location, any subsidiaries, names and functions of corporate officers and directors, annual sales volume, number of employees, and their Standard Industrial Classification or SIC.

If the company you're checking out is a public corporation, it must file with the Securities and Exchange Commission (SEC). To see if a company is listed as public and for general and financial information, contact the SEC at 202-942-8088.

You can also verify information through Dun and Bradstreet (D&B). Most bankers will do this for a small fee. Realize this information is primarily financial. While the government can jail people for not telling the truth, D&B has no such leverage. Consequently, the data may be a sanitized version. Very small firms are not usually registered with them.

Review Chapter 9, "Researching for the Right Opportunity," for additional sleuthing ideas. Every employment interview has a double purpose. The company will probably check your qualifications. You owe it to yourself to make sure *they* measure up.

At first all the busyness will keep you occupied. But what happens when that pales? How do you stay professionally challenged? We have lots of ideas to keep you prospering in paradise. They are in the next chapter.

19

◆

Tactics for Staying
Prosperous and Happy

It's one thing to get caught up in the excitement of moving and launching a new business. But what then? Will you continue to be satisfied—or will the bloom fade from the rose? That depends on you. This isn't lifestyles of the rich and aimless. In this chapter, we'll chat about ways to cultivate personal contentment and keep a sense of exhilaration in your life. We'll also share some small-town strategies for developing and keeping your business at a peak.

COMMUNITY INVOLVEMENT:
REACHING OUT, GETTING IN

Community is back. Civic pride, social consciousness, grassroots activism: these are the lifeblood of towns, large and small. This widespread yearning for community is showing up in our popular culture. It's why nostalgic movies and TV programs about small towns have become a national pastime.

If your company can successfully position itself as a leader in community issues, you'll have tapped into one of the best ways to generate mass appeal and made yourself feel better. Fortunately, in rural America it doesn't take mammoth movements. It can be as simple as sponsoring a charity, using recycled paper or biodegradable chemicals, offering a senior-citizen discount, or donating a small percentage of your sales to a worthy cause. Then make sure what you do is *publicized*.

A word-processing firm donates one cent of every dollar it makes to buy computers for a local school. A clothing store gives its outdated, hard-to-move merchandise to a clearinghouse for the needy. A restaurant donates its leftovers and old-dated products to a church that feeds out-of-work families. An attorney does *pro bono* work one day a month.

Doing good is good for business. In deciding where to invest your time and expertise, choose activities that showcase your competence. For instance, if your business is in the financial area, engage in fund-raising or become the treasurer of a prominent organization. This demonstrates to people that you're proficient with money. If you're an artist, perhaps you should be the person to make the eye-catching posters to announce the chamber of commerce's raffle or membership drive. Is promotional writing your forte? See that you spearhead the writing of the new brochure to publicize the local museum. Sharing your talents strengthens the community and helps you become known.

Consider participation in area government. Rural areas have only 25 percent of the population, yet 75 percent of the local government units in the United States. This enhanced opportunity for citizen involvement also implies an increased role for community leadership. Make your voice heard in local politics.

High on this agenda might be preserving your paradise. Encourage efforts to intelligently control development and the environment so you and your neighbors don't lose the very enticements that attracted you. There's a feeling of personal impact when you participate in shaping the destiny of a small town. From being a helpless observer, you progress to being an active contributor. It's a visible, tangible contribution that can put new meaning in your life.

MINGLE MANAGEMENT: THE ART OF NETWORKING

Networking is nothing more than effective interaction with other people. Polished networking skills equal added professional power. Whether you're at an official networking function, attending a conference, or mingling at a large party, knowing how to "work a room" gives you a business edge and makes the event more fun. This means the ability to circulate, meet, converse, then extricate yourself. Lone Eagles, who purposely want to feather a solitary nest, feel the need to interact with others.

Being prepared is half the secret of successful networking. If you can get a list of attendees beforehand, do so. Decide who you particularly want to chat with. Formulate a short, pithy self-introduction. Saying you are John Jones with the Weaverly Company doesn't cut it. But if you introduce yourself as John Jones and continue by explaining, "We help people analyze their financial goals, then guide them to the most practical and lucrative investment," you've given the other person something to go on.

Please have something to say. Listen to the news, read the daily paper, scan news magazines and general interest periodicals. Taking the initiative and asking the other parties how long they have been in the business, what they do, or where they're from originally is fine. But eventually it's going to be your turn to contribute to the conversation. When schmoozing, find new *angles* that take a fresh look at a topic, *bridges* that connect the current subject to a related one, or *catapults* that jump to a new, unrelated issue. Don't monopolize the discussion, however. A good networker has two ears and one mouth and uses them proportionately.

Always take a hefty stack of business cards. Don't worry about brochures or other promotional materials. You only want to exchange cards (preferably by asking for theirs first). You'll mail other materials as a follow-up procedure. Eat before you go. It's impossible to greet people and converse with a drink in one hand and hors d'oeuvres in the other—and in your mouth.

If you're especially shy, consider volunteering to serve on the welcoming committee. Then you have a "role," a purpose for being friendly. One woman we know considers herself an unofficial hostess at every function she attends. Instead of hanging back and feeling self-conscious, she is proactive and treats people as if they were guests in her home. Another hint is to arrive early and get acquainted with a few people. Then when the room fills up, you won't feel alienated by the crowd.

What if you want to meet and greet people who are already engaged in a discussion? It's not easy to break uninvited into a group. One way is to move physically into their space. Once they notice you, move back slightly. Another approach is to ask permission. You might say, "Excuse me. I'm interested in what you're talking about. May I introduce myself?" Repeat each name as it's said and shake hands firmly.

We've all been in the situation where somebody has captured us and doesn't want to let go. One way to handle this is to say, "Well, it's been great talking to you. I see someone across the room I need to connect with." Then leave. Pronto.

When you want a person's card, simply ask for it. Jot a few notes on the back so you can recall his or her needs and pertinent details later. Be sure to follow up promptly with a call or mailing of materials. When you promise something, do it. By keeping your commitments you prove your reliability and begin to establish rapport.

Suppose you're attending a meeting, workshop, or conference. Where you sit will determine your networking success. Don't plop down next to an associate or friend. You already know that person. Choose an empty chair between two strangers. If you're really serious about networking, change seats at the break to meet more new people.

Actual network clubs flourish in larger cities. The purpose of these organizations is to swap leads. They are also starting to sprout in Small Town USA. In Kalispell, Montana (population 11,000), about 30 local businesspeople meet every week and generate business for each other. Such a club can help you prosper in several ways: Other club members become customers; links are forged and members' friends and clients become your clients; and contact spheres or networking teams evolve. These are noncompetitive businesses that are looking for the same kind of leads you are.

As in life, so in networking, givers get. If you want to manage your mingling successfully, remember this principle.

GROWING YOUR BUSINESS

Ask yourself, "What business am I really in?" Sure you offer goods or services. But that isn't the business you're in. Sound crazy? Read on. The publishers of this book, for example, aren't in the publishing business—they're in the information delivery business. A neighborhood food store may well be in the convenience business. They might decide to make it easier for customers to shop for items besides food: videos to rent or inexpensive gift items. The store might even consider a delivery service. Get the idea?

If you buy an established store, be sure to make any changes gradually. One of the primary reasons for purchasing an existing business is that you inherit a proven customer base. If you change everything right away, these people's loyalty may falter. Tom and Carole Reamer left suburban New Jersey for Spencertown, a hamlet that appeals to weekend escapees from Manhattan. The Reamers bought an old-fashioned country store. Their challenge was to maintain a delicate balance of keeping the locals satisfied while attracting weekenders.

To increase profits, they got rid of the gas pumps. They were a lot of trouble and the insurance was expensive. Next they stopped selling fresh meat; they couldn't compete with a nearby supermarket. While they now stock limited groceries and produce, you can find a variety of other items at their store. If you need anything from a toothbrush to a toilet plunger, this is the place. To satisfy the broader taste of their citified clientele, they added goat cheese, bottled spring water, imported beer, blended coffees, and other gourmet items. To keep locals happy, however, there's still a pour-your-own coffee counter and deli.

Perhaps the most lucrative innovation was adding their own home-baked goods. They bake their own breads, cakes, pies, and cookies. This went over so well, they began making prepared entrees—lasagna, chicken divan, curried beef, chicken pies—which appeal both to vacationers and the townsfolk. The Reamers make a comfortable living. Carole comments, "We don't need as much money here, and we certainly enjoy ourselves more. Besides, you can't put a money value on lifestyle."

Some people forget why they moved to the country and get all caught up in beating the opposition. Do you know the dirty 11-letter word? It's *competition*. When you focus on the competition it detracts from your optimum performance. It places the emphasis on aspects outside of your control. We recommend you compete with *yourself*, rather than others. This challenges you to excel: to be more energetic, more innovative, more service oriented. It focuses your attention on the customer instead of the competitor.

Think of you and your customers or clients as being a privileged partnership. In return for their trust and patronage, they are entitled to the best you can give. According to the U.S. Office of Consumer Affairs, between 37 and 45 percent of people are unhappy with the service they receive. But they don't complain—they simply go elsewhere. Ouch!

Different people want to be served in different ways. Age plays a major role in how they look at service. Mature folks care more about courtesy, security, and how well a professional (such as a doctor, dentist, or attorney) knows them. Middle-aged people want reliability, competence, and access. They look for convenient hours and easy accessibility both physically and by phone. While retirees can take their time shopping, wage earners seek convenience. They buy in a hurry. Young folks look for cheaper prices and in-vogue items.

If you run a retail establishment, it will be feast or famine. During those feast times—when there's an abundance of *them* and too little of *you*—handle it with tact. If you acknowledge people right away, they are usually willing to wait. They see how busy you are. Greet each person with something like: "Good to see you. I'll help you find just what you're looking for (or take your order) as soon as I'm finished with this customer. Thanks for your patience."

Capture names, addresses, and phone numbers of customers. Get an attractive guest book and encourage each to sign it for advance notice of special sales, products, announcements, or new courses being offered. Or jot down the information off their checks. On credit card orders, simply ask for the details.

> Marilyn: When I worked in women's ready-to-wear, I made this part of the sales receipt procedure. Then during slow times, I'd write them a personalized postcard saying something about the item they bought and thanking them for their business. I got lots of positive feedback. Hardly anybody does this. It makes people feel valued.
>
> I also set up a file card system by name, size, and personal preference. When we'd get in a shipment with something that "looked like them," I'd pick up the phone and alert customers about the new item. This really helped build sales.

Developing your own mailing list and putting it into a database is an astute business procedure. You might cull only the most promising customers for a personalized mailing, or go to the whole list to announce something special. You can use mailings to build store traffic, generate goodwill, introduce new items, or ask for referrals.

Profits are waiting for those who nurture their patrons and buy properly. A secret in retail is to keep your inventory lean. Record what you have in stock, then rank items by how fast they move. Get rid of the losers. Check with your trade association to see how many times a year your inventory should turn over. Be sure you don't lag behind the norm. Cut better deals on your purchases by keeping an eye out for discounts. And if you have a lot of merchandise shipped in, consider making your own freight-hauling arrangements and pocketing the volume discount, rather than relying on your suppliers for shipping. When sales slump, remember what acclaimed TV minister Dr. Robert Schuller says: "Tough times never last; tough people do."

OUTSMARTING THE ISOLATION FACTOR

You're only as isolated as you want to be. There are always activities going on, you just have to find them. True, they will be different forms of entertainment than you were used to in the city. But wasn't escaping sophisticated suburbia one of the reasons you moved?

Before writing this chapter, we polled our employees—most of whom have come here from other places—for their ideas on overcoming isolation. Their advice was that being friendly and outgoing opens all doors. Have pleasant conversations with everyone you meet: the service station attendant, bank teller, grocery store cashier. Check out local organizations and clubs that relate to something you like to do. A new face and willing hands are always welcome. Most rural areas have a shortage of people amenable to helping. Join up and jump in! Get on a committee or volunteer for an office right away. Being just a member never gives you as much of an opportunity to get acquainted as does working in small groups. And anything you do socially will also help your business to get known and moving.

Scour the local newspaper for activities. Look not only at the articles, but also at the regular ads, the classifieds, and the "what's happening" section. Read posters and bulletin boards around town to keep up. Attend chamber mixers, potlucks sponsored by service groups, and school performances. If you have children, get involved in the PTA and acquainted with playmates' parents.

For many families, a spiritual connection is the perfect antidote for feelings of isolation. Check the Yellow Pages for churches and synagogues. Visit some and decide which you feel most comfortable with. Sports is another ideal icebreaker. Is there a softball team, snowmobile club, or hiking group you might join?

And don't forget the folks back home. Sending and receiving letters keeps you feeling connected. E-mail is an easy way to have daily contact. Keep pictures of loved ones and friends where you can see them. Spend a few minutes each week in silent, *heartwarming* communion with each of these people. Further keep them in your life by clipping articles and cartoons you see that you know would appeal to them. Drop these items in the mail as a spontaneous "thinking of you" gesture. They may even start reciprocating.

Loneliness is an attitude. It's a negative force that weakens your motivation, stifles your productivity, and squelches your joy. It is combated by positive expectations and specific acts. Having an upbeat outlook and taking action to help you get acquainted provides the cure. Loyal friendships don't happen overnight. It takes time and nurturing to develop these relationships. Give yourself permission to take the time needed to pursue this camaraderie. As the saying goes, "To make a friend you must first be one."

REMAINING MENTALLY STIMULATED

To help you stay sharp, consider getting a brainstorming buddy. Asking for another opinion from a planning partner—especially someone with a different or broader perspective—can prove very rewarding. Approach someone in church or in the community whom you like and respect. Suggest you get together a couple of times a month to share ideas.

Teaching is another method for staying sharp. Whenever we give a seminar, we also learn. As you develop lesson plans or workshop outlines, you automatically hone your own skills. And the questions students sometimes pose—wow! They push you to the outer limits of your own experience and expertise. Opportunities exist in Small Town USA for teaching at community colleges as well as setting up informal classes in your home or a public building. And don't overlook *taking* courses yourself. While the offerings won't be as diversified as they were in the city, there's probably something to interest you. This is another excellent way to meet potential friends.

Subscribe to—and *read*—at least one industry trade journal. This will help you keep up with what is going on in your field. You may want to read the *Wall Street Journal*. If you can't spend the money for a subscription, read it at your local library or online. Use the library in other ways: to take in the latest bestsellers, read general interest magazines, surf the Internet, or join a book discussion group.

Mental stimulation can go in other directions too. Find out about this new land you've claimed as your own. Roam around the back country. Explore! Discover ghost towns, trails, and nature sanctuaries. Seek historical spots. Visit neighboring towns. If you've never been camping, find friends who have and go with them. Buy a birdfeeder and learn the names of new birds. Enjoy the gift of nature that surrounds you.

Perhaps you have an interest you think others would share, but there is no existing group for these people. Start one! Ideas run the gamut from a Great Books discussion group to a Toastmasters club, from a race-walking group to a TOPS club. Put a classified ad in the paper, ask the editor to run a short story introducing your idea, and create flyers to place at strategic places interested people might frequent.

STAYING ABREAST OF YOUR INDUSTRY

Remaining knowledgeable about your industry is more challenging when you live in the country. Eleanor Perry-Harrington tells the story of how she had a small gift shop in a town of 2,000 in Kansas. "I loved it and was settling in nicely. Fortunately, I was invited to go to the gift show in Dallas after awhile," she relates. "There was another world out there. I realized I had gotten into a rut and stagnated. I was jarred back to reality. After that, I made it a point to get out every six months to see what was going on in the big cities."

A hairstylist here in Buena Vista told us of going into Denver each quarter to attend a networking club where salon owners bring their problems. As a first-time businessman, he learned about hiring, taxes, motivating employees, and marketing. He also regularly attends hair shows and educational events sponsored by hair care product manufacturers. When in the city, he stops in and gets acquainted with hairstylists to swap tips and keep in the know about current trends.

We would be remiss if we didn't again point to the Internet as a wonderful tool for keeping up to date. New friends and business colleagues await you online. You can harness top-notch brainpower in your field from all over the world with a little investment of surfing time.

Now that you know how to stay prosperous and happy in the country, take a look at the specific resources we've collected for you in Part Three. We've tried to think about your needs and provide contact points.

Afterword

◆

Thanks for sharing this journey with us. We hope our efforts will make your trip easier, safer, and happier. Writing this book has been sometimes frustrating, usually exhilarating, always probing for us. We've laid our souls bare, sharing what works (easy)—and what doesn't (not so easy).

We're always interested in hearing from our readers. What did you like best about *County Bound!?* How can we improve the next edition? Tell us about your needs, expectations, and experiences.

We are professional speakers who love to share our vision of Countrypreneuring with corporations, associations, government agencies, and private groups. Contact us at the address below about seminars. And naturally we hope you'll want another copy or two as gifts for friends, associates, or loved ones who want to escape the rat race, put down roots, and celebrate a new sense of community.

As you switch from the fast track to a country lane, our wish for you is an easy move, a stress-free transition, and a life changed from endurance to empowerment!

Marilyn and Tom Ross
POB 909-CB, Buena Vista, CO 81211
phone: 719-395-8659, fax: 719-395-8374
e-mail: MarilynRoss@SPANnet.org

PART THREE

---◆---

Resources to Ease Your Relocation and Strengthen Your Business

State Tourism Offices
and Chambers of Commerce

To aid you in your quest for information, below are the state tourism offices and the chambers of commerce for each state. If no statewide chamber exists, the group serving the state's largest city is listed.

Alabama

State Tourism Office
401 Adams Avenue, Suite 126
Montgomery, AL 36104
800-252-2262

Business Council of Alabama
2 N. Jackson Street
Montgomery, AL 36101-0076
334-834-6000

Alaska

State Tourism Office
P.O. Box 110801
Juneau, AK 99811-0801
907-465-2010

State Chamber of Commerce
217 2nd Street, Suite 201
Juneau, AK 99801-1267
907-586-2323

Arizona

State Tourism Office
2702 N. 3rd Street, Suite 4015
Phoenix, AZ 85004
602-230-7733

Chamber of Commerce
1221 E. Osborn Road
Phoenix, AZ 85014-5539
602-248-9172

Arkansas

State Tourism Office
1 Capitol Mall, Dept. 7701
Little Rock, AR 72201
800-643-8383

State Chamber of Commerce
410 S. Cross Street
Little Rock, AR 72203-3645
501-374-9225

California

State Tourism Office
P.O. Box 1499
Sacramento, CA 95812
800-862-2543

Chamber of Commerce
1201 K Street, 12th Floor
Sacramento, CA 95814
916-444-6670

Colorado

State Tourism Office
225 W. Colfax
Denver, CO 80202
800-433-2656

Association of Commerce and
   Industry
1776 Lincoln Street, Suite 1200
Denver, CO 80203-1029
303-831-7411

Connecticut

State Tourism Office
865 Brook Street
Rocky Hill, CT 06067
203-258-4289

Business and Industry Association
370 Asylum Street, 5th Floor
Hartford, CT 06103-2025
860-244-1900

Delaware

State Tourism Office
99 Kings Highway, P.O. Box 1401
Dover, DE 19903
800-441-8846

State Chamber of Commerce
1201 N. Orange Street, Suite 200
Wilmington, DE 19899
302-655-7221

Florida

State Tourism Office
126 W. Van Buren Street
Tallahassee, FL 32399
904-487-1462

State Chamber of Commerce
136 S. Bronough Street
Tallahassee, FL 32302
904-425-1200

Georgia

State Tourism Office
P.O. Box 1776
Atlanta, GA 30301
800-847-4842

State Chamber of Commerce
233 Peachtree Street NE, Suite 200
Atlanta, GA 30303
404-223-2264

Hawaii

State Tourism Office
Empire State Building
350 5th Avenue, Suite 1827
New York, NY 10118
800-353-5846

Chamber of Commerce
1132 Bishop Street, #200
Honolulu, HI 96813-4897
808-545-4309

Idaho

State Tourism Office
700 W. State Street
Boise, ID 83720
800-635-7820

Association of Commerce and
  Industry
802 W. Bannock Street, Suite 308
Boise, ID 83701
208-343-1849

Illinois

State Chamber of Commerce
620 E. Adams
Springfield, IL 62701
800-223-0121

State Tourism Office
311 S. Wacker Drive, Suite 1500
Chicago, IL 60606-6619
312-983-7100

Indiana

State Tourism Office
1 N. Capitol, Suite 700
Indianapolis, IN 46204
800-289-6646

State Chamber of Commerce
1 N. Capitol Avenue, Suite 200
Indianapolis, IN 46204-2248
317-634-3110

Iowa

State Tourism Office
200 E. Grand Avenue, TIA
Des Moines, IA 50309
800-345-4692

Association of Business and
  Industry
904 Walnut, Suite 100
Des Moines, IA 50309-3503
515-280-8000

Kansas

State Tourism Office
700 SW Harrison Street, Suite 1300
Topeka, KS 66603-3702
800-252-6727

Chamber of Commerce and
  Industry
835 SW Topeka Blvd.
Topeka, KS 66612
913-357-6321

Kentucky

State Tourism Office
2200 Capitol Plaza Tower,
   Dept. DA
Frankfort, KY 40601
800-225-8747

Chamber of Commerce
464 Chenault Road
Frankfort, KY 40602
502-695-4700

Louisiana

State Tourism Office
P.O. Box 94291
Baton Rouge, LA 70804-9291
800-334-8626

Association of Business and
  Industry
P.O. Box 80258
Baton Rouge, LA 70898-0258
504-928-5388

Maine

State Tourism Office
P.O. Box 2300, Dept. DA
Hallowell, ME 04347-2300
800-533-9595

Chamber and Business Alliance
7 Community Drive
Augusta, ME 04330-9412
207-623-4568

Maryland

State Tourism Office
217 E. Redwood Street
Baltimore, MD 21202
800-543-1036

Chamber of Commerce
60 West Street, Suite 100
Annapolis, MD 21401
410-269-0642

Massachusetts

State Tourism Office
100 Cambridge Street
Boston, MA 02202
800-447-6277

Association of Chamber of
    Commerce Executives
c/o Waltham West Suburban
    Chamber of Commerce
One Moody Street, Suite 301
Waltham, MA 02154-5521
617-894-4700

Michigan

State Chamber of Commerce
600 S. Walnut Street
Lansing, MI 48933
517-371-2100

State Tourism Office
P.O. Box 30226
Lansing, MI 48909-7726
517-373-0670

Minnesota

State Tourism Office
100 Metro Square, 121 7th Place E
St. Paul, MN 55101
800-657-3700

Chamber of Commerce
30 E. 7th Street, Suite 1700
St. Paul, MN 55101
612-292-4650

Mississippi

State Tourism Office
P.O. Box 1705
Oceanspray, MS 39566-1705
800-647-2290

Economic Council
P.O. Box 23276
Jackson, MS 39225-3276
601-353-0247

Missouri

State Tourism Office
P.O. Box 1055
Jefferson, MO 65102
314-751-4133

State Chamber of Commerce
P.O. Box 149
Jefferson City, MO 65102
314-634-3511

Montana

State Tourism Office
1424 9th Avenue
Helena, MT 59620
800-541-1447

Chamber of Commerce
2030 11th Avenue
Helena, MT 59624
406-442-2405

Nebraska

State Tourism Office
P.O. Box 94666
Lincoln, NE 68509
800-228-4307

Chamber of Commerce and
   Industry
1320 Lincoln Mall
Lincoln, NE 68508
402-474-4422

Nevada

State Tourism Office
Capitol Complex
Carson City, NV 89710
800-237-0774

State Chamber of Commerce
P.O. Box 3499
Reno, NV 89505-3499
702-686-3030

New Hampshire

State Tourism Office
P.O. Box 1856
Concord, NH 03302-1856
603-271-2666

Business and Industry Association
122 N. Main Street, 3rd Floor
Concord, NH 03301
603-224-5388

New Jersey

State Tourism Office
20 W. State Street, CN 826
Trenton, NJ 08625
800-JERSEY-7 (800-537-7397)

State Chamber of Commerce
50 W. State Street, Suite 1310
Trenton, NJ 08608
609-989-7888

New Mexico

State Tourism Office
491 Old Santa Fe Trail
Santa Fe, NM 87503
800-545-2040

Association of Commerce and
   Industry of New Mexico
2309 Renard Place SE, Suite 402
Albuquerque, NM 87106
505-842-0644

New York

State Tourism Office
633 3rd Avenue
New York, NY 10017
800-225-5697

Business Council of New York
  State
152 Washington Avenue
Albany, NY 12210
518-465-7511

North Carolina

State Tourism Office
430 N. Salisbury Street, Dept. 867
Raleigh, NC 27603
800-847-4862

Citizens for Business and Industry
225 Hillsborough Street, Suite 460
Raleigh, NC 27602
919-828-0758

North Dakota

State Tourism Office
Liberty Memorial Building,
  604 East Boulevard
Bismarck, ND 58505
800-437-2077

Greater North Dakota Association
2000 Schafer Street
Bismarck, ND 58502
701-222-0929

Ohio

State Tourism Office
P.O. Box 1001
Columbus, OH 43266-0101
800-282-5393

State Chamber of Commerce
P.O. Box 15159
Columbus, OH 43210-0159
614-228-4201

Oklahoma

State Tourism Office
Marketing Services Division
2401 N. Lincoln Boulevard,
  Room 505
Oklahoma City, OK 73105
800-652-6552

State Chamber of Commerce and
  Industry
330 NE 10th Street
Oklahoma City, OK 73104-3200
405-235-3669

Oregon

State Tourism Office
775 Summer Street NE
Salem, OR 97310
800-547-7842

Association of Oregon Industries,
  Inc.
1149 Court Street NE
Salem, OR 97309
503-588-0050

Pennsylvania

State Tourism Office
453 Forum Building, Dept. PR 901
Harrisburg, PA 17120
800-847-4872

Chamber of Business and Industry
417 Walnut Street
Harrisburg, PA 17101
717-255-3252

Rhode Island

State Tourism Office
1 Exchange Street
Providence, RI 02903
800-556-2484

Greater Providence Chamber of
Commerce
30 Exchange Terrace
Providence, RI 02903-1793
401-521-5000

South Carolina

State Tourism Office
P.O. Box 71
Columbia, SC 29202
803-734-0122

Chamber of Commerce
1201 Main Street, Suite 1810
Columbia, SC 29201-3254
803-799-4601

South Dakota

State Tourism Office
700 E. Wells Avenue
Pierre, SD 57501
800-832-5682

Industry and Commerce
Association of South Dakota
P.O. Box 190
Pierre, SD 57501-0190
605-224-6161

Tennessee

State Tourism Office
P.O. Box 23170
Nashville, TN 37202
800-847-4886

Tennessee Association of Business
611 Commerce Street, Suite 3030
Nashville, TN 37203-3742
615-256-5141

Texas

State Tourism Office
P.O. Box 12728
Austin, TX 78711
800-888-8839

State Association of Business and
Chambers of Commerce
1209 Nucces Street
Austin, TX 78701
512-477-6721

Utah

State Tourism Office
Council Hall, Capitol Hill
Salt Lake City, UT 84114
801-538-1030

State Chamber of Commerce
Association
P.O. Box 6022
Salt Lake City, UT 84106
801-467-0844

Vermont

State Tourism Office
134 State Street
Montpelier, VT 05602
800-837-6668

Chamber of Commerce
P.O. Box 37
Montpelier, VT 05601
802-223-3443

Virginia

State Tourism Office
901 E. Byrd Street
Richmond, VA 23219
800-847-4882

Chamber of Commerce
9 S. 5th Street
Richmond, VA 23219-3823
804-644-1607

Washington

State Tourism Office
P.O. Box 42500
Olympia, WA 98504-2500
800-544-1800

Assn. of Washington Business
1414 S. Cherry Street
Olympia, WA 98501
360-943-1600

Washington, DC

State Tourism Office
1212 New York Avenue, 885 TD
Washington, DC 20005
202-789-7000

Chamber of Commerce
1615 H Street NW
Washington, DC 20062
202-463-5580

West Virginia

State Tourism Office
1900 Kanaha Blvd., Building 6,
    Room B-564
East Charleston, WV 25305
800-225-5982

Chamber of Commerce
1314 Virginia Street East
East Charleston, WV 25330
304-342-1115

Wisconsin

State Tourism Office
P.O. Box 7970
Madison, WI 53707
800-432-8747

Manufacturers and Commerce
501 E. Washington Avenue
Madison, WI 53701-0352
608-258-3400

Wyoming

State Tourism Office
I-25 at College Drive
Cheyenne, WY 82002
800-225-5996

Greater Cheyenne Chamber of
    Commerce
301 W. 16th Street
Cheyenne, WY 82001-4437
307-638-3388

Government Sources

BUSINESS AND COMMERCE

To aid you in finding the answers to questions—or discovering questions you didn't even know you had—we've put together this meaty resource section on business and commerce. It contains references to many government agencies and helpful details about the small business administration.

Department of Commerce
14th and Constitution Avenue NW
Washington, DC 20230
202-482-2000

> **Patent and Trademark Office**
> Washington, DC 20231
> 703-308-4357

> **Bureau of Economic Analysis**
> 1401 K Street NW
> Tower Building, Room 705
> Washington, DC 20230
> 202-606-9900

> **International Trade
>   Administration**
> 14th and Constitution Avenue
>   NW, Room 3850
> Washington, DC 20230
> 202-482-2867

Office of Business Liaison
14th and Constitution Avenue NW
Washington, DC 20230
202-482-3942

Library
U.S. Department of Commerce
14th and Constitution Avenue NW
Washington, DC 20230
202-482-5511

Bureau of the Census
Washington, DC 20233
> Public Information Office
>   301-457-2800
> Data User Services Division and
>   Publications
>   301-457-4100

**Minority Business
  Development Agency**
14th and Constitution Avenue NW,
  Room 6707
Washington, DC 20230
202-482-4547

Atlanta Regional Office
401 Peachtree Street NW,
  Suite 1715
Atlanta, GA 30308-3516
404-730-3300

Chicago Regional Office
55 East Monroe Street, Suite 1406
Chicago, IL 60603
312-353-0182

Dallas Regional Office
1100 Commerce Street, Suite 7B-
  23
Dallas, TX 75242
214-767-8001

New York Regional Office
26 Federal Plaza, Room 3720
New York, NY 10279
212-264-3262

San Francisco Regional Office
221 Main Street, Suite 1280
San Francisco, CA 94105
415-744-3001

Department of Labor
200 Constitution Avenue NW
Washington, DC 20210
202-219-6666

Bureau of Labor Statistics
2 Massachusetts Avenue
Washington, DC 20212
202-606-7828

**Government Contracts for Small
  Business**
Office of Small and Disadvantaged
  Business Utilization
Department of Labor
200 Constitution Avenue NW,
  Room S1004
Washington, DC 20210

OTHER GOVERNMENT AGENCIES

**Chamber of Commerce of the
  United States**
1615 H Street NW
Washington, DC 20062
301-468-5128

Library of Congress
101 Independence Avenue SE
Washington, DC 20540
202-707-2905

U.S. Copyright Office
Library of Congress
Washington, DC 20559
202-707-3000

Internal Revenue Service (IRS)
1111 Constitution Avenue NW
Washington, DC 20224
800-829-1040

Federal Information Center
U.S. General Services
   Administration
P.O. Box 600
Cumberland, MD 21501-0600
800-688-9889

**EPA Small Business
   Clearinghouse Hotline**
Environmental Protection Agency
401 M Street SW
Washington, DC 20460
800-368-5888/703-305-5938

Office of Advocacy
U.S. Small Business
   Administration
409 3rd Street SW, 7th Floor
Washington, DC 20416
202-205-6533

**National Telecommunications
   and Information
   Administration**
Department of Commerce
14th and Constitution Avenue NW
Room 6043
Washington, DC 20230
202-482-2048

**Senate Committee on Small
   Business**
Suite SR-428A
Russell Senate Office Building
Washington, DC 20510-6350
202-224-5175

**House Committee on Small
   Business**
2361 Rayburn House Office
   Building
Washington, DC 20515-6315
202-225-5821

**Federal Communications
   Commission (FCC)**
1919 M Street NW
Washington, DC 20554
202-632-7000

Federal Trade Commission (FTC)
Pennsylvania Avenue and 6th
   Street NW
Washington, DC 20580
202-326-2222

**Interstate Commerce
   Commission**
12th and Constitution Avenue NW
Washington, DC 20423
202-927-7600

SMALL BUSINESS ADMINISTRATION (SBA)

The U.S. Small Business Administration is the primary source of federal government assistance to small businesses. It provides financial help through loans and loan guarantee programs, distributes publications, holds workshops, and offers management assistance and counseling through its various entities. For the local SBA office, see the blue government pages of your phone book or call 800-827-5722.

U.S. Small Business Administration
409 3rd Street SW, Washington, DC 20416
202-205-6605 or 800-827-5722
home page: http://www.sba.gov

Answer Desk Hotline.   Call 800-UASK-SBA (827-5722) for additional resources and recorded information on myriad topics.

Small Business Development Centers (SBDCs).   These centers are organized in all 50 states and typically operate on college campuses. About 600 locations dispense small business counseling in the areas of finance, marketing, technical, and other advice. SBDCs are aimed primarily at start-ups. To find one, contact your local SBA office.

Service Corps of Retired Executives (SCORE).   SCORE is a network of 12,000 retired business executives and professionals who volunteer to help small businesspeople with virtually any problem. Advice is offered on a spot basis or continuing indefinitely. SCORE also sponsors low-cost business management seminars. To locate the office nearest you, call the district SBA office.

Business Information Centers (BICs).   Maintained by the SBA, these centers provide state-of-the-art computers, graphic workstations, CD-ROM technology, and interactive videos for accessing market research databases, planning and spreadsheet software, and a vast library of information. With the BIC library and software, you can craft your own business and marketing plans. BICs are available in SBA district offices.

Regional Offices (SBA)

The SBA has field offices comprised of regional offices, district offices, branch offices, post-of-duty offices, and disaster area offices. Whew! The country has been divided into ten regions, each of which is served by an SBA regional office. Contact the one nearest you for guidance on how to reach the district office. This is the ideal contact point for loan information and management assistance.

Region I
10 Causeway Street, 8th Floor
Boston, MA 02222-1093
617-656-8415

Region II
26 Federal Plaza, Room 31-08
New York, NY 10278
212-264-1450

Region III
Allendale Square, Suite 201
475 Allendale Road
King of Prussia, PA 19406
610-962-3710

Region IV
1720 Peachtree Street NW,
   Suite 496
South Tower
Atlanta, GA 30367-8102
404-347-4999

Region V
300 S. Riverside Plaza, Suite 1975S
Chicago, IL 60606-6617
312-353-5000

Region VI
4300 Amon Carter Boulevard,
   Suite 108
Fort Worth, TX 76155
817-885-6581

Region VII
323 W. 8th Street, Suite 307
Kansas City, MO 64106
816-374-6380

Region VIII
721 19th Street, Suite 400
Denver, CO 80202-2599
303-844-0500

Region IX
455 Market Street, Suite 2200
San Francisco, CA 94105
415-744-2118

Region X
Park Place Building
1200 6th Avenue, Suite 1805
Seattle, WA 98101-1128
206-553-2872

MONEY LENDING AND REAL ESTATE PROPERTY SOURCES

There are numerous sources for obtaining funds and bargain real estate through the U.S. Government. Here is seldom-seen information to help you in this quest.

Federal Deposit Insurance Corporation (FDIC)
Division of Liquidation Offices
Regional and Consolidated Offices

Main Office
Federal Deposit Insurance
  Corporation
550 17th Steet, NW
Washington, DC 20429
(202) 393-8400

Western Office
Federal Deposit Insurance
  Corporation
J-627A-60, P.O. Box 7549
Newport Beach, CA 92658-7549
714-263-7100

Southwest Office
Federal Deposit Insurance
  Corporation
5080 Spectrum
Dallas, TX 75248
214-991-0039

Northeast Office
Federal Deposit Insurance
  Corporation
111 E. River Drive
East Hartford, CT 06108
860-291-4000

Southeast Office
Federal Deposit Insurance
  Corporation
1201 W. Peachtree Street,
  Suite 1800
Atlanta, GA 30309
404-817-2500

Midwest Office
Federal Deposit Insurance
  Corporation
500 W. Monroe
Chicago, IL
312-382-6000

More Real Estate Possibilities

Rural Development
Single Family Housing Division
1400 Independence Avenue SW
MS 0783
Washington, DC 20250
202-720-1474

**Property Management Sales
  Listing**
Department of Veteran Affairs
1120 Vermont Avenue NW
Washington, DC 20421
202-273-5400
Property Management Info Line:
202-418-4270, ext 3338
http://www.onpoint.com/
  vahomes

Federal Grants and Loans

**Economic Development
  Administration**
Public Affairs Office
Washington, DC
202-482-5112
Small business loans for people
  who live in an economically
  depressed area.

Office of Disaster Assistance
Small Business Administration
409 3rd Street SW
Washington, DC 20416
202-205-6734 or 800-488-5323

Inquire at the Office of Disaster Assistance about the two types of disaster loans available from the SBA. "Physical disaster loans" are a primary source of funding for permanent rebuilding and replacement of uninsured disaster damages to privately owned property. "Economic injury disaster loans" provide necessary working capital until normal operations resume after a physical disaster.

Rural Communities Financial Assistance
Farmers Home Administration (FmHA)
U.S. Department of Agriculture
Washington, DC 20250
202-720-4323
Rural development loans and grants for nonfarming purposes.

MISCELLANEOUS INFORMATION

You'll find data here from agriculture to energy, geography to climate, health to human services. There's even a catch-all section of various sources that defy categorization.

Agriculture

Department of Agriculture
14th and Independence
  Avenue SW
Washington, DC 20250
202-720-2791

**National Agricultural Statistics
  Service**
State Statistical Division
14th and Independence
  Avenue SW
South Building, Room 4143
Washington, DC 20250
202-720-3878

Rural Information Center (RIC)
National Agricultural Library,
   Room 304
Beltsville, MD 20705
800-633-7701

**Appropriate Technology Transfer
   for Rural Areas (ATTRA)**
P.O. Box 3657
Fayetteville, AR 72702
800-346-9140 or 501-442-9824

ATTRA falls under the umbrella of the USDA. It specializes in informing farmers, those interested in getting into farming, and agriculture professionals about sustainable agriculture for a cleaner environment and improved profits. Specializing in rural areas, they have resources on a large variety of topics and can search electronic databases or refer you to experts. Free help for everything from truck farming, to raising earthworms, to animal husbandry.

Energy

Department of Energy
1000 Independence Avenue SW
Washington, DC 20585
202-586-6827

**National Energy Information
   Center**
1000 Independence Avenue SW,
   Room 1F-048
Washington, DC 20585-0001
202-586-8800

Geography and Climate

Department of the Interior
1849 C Street NW
Washington, DC 20240
202-208-3100

Bureau of Land Management
1849 C Street NW, Room 5660
Washington, DC 20240
202-208-3801

Geological Survey
1849 C Street NW, MS-2646
Washington, DC 20240
202-208-3888

National Park Service
1849 C Street NW, Room 3424
Washington, DC 20240
202-208-7394

**National Earthquake Information
   Center**
Box 25046, MS 966
Denver Federal Center
Denver, CO 80225
800-525-7848

**National Flood Insurance
   Program**
P.O. Box 159
Lanham, MD 20706
800-638-6620

U.S. Geological Survey—
National Water Information
Clearinghouse
12201 Sunrise Valley Drive
Reston, VA 22092
800-426-9000

U.S. Geological Survey—
Geologic Inquiries Group
12201 Sunrise Valley Drive
Reston, VA 22092
703-648-4383

Coastal Engineering Research
Center
U.S. Army Corps of Engineers
3909 Halls Ferry Road
Vicksburg, MS 39180-6199
601-634-2000

Landslide Information Center
U.S. Geological Survey
MS 966, Box 25046
Denver Federal Center
Denver, CO 80225
303-273-8586 or 800-654-4966
http://geohazards.CR.USGS.gov

National Climatic Data Center
151 Patton Avenue, Room 120
Federal Building
Asheville, NC 28801-5001
704-271-4800

Natural Resources Center
Department of Environmental
Protection
79 Elm Street
Hartford, CT 06106
860-424-3540

Environmental Protection
Agency (EPA)
Public Information Center
401 M Street SW
Washington, DC 20460
202-260-2080

Publications Clearinghouse
Environmental Protection Agency
P.O. Box 42419
Cincinnati, OH 45242
513-489-8190

NCAR Outreach Program
National Center for Atmospheric
Research
P.O. Box 3000
Boulder, CO 80307-3000
303-497-1174 or 303-497-8601

Forest Service
U.S. Department of Agriculture
P.O. Box 96090
Washington, DC 20090-6690
202-205-1760

Hydrologic Information Unit
U.S. Geological Survey
419 National Center
Reston, VA 22092

Health and Human Services

Department of Health and Human Services
200 Independence Avenue SW
Washington, DC 20201
202-619-0257

National Center for Health Statistics
6525 Belcrest Road
Hyattsville, MD 20782
301-436-8500

Health Care Financing Administration
7500 Security Boulevard
Baltimore, MD 21207-5187
410-786-3691

Various Helps

Last Resort Interlibrary Loan
NH Reference Service
Library of Congress
Washington, DC 20540-4720
202-707-5522/Fax 202-707-1389

Uniform Crime Reports
Superintendent of Documents
Government Printing Office
Washington, DC 20401
202-512-1800

Shopping by Mail
Federal Trade Commission
Marketing Practices
6th and Pennsylvania Avenue NW
Washington, DC 20580
202-326-2180 or 202-326-3128

Government Printing Office
Superintendent of Documents
Washington, DC 20401
202-512-1800

Stamps by Mail
U.S. Postal Service
Get address from your local Post Office

Stamps by Phone
800-782-6724

Federal Information Center
P.O. Box 600
Cumberland, MD 21501-0600
800-688-9889

Private Sector Help

HOME-BASED BUSINESSES

For the work-from-home crowd, here are resources to make your heart race. You need never feel isolated again.

American Home Business Association
4505 S. Wasatch Boulevard
Salt Lake City, UT 84124
801-273-5450

Home Office Computing **Magazine**
P.O. Box 51344
Boulder, CO 80321-1344
303-604-1464

National Association of Home Based Businesses
Newspaper: *Home Based Business*
10451 Mill Run Circle
Owings Mills, MD 21117
401-363-3698

National Association for the Cottage Industry
Newsletter: *The Cottage Connection*
P.O. Box 14850
Chicago, IL 60614
312-472-8116

TELECOMMUTING

These sources may be of interest if you want further information on the field of telecommuting.

Management and Synergy Planning
E.M. and Linda T. Risse
12501 N. Lake Court, Suite 100
Fairfax, VA 22033
703-968-4300 or 703-968-4302

Global Telematics
John S. Niles, President
322 NW 74th Street
Seattle, WA 98117-4931
206-781-9493
e-mail: jniles@nci.com

The Gordon Report
Gil Gordon
Telespan Publishing
50 A West Palm Street
Altadena, CA 91001
908-329-2266

The Kern Report
Coralee Smith Kern
P.O. Box 14850
Chicago, IL 60614
312-472-8116

EDUCATION

If you seek schooling options for your children, the sources listed below may be of interest.

Alternative vs. Traditional Schools
ERIC Clearinghouse on Educational Management
University of Oregon
1787 Agate Street
Eugene, OR 97403-5207
800-438-8841

Rural Education and Small Schools Clearinghouse
ERIC Clearinghouse on Rural Education and Small Schools
Appalachia Educational Laboratory, Inc.
P.O. Box 1348
Charleston, WV 25325-1348
800-624-9120

TELEPHONE INFORMATION

Here are toll-free phone number options. Prices on such services have dropped significantly over the past few years. For information call:

AT&T: 800-222-0400
US Sprint: 800-877-4000
MCI Telecommunications: 800-888-0800

LENDING SOURCES

Finding money isn't easy. To simplify this task, we've listed here firms willing to consider financing franchises and some other enterprises.

American National Bank
1361 Euclid Avenue
Cleveland, OH 44115
216-622-7676

American Pacific State Bank
15260 Ventura Boulevard,
   Suite 1600
Sherman Oaks, CA 91403
818-783-9943

Bank of Commerce
9918 Hibert Street, #301
San Diego, CA 92131
619-536-4545

Bank of Yorba Linda
25431 Cabot Road, Suite 204
Laguna Hills, CA 92653
714-452-0922

Brenner Financial Services, Inc.
1100 West St. Germain
St. Cloud, MN 56301
612-255-7132

California United Bank
16030 Ventura Boulevard
Encino, CA 91436
818-907-9122

**CDC Small Business Finance
   Corporation**
P.O. Box 882228
San Diego, CA 92168
619-291-3594

The Chase Manhattan Bank, N.A.
Two Chase Manhattan Plaza,
   12th Floor
New York, NY 10081
212-552-8903

Citibank, N.A.
One Count Square, 40th Floor
Long Island City, NY 11120
718-248-9011

**Commercial Bank of San
   Francisco**
333 Pine Street, 4th Floor
San Francisco, CA 94104
415-627-0303

Corestates Bank, N.A.
467 Pennsylvania Avenue,
   Suite 107
Ft. Washington, PA 19034
215-628-3634

Danvers Savings Bank
One Conant Street
Danvers, MA 01923
506-777-2200

Emergent Business Capital, Inc.
121 West Dewey, Suite 210
Wichita, KS 67202
316-263-1001

Enterprise Capital, Inc.
1485 South County Trail
East Greenwich, RI 02818
401-886-4600

First Union National Bank
1500 S. Dale Mabry Highway,
   3rd Floor
Tampa, FL 33629
813-258-7071

First Western SBLC, Inc.
17290 Preston Road, 3rd Floor
Dallas, TX 75252
214-380-0044

Firstar Bank of Sheboygan, N.A.
P.O. Box 328
Sheboygan, MI 53082-0328
414-459-6908

Guardian State Bank
142 East 200 South
Salt Lake City, UT 84111
801-531-3408

Heller First Capital Corporation
500 W. Monroe Street, 15th Floor
Chicago, IL 60661
312-441-7404

Imperial Bank
9920 S. La Cienega Boulevard
   14th Floor
Inglewood, CA 90301
310-417-5790

Landmark Bank
2099 S. State College Boulevard
Anaheim, CA 92806
714-935-2535

Liberty National Bank
P.O. Box 1160
Huntington Beach, CA 92647-1160
714-895-2929

The Money Store Investment
   Corporation
P.O. Box 13667
Sacramento, CA 95853-3667
916-446-5000

National Republic Bank of
   Chicago
1201 W. Harrison Street
Chicago, IL 60607
312-738-4913

Orange National Bank
274 N. Glassell Avenue
Orange, CA 92666
714-771-4000, ext. 350

Sacramento Commercial Bank
P.O. Box 862
Sacramento, CA 95812-0862
916-443-4700

South Shore Bank of Chicago
7054 S. Jeffery Boulevard
Chicago, IL 60649
312-753-5671

Stillwater National Bank
P.O. Box 1988
Stillwater, OK 74076
405-372-2230

Stultz Financial
1420 Bristol Street N, Suite 230
Newport Beach, CA 92660
714-476-8244

Suarez Consulting
7355 West 97th Place
Westminster, CO 80021
303-430-5965

Truckee River Bank
P.O. Box 61000
Truckee, CA 96160
916-582-3000

U.S. Bank
P.O. Box 4412
Portland, OR 97208-4412
503-275-6439

Zions First National Bank
One S. Main Street, 259-K2
Salt Lake City, UT 84111
801-524-4870

Source: This Lending Sources List was compiled by the National Association of Government Guaranteed Lenders, Inc. It is reprinted from the *Franchise Opportunities Guide,* published by the International Franchise Association, 1350 New York Avenue NW, Suite 900, Washington, DC 20005, 202-628-8000.

ASSOCIATIONS

There are hundreds of associations that are helpful to entrepreneurs. It's impossible to list all of them here. Instead we've selected a few you may find worthwhile.

American Society of Association Executives
Information Central
1575 I Street NW
Washington, DC 20005-1168
202-626-2723

National Association of Manufacturers
1331 Pennsylvania Avenue NW, Suite 1500 North
Washington, DC 20004-1790
202-637-3000

National Coalition for Advanced Manufacturing
1331 Pennsylvania Avenue NW, Suite 1410 North
Washington, DC 20004
202-622-8960

National Business Incubation Association
Dinah Adkins, Executive Director
20 E. Circle Drive, Suite 190
Athens, OH 45701
614-593-4331

International Franchise Association
1350 New York Avenue NW, Suite 900
Washington, DC 20005-4709
202-628-8000

Direct Marketing Association
120 Avenue of the Americas
New York, NY 10036-8096
212-768-7277

SELECTED SUPPLIERS

Want an inexpensive way to check out a locale? These organizations specialize in matching home swapping. Perhaps you can trade your home for that of someone else for a few weeks.

Intervac U.S.
415-435-3497

Vacation Exchange Club
602-972-2186

For ways to power an independent lifestyle, here are a couple of vendors that can get you started.

Photocomm, Inc.
7681 E. Gray Road
Scottsdale, AZ 85260
800-223-9580

Backwoods Solar Electric
  Systems
Steve Willey
8530 Rapid Lightning Creek Road
Sandpoint, ID 83864
208-263-4290

Topographic maps, specialized maps, even aerial photography overviews can be obtained to help you make wise decisions. If you were considering investing in a large piece of land, for instance, certain maps can help you judge the terrain, etc. Here are some sources for obtaining these tools:

U.S. Geological Survey—
  Topographic mapping and
  aerial photography
12201 Sunrise Valley Drive
Reston, VA 22092
800-USA-MAPS

DeLorme Mapping
P.O. Box 298
Freeport, ME 04032
800-227-1656

Federal Emergency Management
  Agency
Flood Map Distribution Center
6730 Santa Barbara Court
Baltimore, MD 21227-5832
800-358-9616

Also the Library of Congress (202-707-5000) has a cartographic collection that houses some 4 million maps, more than 50,000 atlases, plus globes and related reference books. Information derived from satellites can also be obtained.

Geography and Map Division
Library of Congress
Washington, DC 20540-4720
202-707-5000

MANUFACTURERS' REPRESENTATIVE ASSOCIATIONS

Here's a helpful listing of product- or market-specific associations that have reps who may be interested in carrying what you manufacture. The salespeople who belong to these various groups sell everything from books to safety equipment, sporting goods to home furnishings.

Agricultural and Industrial
  Manufacturers Representatives
  Association
Frank Bistrom, Executive Director
5818 Reeds Road
Mission, KS 66202
913-262-4510

American Beauty Association
Paul Dykstra, Executive Director
401 N. Michigan Avenue
Chicago, IL 60611
312-644-6610, ext. 3285

American Lighting Association
Richard D. Upton, President
P.O. Box 580168
Dallas, TX 75258-0168
214-698-9898

Armed Forces Marketing Council
  Manufacturers Representatives
Rip Rowan, Executive Director
1750 New York Avenue NW,
  Suite 340
Washington, DC 20006
202-783-8228

Association of Industry
  Manufacturers Representatives
Mr. Carmen DiPadova, Executive
  Director
222 Merchandise Mart Plaza,
  #1360
Chicago, IL 60654
312-464-0092

Association of Visual
  Merchandise Representatives
Tom Raguse, President
307 Cove Creek Lane
Houston, TX 77042-1023
713-782-5533

Automotive Parts Association
Bob White, Chairman
c/o Bob White Associates
3 Cypress Lane
Berwyn, PA 19312
301-654-6664

Automotive Service Industry
Association
Gene Gardner, President
25 Northwest Point Boulevard,
#425
Elk Grove Village, IL 60007
708-228-1310

Broker Management Council
William Bess, Executive Director
P.O. Box 150229
Arlington, TX 76015
817-465-5511

Bureau of Wholesale Sales
Representatives
Mike Wolyn, Executive Director
1801 Peachtree Road NE, Suite 200
Atlanta, GA 30309
800-877-1808

Construction Industry Sales
John Hancock, Secretary/Manager
202 E. Huron Street, Suite 204
P.O. Box 1021
Ann Arbor, MI 48106
313-769-8169

Costume Jewelry Salesman's
Association
Michael Gail, President
389 Fifth Avenue
New York, NY 10016
212-532-7595

Electronics Representatives
Association
Raymond J. Hall, Executive Vice
President/CEO
20 E. Huron Street
Chicago, IL 60611
312-649-1333

The Foodservice Group, Inc.
Kenneth W. Reynolds,
Executive Director
P.O. Box 76533
Atlanta, GA 30358
404-977-1476

Health Industry Representatives
Association
Frank Bistrom, Executive Director
5818 Reeds Road
Mission, KS 66202
913-262-4513

Incentive Manufacturers
Representatives Association
Karen Renk, Executive Director
1805 N. Mill Street, Suite A
Naperville, IL 60563
708-369-3466

Infant's Furniture
Representatives Association
Jerry Jones, President
4501 N. High Street, Suite B
Columbia, OH 43214
800-969-1985

International Association of
Plastics Distributors
Carol Wagner, Executive Director
4707 College Boulevard, Suite 105
Leawood, KS 66211-1611
913-345-1005

**International Home Furnishings
Representatives Association**
Kelly R. Crisco, CMR Executive
 Director
P.O. Box 670
High Point, NC 27261
910-889-3920

**International Housewares
Representatives Association**
William Weiner, Executive
 Director
20 E. Huron Street
Chicago, IL 60611
312-266-7377

**International Manufacturers
Representatives Association**
Mert Dale
P.O. Box 702-678
Tulsa, OK 74170
918-743-5443

**Manufacturers Representatives
of America**
(Specific products include: paper,
 plastic sanitary supply
 products)
William Bess, Executive Director
P.O. Box 150229, 1903 Turf Club
 Road
Arlington, TX 76015
817-465-5511

**Marketing Agents for Food
Service Industry**
Brad Parcells, Executive Director
Smith, Bucklin & Associates, Inc.
401 N. Michigan Avenue
Chicago, IL 60611
312-644-6610, ext. 3311

**Mechanical Equipment
Manufacturers Representatives**
William Marano
c/o Engineering Center
11 West Mt. Vernon Place
Baltimore, MD 21201
301-574-2727

**National Association General
Merchandise Representatives**
Jack Springer, Executive Director
Smith, Bucklin & Associates, Inc.
401 N. Michigan Avenue
Chicago, IL 60611
312-644-6610

**National Association of
Publishers Representatives**
Ralph Woodward, Secretary
P.O. Box 2436
Framingham, MA 01701
508-877-5328

**National Electrical
Manufacturers Representatives
Association**
Henry P. Bergson, Executive Vice
 President
200 Business Park Drive, Suite 301
Armonk, NY 10504
914-273-6780

**National Food Brokers
Association**
Robert Schwarze, President
2100 Reston Parkway, Suite 400
Reston, VA 22091-1208
703-758-7790

**Office Products Representatives
Alliance**
301 N. Fairfax Street
Alexandria, VA 22314
800-542-6672

Professional Picture Framers Association
Rex P. Boynton, Executive Director
4305 Sarelien Road
Richmond, VA 23231-4311
800-832-7732

Professional Reps Organization
Bill Moore, President
c/o John Ficarra & Associates
P.O. Box 339
Sharon, MA 02067
315-255-2879

Safety Equipment Manufacturers Agents Association
George Hayward, Executive Director
7200 Paddison Road
Cincinnati, OH 45230
513-231-4266

Sales Associates of the Chemical Industry
Patrick Vazquez, President
c/o A.L. Laboratories
1 Executive Drive
Fort Lee, NJ 07024
201-947-7774

Sporting Goods Agents Association
Lois E. Halinton, Executive Director
P.O. Box 998
Morton Grove, IL 60053
708-296-3670

Stationery Representatives Association
M.S. Kellner, Managing Director
230 Park Avenue
New York, NY 10169
212-687-2484

Tackle/Shooting Sports Association
Joe Kuti
1033 N. Fairfax Street, Suite 200
Alexandria, VA 22314
703-519-9691

Source: List provided by Manufacturers' Representatives Educational Research Foundation (MRERF), Dr. Marilyn Stephens, Executive Director, P.O. Box 247, Geneva, IL 60134, 708-208-1466

Bibliography/Recommended Reading

Backyard Market Gardening by Andy Lee, Good Earth Publications

Best Home Businesses for the `90s by Paul and Sarah Edwards, Jeremy P. Tarcher, Inc.

Big Ideas for Small Service Businesses by Marilyn and Tom Ross, Communication Creativity

Boom Counties by Jack Lessenger, PhD, SocioEconomics

Catalog of Catalogs, The by Edward L. Palder, Woodbine House

Clicking by Faith Popcorn and Lys Marigold, Harper Collins

Company Relocation Handbook by William Gary and Sharon Kaye Ward, PSI Research

Complete Guide to Self-Publishing, The by Tom and Marilyn Ross, Writers Digest Books

Country Careers by Jerry Germer, John Wiley & Sons, Inc.

Creative Cash by Barbara Brabec, Barbara Brabec Productions

Discover the Good Life in Rural America by Bob Bone, Communication Creativity

Finding and Buying Your Place in the Country by Les Scher and Carol Scher, Dearborn Financial Publishing, Inc.

Follow Your Bliss by Hal Zina Bennett, PhD, and Susan J. Sparrow, Avon Books

Handmade for Profit by Barbara Brabec, Evans

How to Find and Buy Your Business in the Country by Frank Kirkpatrick, Storey Communications

How to Find Your Ideal Country Home by Gene GeRue, Heartwood Publications

How to Set Your Fees and Get Them by Kate Kelly, Visibility Enterprises

Moving to Small Town America by William Seavey, Dearborn Financial Publishers, Inc.

Moving to the Country Once and for All by Lisa Rogak, Country Roads Press

National Directory of Newspaper Op-Ed Pages by Marilyn Ross, Communication Creativity

New Corporate Frontier, The by David A. Heenan, McGraw-Hill, Inc.

100 Best Small Towns in America, The by Norman Crampton, Prentice Hall General Reference

Penturbia by Jack Lessenger, PhD, SocioEconomics

Places Rated Almanac by Richard Boyer and David Savageau, Prentice Hall Travel

Popcorn Report, The by Faith Popcorn, Doubleday Publishers

Publicity Manual, The by Kate Kelly, Visibility Enterprises

Rating Guide to Life in America's Small Cities, The by G. Scott Thomas, Prometheus Books

Retirement Places Rated by David Savageau, Prentice Hall Travel

Small Town Bound by John Clayton, Career Press

Small Town Operator by Bernard Kamoroff, CPA, Bell Springs Publishing

Successful Direct Marketing Methods by Bob Stone, NTC Business Books

Technotrends by Daniel Burrus with Roger Gittines, HarperBusiness

Third Wave, The by Alvin Toffler, Bantam Books

Trauma of Moving, The by Audrey T. McCollum, Sage Publications

Vacation Home Exchange and Hospitality Guide, The by John Kimbrough, Kimco Communications

What Color Is Your Parachute? by Richard Nelson Booles, Ten Speed Press

Working from Home by Paul and Sarah Edwards, Jeremy P. Tarcher

You Can't Plant Tomatoes in Central Park by Frank Ruegg and Paul Bianchina, New Horizon Press

Index

About the Authors

Marilyn and Tom Ross live what they write about in *Country Bound!* In 1980, they traded a suite of offices overlooking southern California's Pacific Ocean for a remote 320-acre horse ranch nestled in the Rocky Mountains. Finding that too isolated, they now live in a small Colorado mountain town.

They have collaborated on six previous books. Their best-selling marketing guide, *Big Ideas for Small Service Businesses,* was selected as one of the 30 best business books of the year by Soundview Executive Book Summaries. In addition to writing books and articles, the Rosses are in demand as professional speakers. Members of the National Speakers Association, Marilyn and Tom present seminars and do training workshops for major corporations, private organizations, and trade associations. They speak about entrepreneurship, marketing, publishing, and rural relocation.

This pair has been noted and quoted in publications across the land: the *Wall Street Journal, U.S. News & World Report,* and the *New York Times* have written about them and their work. Additionally, they've been featured twice on NPR's "All Things Considered."

In 1993 the Rosses were tapped to be senior associates of the prestigious Center for the New West, a Colorado-based think tank. Their areas of specialization are rural entrepreneurship and home-based businesses. They also serve on the National Advisory Board of the American Home Business Association.

As consultants, they work with clients from coast to coast—primarily by phone, fax, mail, and overnight delivery service. Through About Books, Inc., Tom and Marilyn help professionals package their specialized knowledge in book form to give them greater visibility and credibility. Sister company Accelerated Business Images is a public relations firm. It specializes in developing customized quick-fix programs with long-lasting results.

They are both listed in the 23rd edition of *Who's Who in the West*. And between them, this dynamic pair is also included in *Who's Who of American Women, The International Businessmen's Who's Who*, and *Men and Women of Distinction*. Their writing careers are detailed in *Working Press of the Nation, Who's Who in U.S. Writers, Editors & Poets, Contemporary Authors,* and *The International Authors and Writers Who's Who*.

New
CD-ROM Money Maker Kits from Dearborn Multimedia

Book & CD-ROM Set

A DEARBORN MONEY MAKER KIT

THE MORTGAGE KIT

THE MORTGAGE KIT

THIRD EDITION

- SELECT THE RIGHT LOAN
- NEGOTIATE THE BEST TERMS
- LOCK IN THE LOWEST RATE
- UNDERSTAND ALL YOUR OPTIONS

THOMAS C. STEINMETZ
PHILLIP WHITT

Features:

- *25 minute video help with the author*
- *12-28 interactive printable forms per CD-ROM*
- *On-Line glossary of terms*
- *Quick-start video tutorial*
- *Interactive printable book on CD-ROM*
  (Print out sections you like for closer reading or writing notes.)

Start Enjoying Greater Financial Freedom Triple Your Investment Portfolio

SAVE Thousands on Real Estate as a Buyer or Seller

Successfully Start & Manage a **NEW** Business.

Give the Gift of Country Freedom to Your Friends and Loved Ones!

ORDER FORM

❏ **YES,** I want _____ copies of *Country Bound! Trade Your Business Suit Blues for Blue Jean Dreams* at $19.95 each, plus $5.00 shipping per book.

_____ Check/money order enclosed • Charge my _____ VISA _____ MasterCard

Name _____ Phone (____)_____ ___

Organization (if applicable) _____

Address _____

City/State/Zip _____

Card # _____ Exp. _____ Signature _____

Check your leading bookstore or call credit card orders to:
1-800-829-7934 anytime
or fax your order to: 312-836-1021 ATTN: EMJ

Please make your check payable and return to:
Dearborn Financial Publishing, Inc.
Department EMJ
155 North Wacker Drive
Chicago, IL 60606-1719